CHEN DUXIU

Chen Duxiu

FOUNDER OF THE CHINESE COMMUNIST PARTY

BY LEE FEIGON

PRINCETON UNIVERSITY PRESS

Published by Princeton University Press, 41 William Street,
Princeton, New Jersey 08540
In the United Kingdom: Princeton University Press,
Guildford, Surrey

Library of Congress Cataloging in Publication Data will be
found on the last printed page of this book

ISBN 0-691-05393-6

This book has been composed in Linotron Sabon

Clothbound editions of Princeton University Press books
are printed on acid-free paper, and binding materials are
chosen for strength and durability. Paperbacks,
although satisfactory for personal collections, are not usually
suitable for library rebinding.

Printed in the United States of America by
Princeton University Press
Princeton, New Jersey

To My Parents, Gershon and Ethel Feigon,
for their help and their kindness.
Their devotion to learning and ideas
has been an inspiration to me.

CONTENTS

ABBREVIATIONS

AHSHB	*Anhui suhua bao* [Anhui Vernacular Paper]
DXWC	*Duxiu wencun* [Chen Duxiu's Collected Writings]
KMT	Guomindang
MZPL	*Meizhou pinglun* [Weekly Critic]
QN	*Qingnian* [Youth]
XQN	*Xin Qingnian* [New Youth]

Chen Duxiu, the man who led the New Culture movement and founded the Chinese Communist party, was a towering presence in modern Chinese history. In attempting to measure his influence, the standard one-dimensional comparisons are not sufficient. Too often, Chen and other modern Chinese political figures have been judged purely in terms of their thought, divorced from the deeds they helped inspire. By these criteria, many modern Chinese theorists seem considerably less rigorous than the Westerners to whom they have been compared. How many times, for instance, has it been said that the turn-of-the-century Chinese reformer, intellectual, and political leader Liang Qichao (1873–1929) was just as profound as his contemporary, Max Weber, in his critiques of the failure of European civilization following World War I? Comparisons such as that of Liang to Weber often take on a defensive tone that suggests that it is somehow astonishing that Chinese thinkers, too, can be profound.

But Chen Duxiu, like other important Chinese political figures, never considered spending year after year in the British Museum trying to work out his ideas and discipline his thought, as did someone such as the Communist philosopher Karl Marx. Ideas in China earned one respect and hence the potential for engaging in political action—the ultimate object of all thought. Since theory gave one a political following, there were few political theorists (at least within the Confucian tradition) who did not serve, at one stage or another of their careers, as officials or political actors.

Why, therefore, should these Chinese thinker-politicians be compared with Western intellectuals rather than with Western politicians? It is common to compare the thoughts of Chen Duxiu with those of Karl Marx but not with those of politicians such as Gerald Ford or Dwight Eisenhower. When seen in this light, the thought of Chen, Mao, and the others would seem disciplined beyond belief.

It is true that there are the examples of Lenin and Trotsky, who were thinkers as well as political actors. And in fact Chen and even Mao are more often compared with these political leaders than with Marx; this study makes the same comparison. To the extent that Lenin and Trotsky wrote primarily to legitimize their cause among their followers and convince them to take action, their theoretical writings (if they were in fact theory and not simply tactics) may be compared to those of Chen or Mao.

The breadth of Chen Duxiu's works was, however, far greater than that of his Russian counterparts. The tradition of the Chinese intellectual, which Chen followed, was that of the generalist who had to prove himself in many areas of Chinese social and cultural life before he could develop a following. Potential Russian political and intellectual leaders did not have to face such a test.

This need for Chinese intellectuals to immerse themselves in their society to establish credentials may partially explain the tendency noted by Benjamin Schwartz that the Chinese radical intelligentsia were far less alienated from their society than the Russian intelligentsia.[1] Unlike Lenin or Trotsky, Chen may be said to have thought and breathed Chinese culture throughout his entire life. He was not simply concerned with political theory but made contributions to traditional philological scholarship, literature, and the arts; he also helped introduce Western geographical, military, and scientific concepts to China. Though Chen may not have contributed as much to any one field as did Lenin or Trotsky, the range of his contributions far exceeds anything contemplated by these great Russian leaders.

In the end, Chen simply could not keep up with his own accomplishments. Traditionally, political alliances in China have been more casual and personal, dependent as they were

---

[1] Benjamin Schwartz, "The Intelligentsia in Communist China: A Tentative Comparison," *Daedalus*, Summer 1960, pp. 604–21.

on the intellectual legitimacy of the leader. Chen was the first to use his personal legitimacy to build a disciplined bureaucratic political organization. But having acquired legitimacy under the traditional system, he never quite felt comfortable with that organization, nor could he control it. When faced with a similar problem, Mao chose to tear down the organization he had constructed rather than allow himself to be pushed from the scene, as was Chen. Though Chen's personal legitimacy ultimately was destroyed, his influence, spreading over many areas of Chinese culture and society, was indelible.

Thus, if we multiply the standard one-dimensional assessments of the depth of Chen Duxiu's thought by the enormous breadth of his interests over so many cultural areas, and by the wide span of time over which his influence has lasted, the three-dimensional reality of Chen's being and importance can be seen as imposing indeed.

In making this study, I am indebted to more people than I could possibly remember to thank. But there are three people whose generosity and insights have probably contributed more to this book than I have. The first of these is my wife Leanne. It is customary in studies of this kind to put in a note of thanks to one's spouse, especially when she or he has helped with typing or editing. In my case, the aid and support Leanne has given me has been enormous. Leanne has spent days and nights, sometimes to the wee hours of the morning, assisting me with this study at the expense of her own work. She is my best friend, confidante, and critic.

I also owe more than I can explain in an acknowledgment page to Maurice Meisner. Maurie has been a teacher and adviser to me, helping me with grants and letters, providing me with suggestions on new approaches to take, and giving me encouragement when I needed it. Maurie has also been a guiding light in helping me get back on course when I went off on ridiculous tangents or took a wrong turn.

The third person to whom I want to give a special note of appreciation is Professor Lin Maosheng of the Department of Party History of the People's University in Beijing. Professor

Lin was extraordinarily generous to me with both his time and his ideas during my stay in China in the 1980–81 academic year. Although our ideas and approaches to Chen were often different and there was much material that he was unable to show me, Professor Lin spent several months of his time discussing his ideas on Chen Duxiu with me and allowing me to benefit from the insights gained from his thirty years of research on the topic. He is a true teacher and scholar, and I am enormously indebted to him.

Additionally, there are numerous librarians and scholars, most of whose names I never knew, who have aided me in my research in libraries throughout the United States, Taiwan, Japan, Hong Kong, and China. There are also dozens of other people who have either kindly shared experiences with me or have given me ideas for new sources of information. I would particularly like to thank Joe Miller, whom I have never met but who went to great trouble to send materials from Australia to China for me. I am also grateful to Cha Shijie and Zhao Yashu for helping me during my stay in Taiwan. Additionally, I would like to thank Yang Youwei, my Chinese teacher in Taiwan, who first interested me in Chen Duxiu and personally copied the original articles on Chen Duxiu that I used in beginning the research on my Ph.D. dissertation for the University of Wisconsin, Madison.

A number of people who have seen parts of this manuscript shared their ideas on it with me. Roger Bowen, Ben Elman, Wang Fanxi through the kind intercession of Gregor Benton, Herman Mast, and Richard Kagan have all given me valued suggestions for changes. A great deal of the material covered in this study would have been missed without the aid of Ding Yeo. I was fortunate in having the benefit of her insights and fortitude first in Taiwan and then in the U.S., when she became a graduate student at the University of Wisconsin and later at Harvard. Many of my most important contacts came as a result of the intercession of Ding Yeo. I would also like to thank Chu-chu Liang and Joan Langley for their aid with the calligraphy. I want to thank Miriam Brokaw for her patience and support and Alice Calaprice for her careful editorial comments and advice. Finally, I would like to thank Kathy Childs, who helped assemble the bibliography and index for me.

This study has been completed as the result of a Fulbright research grant to China for 1980–81 and as the result of earlier grants to Taiwan from the University of Wisconsin, NDEA Title VI, and Colby College.

Once again, I would like to thank my wife, Leanne, and my two daughters, Maia and Brooke.

November 19, 1982
China, Maine

CHEN DUXIU

CHAPTER ONE

PERSPECTIVES ON CHEN DUXIU

The year 1879 marked the birth of two men who would exercise enormous influence over the shape of modern history, Leon Bronstein in Russia and Chen Duxiu in China. Acutely aware of the "backwardness" of their homelands in relation to the advanced industrial states of Western Europe, both men would be concerned with the adaptation of Marxism under these conditions and would play seminal roles in the establishment of the Communist parties of their respective countries. Furthermore, Leon Bronstein and Chen Duxiu would both be identified with the cosmopolitan or internationalist wings of their parties in an era in which "socialism in one country" came to be a Marxist-Leninist orthodoxy. The two were finally expelled from the parties they had helped establish and both were vilified by their former comrades. Yet despite their shared birth year and similar historical roles, these two figures differed greatly in their eventual fame.

The revolutionary theories and actions of Leon Bronstein, later known as Trotsky, created profound controversy and continue to excite interest to this day, not only in the Soviet Union but in the entire world. Chen Duxiu has rarely been credited for his ideas and activities in China or in the West, even though his contributions to the Chinese Revolution were of at least equal importance. Indeed, his influence cannot be understated: with the possible exception of Mao Zedong, it would be hard to find someone whose ideas and actions have had greater consequences for modern Chinese history than Chen Duxiu. His contributions included everything from the introduction of punctuation in Chinese writing to the establishment of the Chinese Communist party. He helped to guide the Republican revolution that overthrew the Qing dynasty in 1911, he was the major leader of the New Culture movement between 1915 and 1919, and he served as the first secretary-general of the Chinese Communist party. Still, Chen Duxiu was pushed into a political no man's land. Rejected by those with whom he had worked most closely, he died in obscurity. The Chinese Communists hounded him out of the very party he had helped found—ironically, for his Trotskyist beliefs—in 1929, condemning him as an "opportunist" and "renegade." On the other side, the Chinese Nationalist regime, which once touted Chen's late-in-life reconversion to the principles of democracy, still shuns him not only for his Communist activities but also for his earlier role as a zealous opponent of Chinese tradition.

Trotsky also is considered a nonperson today by the Russian Communist party that he once led. Within the Soviet Union all references to his name and deeds have been removed from the official history of the Bolshevik Revolution. But Trotsky before his fall was a successful revolutionary who helped create one of the major upheavals of this century. Thus Trotsky's actions, even after his exile from the land of his birth, drew headlines throughout the world. Chen, by way of contrast, was a revolutionary failure. After 1927 his name was mentioned even less outside of China than inside the country.

But Chen's failure to lead a successful revolution is only a partial reason for the lack of attention that has been paid to Chen outside of China. Unlike Trotsky, whose revolutionary ideals were formed in no small part because of his alienation from the mainstream of Russian society, Chen's revolutionary goals were largely a product of his immersion in Chinese society.

One of the major points of this study is that although Chen was known for his relentless attacks on Chinese tradition, his success as a revolutionary was achieved precisely because of his ability to manipulate the tradition he was attacking. This is not surprising. Unlike most well-known foreign revolutionaries such as Trotsky or the generation of Chinese revolutionaries that followed Chen Duxiu, Chen and the Chinese of his generation were absorbed in the traditions of their society.

As Maurice Meisner has put it: ". . . the very intensity of his assault on traditional values and his strident calls for Westernization reflected the influence that those values once exerted on him."[1]

Chen's reliance on Chinese tradition at the same time as he was attacking it has not been very well understood by most who have studied Chen. The failure to understand this point has affected our understanding of the entire period of history that Chen influenced. A prime example of this can be seen in the common scholarly view of Chen's role in the New Culture movement, when Chen led a withering attack on virtually all aspects of Chinese tradition. Ironically, this aspect of Chen's life that has been explored the most has been understood the least.

Most studies of the New Culture movement period have failed to ask why Chen's critique of many features of the traditional society were so persuasive to a generation of people who grew up in that tradition. Assuming the appeal of Western values, these studies have been content with taking Chen's attacks on the old culture at face value, identifying Chen as an all-out Westernizer who advocated science and democracy as the solution to China's woes. Benjamin Schwartz, writing in his pioneering study of Chen in 1951, called Chen "a man deeply involved in the situation of his country who has jettisoned traditional Chinese solutions and is anxiously looking Westward for new solutions. . . . Chen's avowed aim is to eliminate the traditional Chinese pattern of life and thought and to substitute a modern, Western pattern of life and thought."[2] This dislike for his own tradition, Schwartz asserted, led Chen to distrust narrow patriotic sentiment because he, "like many European liberals," regarded it as an anachronism, one which was apt to lead to the exaltation of "nationalism."[3] Since 1951, Western historians of China have

[1] Maurice Meisner, *Li Ta-chao and the Origins of Chinese Marxism*, p. 45.

[2] Benjamin Schwartz, "Ch'en Tu-hsiu and the Acceptance of the Modern West," *Journal of the History of Ideas*, Jan. 1951, p. 63.

[3] Ibid.

been virtually unanimous in their agreement with Schwartz's description of Chen.[4] Indeed, it has become axiomatic to assert that during the period from 1915 to 1921, Chen was the key representative, or at least a major proponent, of Western "liberal" values. Moreover, most would agree with Schwartz's contention that Chen represented international or cosmopolitan tendencies during an era characterized by its vehement nationalism.[5]

To be sure, Professor Lin Yu-sheng has recently attempted to show what he calls the "cultural intellectualist" assumptions of Confucianism in what he sees as Chen's insistence on the priority of intellectual over social change prior to 1921.[6] Still, even Professor Lin agrees that Chen was a radical iconoclast who was interested in the introduction of Western ideas into China.

Most Chinese Communist writers have likewise viewed Chen Duxiu's role during the initial stages of the May Fourth period as that of a cosmopolitan intellectual interested in introducing Western bourgeois ideas of "science and democracy" into China during the so-called "bourgeois-democratic" phase of the Chinese Revolution.[7] To be sure, not all Chinese Communist authors have felt Chen's legacy from this period to be a positive one. Ever since Chen's expulsion from the party in 1929, most Chinese Marxist historians have been very uneasy about just how to assess Chen's obviously massive contri-

[4] See, for instance, Chow Tse-tsung, *The May Fourth Movement*; also Thomas Kuo, *Ch'en Tu-hsiu and the Chinese Communist Movement*; D.W.Y. Kwok, *Scientism in Chinese Thought*; Jerome Grieder, *Hu Shih and the Chinese Renaissance: Liberalism in the Chinese Revolution, 1917–n1937*, idem, *Intellectuals and the State in Modern China*; and Meisner, *Li Ta-chao*.

[5] For the most recent and eloquent exposition of this, see Grieder, *Intellectuals and the State*.

[6] Lin Yu-sheng, *The Crisis of Chinese Consciousness: Radical Antitraditionalism in the May Fourth Era*.

[7] For a good survey of Chinese Communist attitudes toward Chen Duxiu, see Lin Maosheng, "Guanyu Chen Duxiu yanjiu de yixie wenti" [A few problems in researching Chen Duxiu], in *Zhongguo renmin daxue dangshixi dangshi jinxiuban jianggao* [An outline of a lecture for a class of advanced studies in party history for the party history department of People's University], no. 6, Sept. 23, 1980.

butions to the early years of the Chinese Revolution. This was most apparent during the years of the Cultural Revolution in the late sixties, when it was claimed that "every pore on Chen Duxiu's body was stained with the blood of the people."[8] During this time those who had previously implied in writing or even sometimes in conversations that "Chen had made some positive contributions during the May Fourth period" were criticized, and "some were even expelled from the party for this reason."[9]

This harsh assessment of Chen's activities prior to 1919 has been generally repudiated in China since 1976. An article in the *Liberation Daily* in 1979 attempted to sum up the attitude toward Chen: "It was Chen Duxiu who criticized the old feudal ethic, propagated the new thought, and founded the literary revolution. He was the most influential leader and 'bright star' of intellectual circles during the May Fourth period."[10] With cosmopolitanism again in vogue and with an interest in Western ideas and technology once more fashionable in China, the party has again begun to evaluate positively what it considers to be Chen's earlier role in popularizing Western ideas in China.

But if Chinese historians of Chen's New Culture movement activities would appear to have again shifted to a generally sympathetic view of his supposed role in Westernizing Chinese thought, their Soviet counterparts are still skeptical. Not surprisingly, Russian historians do not tend to be impressed by what others see as Chen's fascination with Western bourgeois democratic ideas and institutions. Soviet historians tend to stress the period after 1919 when Chen came under the influence of the Bolshevik Revolution and became one of the first

[8] Lin Maosheng, "Dui Chen Duxiu pingjia de jige wenti" [Several problems in evaluating Chen Duxiu], in Hu Hua, ed., *Zhongguo xiandaishi jiaoxue cankao ziliao [Reference materials for teaching and studying about modern Chinese history]*, no. 1 (Beijing, 1981), p. 47.

[9] Ibid.

[10] "Ruhe pingjie Chen Duxiu de gong yu guo?" [How do we evaluate the contributions and faults of Chen Duxiu?], *Jiefang junbao [Liberation Army News]*, Oct. 14, 1979.

in China to advocate proletarian revolution. Indeed, at least one recent study of the May Fourth period has suggested a persistence of Confucian ideas in the literature of the New Culture movement that began in 1915 with Chen's publication of *Youth*, or *New Youth*, magazine.[11]

Although this approach might seem novel, a recent Japanese study by Matsumoto Hideki has gone even further in the same direction. To be sure, Matsumoto, like most Western and Chinese writers, sees Chen as engaged in transforming the spiritual consciousness of Chinese youth by attempting to "elevate European and American ideas of science and democracy" within China.[12] But Matsumoto traces the primary distinctions raised by Chen in carrying out this goal to the ideas of earlier, more traditional Chinese scholars. In particular, Matsumoto traces Chen's ideas to his youthful association with Zhang Binglin, the great Confucian scholar who in the pre-1911 period was a revolutionary associate of Chen Duxiu.[13]

Although most have taken for granted the radicalism of Chen's ideas, Matsumoto asserts that both Chen and Zhang shared a "scholar-gentry (*shi dafu*) consciousness" that underlay what he calls the "conservatism" of many of Chen's positions.[14] Matsumoto does not really explain why he feels that Chen and Zhang had a "scholar-gentry consciousness" or why he would characterize some of Chen's ideas as conservative, but he does suggest that although Chen and Zhang end up on opposite sides during the Republican period, Chen may have derived from Zhang Binglin his notion of a distinctive Chinese (and European) national consciousness. For although by 1915 Chen Duxiu, like Zhang, clearly felt that Chinese culture needed to be changed, he also felt that culture

[11] K. I. Golygina, *Theory of Elegant Literature in China* (Moscow, 1971). This is discussed briefly in E. Stuart Kirby, *Russian Studies of China.*

[12] Matsumoto Hideki, "Shin bunka undo ni sura chin Dokushu no rikyo shiron" [Chen Duxiu's critique of Confucianism during the New Culture movement]. *Ritsumeikan Bunganku*, 299 (May 1970).

[13] Ibid.

[14] Ibid.

could be reduced to an inherited set of values, or a "national essence."[15]

In fact, around the turn of the century, Chen had been part of a movement led by Zhang Binglin and Liu Shipei, another scholar-radical later turned conservative, to restore China's national essence. A number of American writers have lately studied the National Essence movement, seeing it in the decade after the 1911 Revolution as a conservative "countercurrent" to the New Culture movement led by Chen Duxiu.[16] What these writers have not noted (nor were they particularly concerned with this issue) is the similar historical footing of Chen Duxiu and the so-called conservative National Essence scholars, against whom Chen turned after 1911. For as Matsumoto points out, even after Chen broke with the members of the National Essence movement, he continued to be influenced by the ideas and values of this movement.[17]

Many of the positions Chen took during the New Culture movement period were a result of his opposition to the proposals for the establishment of a Confucian religion by the former reform movement leaders Kang Youwei and Liang Qichao. As Matsumoto implies, Chen's anti-Confucian rhetoric owed much to the attack by National Essence movement leader Zhang Binglin on Kang Youwei, Liang Qichao, and other members of the so-called Gongyang school that began in the early 1900s.[18] Zhang, and then a decade later Chen, vehemently disagreed with Kang's notion that Confucianism was a national religion similar to that of Christianity in the West.

This disagreement between Kang and Zhang (which was later joined by Chen Duxiu) was in many ways a continuation of a discussion that had been going on for several centuries between the followers of the so-called New Text movement, represented in the late nineteenth and early twentieth centuries

[15] Ibid.
[16] Charlotte Furth, ed., *The Limits of Change: Essays on Conservative Alternatives in Republican China*, pp. 30–31.
[17] Matsumoto Hideki, "Shin bunka."
[18] Ibid.

by Kang Youwei and his followers, and the adherents of the Old Text movement, represented in modern times by Zhang Binglin. The Old Text adherents, who pioneered the *kaozheng* or evidential method of scholarship, desired to return to what they considered to be the authentic Confucian tradition; in the process they managed to demolish many of the neo-Confucian orthodoxies that had been taken for granted in China since at least the Song dynasty (960–1279). The Old Text adherents were particularly opposed to what they felt to be the metaphysical assumptions of the neo-Confucian doctrine, seeing them as adulterations introduced into Confucian doctrine as a consequence of Buddhist influence. Old Text scholars pioneered a more critical and rational view of Confucian tradition as well as rigorous standards of scholarship that may have made it easier for later Chinese to accept Western democratic and scientific ideas critical of the traditional Confucian orthodoxy.[19]

Certainly, the critiques of the Old Text proponents influenced their New Text opponents and vice versa. A shared sense of values was evident in the twentieth century when both sides sometimes joined forces in their opposition to the problems posed for China by Western imperialism. Both Chen Duxiu and Zhang Binglin, for instance, were at one time followers of their later enemy Kang Youwei. It is therefore not surprising that in attacking Confucianism, Chen Duxiu often took for granted the definitions of Confucianism put forward by his opponents. As Matsumoto asserts, Chen's later attacks on Confucian ritual as inseparable from the Confucian tradition showed the influence of Liang Qichao, who in his Confucian writings emphasized the stress on rites of Confucius's disciple Xun Zi.[20]

Matsumoto's demonstration of Chen's indebtedness to Liang Qichao and Zhang Binglin suggests an interesting avenue of inquiry. The writings of Japanese writers such as Matsumoto, along with the ideas of the Soviet historians mentioned above,

[19] Benjamin Elman, *From Philosophy to Philology: Intellectual and Social Aspects of Change in Late Imperial China.*
[20] Matsumoto Hideki, "Shin bunka."

provide an important supplement to the works of Western scholars who have recently studied long-ignored conservative Chinese figures such as Zhang Binglin, Liu Shipei, and Liang Shuming.[21] Taken together the studies of these recent historians make it clear that the relationship of Chen Duxiu (and by association the entire New Culture movement) to his tradition and to Western ideas is far more complicated than past historians have suggested. Placed within this context, many of the stereotypes about Chen disappear.

Chen was not simply a Westernized intellectual. Contrary to most previous Chinese and Western biographers of Chen, I maintain that during the period in which he edited the journal *New Youth*, the major focus for the New Culture movement, Chen in fact was an ardent nationalist whose seeming cosmopolitanism was skin-deep at best. But Chen opposed those nationalist proposals that he felt would not preserve what he deemed the true essence of the Chinese nation. Similarly, he advocated Western ideas that he felt could help to retain a real Chinese essence. The ideas of "science and democracy," which Chen is often credited with introducing or at least popularizing in China, were already prevalent by the time that Chen began the New Culture movement. In fact, such notions were originally introduced by the very people Chen attacked in his New Youth writings for having perverted these ideas—Kang Youwei, Liang Qichao, and their followers. (Attacking people for betraying their own ideals was to become a common trait in Chinese Communist history.) Chen retained the Old Text movement's antipathy to Kang's proposals for a Confucian religion. Additionally, he felt that Kang's attempt to show the compatibility between Confucianism and "science and democracy" would result in a negation of Western ideas. Like Zhang Binglin and other Old Text scholars, Chen felt

---

[21] Charlotte Furth, "The Sage as Rebel: The Inner World of Chang Pinglin," in *The Limits of Change*. Also, Martin Bernal, "Liu Shih-p'ei and National Essence," in *Limits of Change*. Also, Laurence Schneider, "National Essence and the New Intelligentsia," in *Limits of Change*. See also Guy S. Alitto, *The Last Confucian: Liang Shu-ming and the Chinese Dilemma of Modernity*.

that the proposals of his opponents, especially Kang Youwei, were incompatible with the true needs and ideals of the Chinese people and nation.

But I am not simply writing to show that Chen Duxiu's role in history during the New Culture movement was more complicated than previous writers have suggested. The failure to understand corrrectly Chen Duxiu's role in this movement has in turn led to a basic misunderstanding of the history of the early Chinese Communist party and in a more general sense to a failure to appreciate fully the continuities and discontinuities in modern Chinese history.

The debate over continuity has been defined largely by the often misinterpreted works of the late Joseph Levenson. Essentially, Levenson's works can best be understood in terms of his own metaphor of "new wine into old bottles."[22] Levenson's point was that the content and intent of twentieth century Chinese political and social reform is so different from that of the traditional society that one has to talk about a radical discontinuity or break in modern Chinese history. No matter what the bottle looks like, the wine is different. This change, in Levenson's opinion, was a result of the impact of Western imperialism. Levenson felt that the difficulties of the Chinese social and political establishment in repelling Western incursions into China forced the Chinese to adopt many of the methods, and subsequently even ideas, of Western society. Unfortunately Levenson's penchant for belittling the attempts of modern Chinese reformers to search for parallels in Chinese and Western history, as well as his fondness for exposing the futility of any effort at salvaging Confucian values that might be compatible with Western ideas, have given many the notion that Levenson virtually denied any Chinese context to modern Chinese history. This misconception has been exacerbated by the Western sensibilities that pervaded Levenson's works; many readers have inferred—quite falsely—that Levenson was gloating that the West had in effect defeated the East.[23]

[22] Joseph Levenson, *Confucian China and Its Modern Fate*, vols. 1–3.
[23] For a good discussion of the pros and cons of Levenson's work, see Maurice Meisner and Rhoads Murphey, eds., *The Mozartian Historian: Essays on the Works of Joseph R. Levenson.*

While a number of recent American historians have tended to see Levenson in this way, at least one Soviet commentator, who is better able to understand Levenson's works than his American counterparts, has suggested that Joseph Levenson (and Maurice Meisner) were among the few "bourgeois" historians who have "been disturbed" by the overly "idealistic" manner in which the history of traditional Chinese society is usually portrayed.[24] To be sure, the writer is still critical of Levenson's work, seeing it as another example of Western bourgeois Sinology. Still, Soviet authors would appear to have had no trouble in understanding the basic premise underlying Levenson's works. Levenson began with the assumption that Chinese thinkers were faced with the fact of Western material superiority and the resulting ability of the West to invade China and offer an alternative to the existing political and social elites. Levenson is therefore not implying (and certainly not gloating) that Chinese thought could not stand up in the face of Western ideas. Rather, he is examining the dilemmas faced by the Chinese elite who in Levenson's view were confronted by superior Western military and economic might and felt compelled to seek new ideas to reestablish their own position and preserve the independence of their country.[25]

Although Levenson's writings have been misunderstood, they still have dominated the debate over continuities in modern Chinese history. Much recent scholarship has been devoted to showing the persistence of traditional ideas or institutions in modern China and proving that many Chinese were seriously concerned with problems very similar to those with which Western thinkers are usually identified. But many of these attempts to refute Levenson have forgotten that Levenson himself suggested that it is only the wine and not the bottles that have changed.[26]

In the rush to refute Levenson, people seem to have ignored the obvious. One of the underlying themes of this study is

[24] L. A. Bereznii, A Critique of American Bourgeois Historiography on China: Problems of Social Development in the Nineteenth and Early Twentieth Centuries, p. 8.
[25] Joseph Levenson, Confucian China, vol. 1.
[26] Ibid.

that those Chinese most receptive to Western ideas were those who had themselves earlier been drawn to Chinese ideas that were iconoclastic in terms of Chinese tradition and bore much similarity to the Western ideas they were later to advocate. As already mentioned, as a youth Chen Duxiu was very involved with those Confucian iconoclasts of the *kaozheng* (evidential research) school who, as Benjamin Elman has demonstrated, had begun to repudiate many traditional neo-Confucian ideas well before the arrival of the West.[27] Although this background seems startling at first glance for a man to be identified later with Western ideas, it should be obvious that those involved with Western ideas would have been interested earlier in similar Chinese ideas. Yet in spite of the recent search for continuities in Chinese thought, no one has previously bothered to point this out.

Still, as this study seeks to show, Chen's iconoclasm would have been a very lonely undertaking had there not been a group of influential people who had reason to support his ideas. It should also not be surprising that many among those at the upper levels of Chinese society were discontented with the official system. Several centuries earlier, the *kaozheng* movement had originated in the middle of the Qing dynasty among southern merchant families with official connections. By the late nineteenth or early twentieth century, groups such as those which had once backed the *kaozheng* movement were even more willing to lend support to new heterodox groups. Some members of these groups were involved in specialized, particularistic pursuits that did not always receive what they considered to be adequate recognition from the official government ideology. Others were simply dissatisfied with their own political and social power and perhaps enjoyed experimenting with new ideas. The traditional and, later, Western iconoclastic values that Chen advanced (and initially claimed were mutually compatible) were those that appealed to the interests of these groups, with which Chen identified both because of birth and inclination.

[27] Elman, *From Philosophy to Philology.*

The changes advocated by Chen were those that he felt were necessary for China to meet the challenge of the West. But some of these changes were also beneficial to a substantial portion of the Chinese elite, particularly those legions of clerks, merchants, military men, and others who might not have received sufficient credit under the old system. Change, in the form of Western technology and thought, gave to many of these people new tools with which to carry out their jobs more efficiently, while at the same time affirming the importance of those engaged in these specialized particularist concerns. Chen Duxiu began his career, in effect, as a spokesperson for this group. But while his protests and ideology grew out of this tradition, Chen came to oppose the political and social order that most of these people (i.e., the traditional iconoclasts and their merchant and gentry allies) were willing to accept after 1911.

Viewed within this context, Chen's New Culture movement ideas can be seen as a repudiation of the ideas of his early associates who now eschewed further change, and his activities were in many ways an attempt to remind his earlier associates of their previous iconoclasm. Chen's writings were also an attempt to reach a new body of youth, who he hoped would be as iconoclastic as he and his peers had been in their own younger days. Chen's *New Youth* writings came at a time when his earlier associates—Zhang Binglin, Liu Shipei, and Sun Yuyun, among others—had become fearful of radical political change. Although all these people had been radicals, they were now no longer willing to tinker very much more with the traditional political and social structure. To counter these former associates, Chen attempted to appeal to the new generation of students during the 1915 to 1919 period.

The failure to understand properly that Chen's appeals to this new student group were influenced by his relations with his former radical associates has clouded our understanding of the problem of continuity in modern Chinese history. It has also created misconceptions in understanding the development of the Chinese Communist party, particularly Chen's role in the establishment of that party. To be sure, there has been little agreement on Chen's place in the early history of the party. He has been considered so controversial by most Chinese and even by some Western scholars that his accomplishments in founding the party have sometimes been ignored or slighted.

Among Western historians, the majority view has once again taken its cue largely from the pioneering writings of Benjamin Schwartz.[28] Schwartz has concluded that Chen Duxiu turned to Marxism because of his disappointment with the Western powers' betrayal of China's interests at the Paris Peace Conference of 1919, when German rights in China's Shandong province were transferred to the Japanese. Looking for an alternative to Western democratic ideas, Chen was attracted by the message of "scientific" socialism that pervaded Marxist doctrine. The idea of a scientific solution to society's problems combined with the message of economic development that emanated from the Bolshevik Revolution gave Chen and his comrades, in Schwartz's view, hope for a prescription to the woes of Chinese society.[29] This is a view of Chen as a cosmopolitan with a great deal of belief in foreign, especially Western, ideas and methods. Schwartz has theorized that it was Chen's faith in foreign powers that made him ultimately willing to yield to Comintern discipline and allow himself to be manipulated by his Soviet advisers who wanted the infant CCP to conclude a United Front in 1923 with the Guomindang (KMT), the party of Sun Yatsen and Jiang Kaishek. When the United Front collapsed in 1927, Chen was made its scapegoat.

Still, Schwartz's view credits Chen with more independence of thought than does the view of Guomindang writers who, although somewhat sympathetic to Chen's account of how he was vilified by the Comintern after 1927, still see Chen as a tool of the Russians. Few Guomindang historians, when writing about Chen Duxiu's Communist activities, have not mentioned—or more often, quoted from—the report delivered to Sun Yatsen in November of 1923 in which eleven right-wing

[28] Benjamin Schwartz, *Chinese Communism and the Rise of Mao*, esp. chaps. 1–3.
[29] Ibid.

KMT members opposed to Chinese Communist Party (CCP) admission into the KMT charged that Chen Duxiu was leading a Russian-organized effort to subvert the KMT and to take over the leadership in that organization.[30]

Chinese Communist historians seem to take the opposite point of view from their Guomindang counterparts. Until recently, they have felt that Chen's problem was that he failed to heed Comintern advice. But this, in the view of Communist writers, was not as a result of Chen's independence of thought. Some, as already mentioned, have felt that Chen was simply an agent of the KMT;[31] in the thirties, Communist writers even accused Chen of being a Japanese spy.[32] Most Communist historians, however, have felt that Chen was simply enamored with Western bourgeois ideas, so much so that he refused to abandon the alliance with the Guomindang long after it had stopped serving any purpose. The orthodox line on Chen has followed fairly closely the accusations made against him in 1931 by Cai Hesen, who blamed Chen for allowing the KMT to assume the leadership in the national revolution, for neglecting the proletariat, and in particular for slighting the peasantry, whom Cai felt Chen regarded as "reactionary" and "superstitious."[33]

Lately, as the ideological climate in China has changed, Chinese Communist historians have moved closer to the view of their Guomindang and American counterparts. Recent articles have suggested that many of the problems of the United Front for which Chen has been blamed were a result of Comintern errors.[34] This position thus implicitly concedes that the

[30] Zhongguo guomindang zhongyang jiancha weiyuan hui [Chinese Guomindang Central Control Commission], *Danhe gongchandang liangda yaoan* [*Two important documents impeaching the Chinese Communist party*].

[31] For a discussion of this, see Lin Maosheng, "Dui Chen Duxiu."

[32] This is discussed in chapter 7.

[33] Cai Hesen, "Dang de jihui zhuyi shi" [The history of party opportunism], in *Chise dangan* [*Red documents*], ed. Li Minhun (Beijing, 1928).

[34] Lin Maosheng, "Dui Chen Duxiu"; idem, "Guanyu Chen Duxiu." See also Wang Yongchun and Chen Jiaxia, "Chen Duxiu zai guogong hezuo wenti shang de sixiang bianhua" [The transformations in Chen Duxiu's thoughts

Comintern had a major role in the early history of the party. But it does not get Chen Duxiu off the hook—it still views him as overly enamored, or at least too trusting, of the Russians. The Russians, not surprisingly, are also unwilling to let Chen off the hook. Most Russian authors still tend to follow the orthodox line on Chen that came out of the 1929 conference on "Chen Duxiuism" held in the Soviet Union in order to defend the Stalinist position on the failure in 1927 of the first CCP-KMT United Front. At this conference, Chen was said to have taken a "Menshevik" road as regards the Chinese revolution.[35] In particular, he was accused of having refused to carry out the policy of agrarian revolution after 1925. At this meeting, the former Comintern agent to China, Borodin, went even further, maintaining that Chen Duxiu and the Shanghai leadership of the party had since 1923 pursued a policy that ignored the agrarian revolution, believing that the major issue facing the country was that of imperialism.[36] I will argue in this book that this view of Chen as one who opposed the agrarian revolution is in general an unfair one, but it is the view that has prevailed in China and in the Soviet Union since the late 1920s. Ironically, Borodin's attempt—circumspect as it was—to show a fundamental disagreement between the part of the party he controlled and that over which Chen Duxiu maintained dominance was ignored and attacked, although I will argue here that there was some substance to Borodin's charges in this regard.

Recently a new view of the Chinese revolution has also surfaced in the Soviet Union, implying that Chen has been

on the question of cooperation between the Communists and the Nationalists]. *Dangshi yanjiu* 5 (Oct. 28, 1980). Also Tao Kangle, "Dui Chen Duxiu youqing jihui zhuyi luxian xingcheng de yidian renzhi" [A little understanding of the circumstances behind Chen Duxiu's right-wing opportunism], *Dangshi yanjiu* 5 (Oct. 28, 1980): 31–37.

[35] The principal spokesman for this position was Pavel Mif. For a discussion of this conference see Dan Jacobs, *Borodin: Stalin's Man in China*, pp. 306–12.

[36] Ibid. See also Lydia Holubnychy, *Michael Borodin and the Chinese Revolution, 1923–1925*, pp. 319–20.

guilty of leftist, not rightist, errors.[37] This view, which seeks to explain Chen's later Trotskyist activities and also to trace the problems of Maoism back through the early history of the party, has attempted to explain Chen's problem as a result of his belief in the possibility of an immediate socialist revolution for China without the necessity of a bourgeois stage to the revolution. It is as a consequence of his belief in the possibility of telescoping the revolution that Chen is said to have refused to consider alliances with the peasantry or any group other than the urban proletariat.

Whatever other problems it might have, this theory does consider Chen as an independent revolutionary theorist. In this it departs from all other interpretations of Chen; as different as the various interpretations of Chen are, they all share in common a tendency to perceive him as foolishly romantic in terms of his perception of the Chinese revolution and as overly infatuated with Western or at least foreign theories and ideas. One of the points of this study is that this image of Chen does not hold up under close scrutiny. This is not to say that the ideas of all previous writers on Chen have been completely incorrect, but that they have been derived in no small part from a misconception of Chen's role in the New Culture movement. Once it becomes clear that Chen was not simply an unthinking believer in Western solutions and ideas for China, it becomes easier to examine the murky ground surrounding Chen's decision to become a Marxist.

As I will demonstrate, Chen's Marxist ideas did not develop as suddenly as most have previously insisted. Like many traditional Chinese intellectuals—particularly those conservative liberals like Liang Qichao, Dai Jitao, and others—who had influenced him since 1915, Chen was captivated by socialism in the postwar period, seeing it as an alternative to capitalism that could utilize some of the existing Chinese social structure;

---

[37] "Novye materialy of pervom s'ezde Kommunisticheskoi Partii Kitaia" [New Materials on the First Congress of the Communist Party of China], *Norody Azii i Afriki [Peoples of Asia and Africa]* 6 (1972): 150–58. Although this article does not by itself seem all that suggestive, it created a great amount of discussion when I was in China in 1980–81.

Chen and his colleagues had been developing this point with regard to socialism since the early 1900s. Unlike his more conservative colleagues, however, Chen was willing to break with traditional political institutions to implement these ideas. Thus Chen, alone among his colleagues, willingly accepted Comintern aid in developing the first Chinese Communist party.

Chen did not accept this aid because of a simple naive faith in Soviet or Western solutions, as has sometimes been implied. Rather, Chen was aware of the very real help that the Comintern could give him and of the need to direct the Chinese radical youth—to whose needs he was always very sensitive—who were already breaking with the social and political institutions of the past. And in spite of his deep suspicions of Soviet intentions, Chen found himself enmeshed in the web of mechanisms created by the Soviet technicians who offered to help Chen in the construction of the party and in the increasing hostility of a youth movement that had a propensity to turn on leaders who appeared to falter or compromise. The traditional relationship that Chen had formed with his student followers in the years prior to 1922 did not serve very well once he and his followers were enveloped by the party organization, a lesson future Chinese leaders also were to learn.

When Chen finally turned to the formation of a Trotskyist group, it was not (as again almost all writers on Chen have implied), as a desperate reaction to his own expulsion from the party he had created. Having been disavowed by the Comintern, Chen did not simple-mindedly feel that he needed a new foreign inspiration. Rather, he had on his own begun to develop many ideas similar to those of Trotsky. Moreover, Chen also desired to continue his relationship with the urban intellectual youth he had once led so well. In the process, he was to articulate some of the complaints harbored by leftist intellectuals against the official party since that time. Chen's Trotskyist followers were the inheritors of the legacy of these urban intellectuals with whom Chen had been working since the early 1900s and who contributed so many ideas to the formation of dissent within the Chinese Communist party.

In the end Chen, like Trotsky, found himself misunderstood and denigrated by the very group he had helped found. But both men left a towering legacy in their respective countries. In a way, it is Chen's legacy that is the greater. If it is rare enough to find an individual who is able to supplant the values with which he was raised and to have an effect on changing the traditional values of his society, it is even rarer that a person is able to have an impact on more than one field, as did Chen Duxiu, who influenced not only the political but also the cultural and intellectual life of modern Chinese society. The scope of Chen's influence is all the more impressive when one notes that, practically alone among his contemporaries, Chen was a major figure through three separate periods of modern Chinese history: the pre-1911 Republican revolutionary period, the period of the May Fourth movement, and the period of the early history of the Chinese Communist party.

That one person could have such a great impact over such a broad historical field says much about the China of the early 1900s. It was probably only in China—and certainly not in the Russia of Trotsky—that one person could still have so much influence over both culture and politics. A division between culture and politics had not yet occurred in early twentieth-century Chinese society. In fact, the traditional association of intellectual and political activities in China led to a situation in which cultural concerns were expected of those involved in politics, so that the two were even more closely connected than in other premodern societies.

This close connection between culture and politics explains why Chen's cultural innovations gave him such great political influence over Chinese student youth. Bred to believe that they had a unique role to play in Chinese society and suddenly released from many of the fetters of their past, Chinese youth have proved to be the moving force in all the major changes that have occurred in Chinese society in the twentieth century. Chen was the chief theoretician and leader of this youth revolution in China in the earlier part of this century. Just as he was able to draw on the roots of traditional Chinese iconoclasm to legitimize his break with traditional Chinese ideas, so was he able to utilize the traditional roots of his influence among the youth to lead them in a radically new direction.

Taking advantage of the political respect traditionally given to cultural leaders, Chen infused these youth with a new sense of mission and purpose in transforming Chinese society, eventually leading them to communism. Even after he left the party, Chen continued to excite a small minority of party youth with demands for democratic reforms within the party and for the independence of artistic and literary activities. He in effect defined a special place for Chinese youth in the Marxist ideas he brought to China.

CHAPTER TWO
AWAKENING YOUTH

Chen Duxiu's life has always been clouded by an air of mystery, further thickened by constant rumor. This is partly to be expected in a man whose attitudes to the past were so ambivalent and paradoxical and who exhibited an extreme reluctance to discuss his private affairs even with his friends. In his later years, however, Chen decided to overcome this reticence and begin writing an autobiography with the idea of illustrating for others, through the story of his own struggle, the amount of effort necessary among members of his generation to overcome the weight of the past.[1]

But even in this document, which was never completed, Chen Duxiu confesses that he remembers little about his childhood and family and does not care to question friends and

[1] Chen Duxiu, *Shian zizhuan* [Chen Duxiu's autobiography], pp. 23–47. This has been translated by Richard Kagan, *China Quarterly*, 50 (April–June 1972): 301–14. The autobiography was written in mid-1937 while Chen was in prison. It was first published in the *Yuzhou feng* [*Universal Wind*]. Although the original plan was to write the story of Chen Duxiu's life through the May Fourth period, his writing was interrupted when he was unexpectedly let out of jail as a result of the establishment of the Second United Front between the KMT and the CCP. For the story of the writing of the autobiography, see Feng De, "Guanyu shian zizhuan" [Regarding Chen Duxiu's autobiography], *Gujin* [*Old and New*] 6 (Feb. 20, 1942). Zheng Xuejia has claimed that Chen wrote more than the two chapters that were published. But during extensive interviews in China in 1980–81 with people who have been doing research on Chen Duxiu or were close to Chen before his death, I turned up no one who had any knowledge of these extra chapters. This reconfirms what Tai Jingnong told me in an interview in Taipei in January 1975. Tai, who was close to Chen before he died, said that he did not believe that Chen had written any more of the autobiography than was published. For Zheng Xuejia's version of the story, see "Ban xin qingnian qian Chen Duxiu shenghuo de pianduan" [Fragments of Chen Duxiu's life prior to the publishing of *New Youth*], in *Zhonggong xingwang shi* [*The history of the rise and fall of the Chinese Communist party*], vol. 2, p. 764.

relatives in an effort to freshen his memory. Instead, he has
decided to concentrate only on those events that have left a
deep impression on him.

"FATHERLESS CHILD"

The first of these recollections is that he was a "fatherless
child" educated by an overly strict grandfather.[2] In his autobiography, Chen stresses that his father died when Chen
was only a few months old (a loss repeated, coincidentally,
in the early lives of almost every other future leader of the
May Fourth movement),[3] and that since he never really knew
his father at all, his iconoclastic revolt against Chinese tradition could in no way have been a revolt against his father,
as claimed by some of his contemporaries.[4]

But Chen was hardly the lonely orphan of humble origin
that he portrayed himself to be in his autobiography. Chen's
father, who had been a minor official and a tutor to a wealthy
family in Suzhou, died when Chen was actually two years—
not two months—old,[5] after which Chen was adopted by his
paternal uncle,[6] whose beneficent influence offset the harshness of Chen's grandfather-teacher, who died when Chen was

[2] Chen Duxiu, *Shian zizhuan*, p. 24.

[3] Lu Xun, Li Dazhao, Ba Jin, and Fu Sinian are just a few of the people
to whom this description applies.

[4] Chen Duxiu, *Shian zizhuan*, pp. 24–25.

[5] "Chen Yanzhong xiansheng zhuan" [A biography of Mr. Chen Yan-
zhong], as excerpted from the family genealogy and carried in Anqing shi
lishi xuehui [Anqing municipal historical committee] and Anqingshi tushuguan [Anqing municipal library], joint eds., *Chen Duxiu yanjiu cankao ziliao
[Research materials on Chen Duxiu]*, vol. 1, pp. 63–64. Also "Chen Yanzhong zhuan" [Biography of Chen Yanzhong], excerpted from the *Huaining
District Gazette* in ibid., p. 65. Also Zhang Dong, Xie Xunsheng, and Shi
Dunnan, "Chen Duxiu jiashi gaolue" [A brief study of Chen Duxiu's family
history], in ibid.

[6] "Fangwen Chen Songnian tanhua jilu" [Record of an interview with Chen
Songnian], May 25–26, 1979, draft prepared in manuscript form, confirmed
and signed by Chen Songnian. This information has also been noted by a
number of other sources, including almost all of Chen's family and close
friends. I first became aware of it in January 1975, after an interview with
Tai Jingnong.

ten. Chen's uncle had no children of his own, and he and his wife were very close to Chen and his older brother and were to remain so until their deaths—the uncle, Chen Xifan, passing away in 1913, his wife surviving until the late 1930s. Moreover, Chen's uncle was a powerful official who managed to accumulate a considerable amount of wealth during his tenure in office.[7]

To be sure, in not mentioning his adopted father, Chen may have been attempting to keep a pledge he made to his uncle in the early 1900s, when his uncle pretended to have Chen's name removed from the family genealogy as a result of the nephew's revolutionary activities. Chen thereafter publicly insisted that he no longer had anything to do with the family businesses, though this was merely a front designed to prevent the government from meddling with the family fortune in revenge against Chen Duxiu's antigovernment activities.[8] In spite of this ruse, much of Chen's uncle's fortune was plundered by government troops who raided the family house in 1913 and 1927 in Anqing,[9] the capital of Anhui at that time, because of Chen's radical involvements. In writing his autobiography, Chen may have been reluctant to jeopardize further the finances of his stepmother and his children; one of his sons was at that time attending college in Beijing, his education being financed by the income from the family antique shop in that city.[10]

Still, in describing himself as a lonely orphan raised until

[7] "Chen Xiawen tan Chen Duxiu" [Chen Xiawen discusses Chen Duxiu], as interviewed by Chen Songnian, Zhang Dong, and Wen Fengyan in *Chen Duxiu yanjiu cankao ziliao*, 1: 92–95. See also "Zaifang Chen Songnian tanhua jilu" [Another record of an interview with Chen Songnian], November 1979, in *Anhui gemingshi yanjiu ziliao* [Materials on the history of the revolution in Anhui], vol. 1, ed. Anhuisheng shehui kexuesuo lishi yanshi [Anhui provincial social science group historical research bureau], pp. 9–10. Finally, see "Guanyu jiachan xingbai de huiyi" [Recalling the rise and fall of the family fortune], draft of an interview with Chen Songnian from July 29, 1980.

[8] Zhang Jun et al., "Chen Duxiu jiashi gaolue," p. 192.

[9] Ibid. See also Chen Xiawen, "Chen Xiawen tan Chen Duxiu." Also Chen Songnian, "Zaifang Chen Songnian tanhua jilu."

[10] Chen Songnian, "Guanyu jiachan xingbai de huiyi."

he was ten by an opium-smoking, tyrannical grandfather, Chen was probably also attempting to maintain his public image as a dedicated revolutionary rather than as the rich scion of an official family. The grandfather Chen described in his autobiography bore a striking resemblance to the grandfather in Ba Jin's *The Family (Jia)*, a novel that became a classic for the Chinese youth in the 1920s and 1930s who were in rebellion against the ethos of the old society.[11] In both works, the grandfathers' corrupt hypocritical moralism seems to exemplify the problems of the old Confucian order. Even if Chen's grandfather, who appeared to his contemporaries to be a cultured and learned man, was indeed as fierce as Chen portrayed him to be, still we must ask why Chen chose to write about him at such length in his autobiography. One likely explanation is that Chen, as we will see, was obsessed with maintaining the loyalty and admiration of a youthful radical audience; his descriptions of the meanness of his grandfather played to the antipatriarchal passions of that audience. (At almost the same time Mao Zedong, who was similarly interested in gaining a loyal following among Chinese youth, was dictating an autobiography in which he depicted himself as the rebellious victim of a tyrannical father.)[12]

Most of those who embraced this antifeudalism were themselves strongly influenced by the values of their own family, and Chen was no exception. In spite of Chen's self-description as an opponent of the traditional ideals of his family, there are hints that his family was very important in helping to shape his lifelong attitudes toward both the West and the Chinese official class. His genealogy[13]—his father and grandfather were teachers and minor officials, another uncle had been a minor official, and before then his ancestors had been mostly peasants—suggests an up-and-coming family who had improved its standing through hard work and enterprise, not through official connections. The local annals confirm that

[11] For a discussion of this, see Olga Lang, *Pa Chin and His Writings: Chinese Youth Between Two Generations.*
[12] Edgar Snow, *Red Star Over China*, pp. 121–34.
[13] Zhang Dong et al., "Chen Duxiu jiashi gaolue."

Chen's uncle was an unpretentious man with a common touch.[14] A *juren* of relatively humble origin, the uncle rose to be the chief magistrate of Liangyang *zhou* or region.[15] (Today this area encompasses much of Liaoning province, including the city of Shengyang.) This rapid rise on the part of someone with such an undistinguished background suggests a master of administrative and personal details. One would expect that Chen's uncle would also have a certain disdain for those in the upper-level scholar-gentry class who depended on his practical knowledge to maintain their power; these were the same elites Chen would attack so vehemently throughout his career.

Certainly Chen's uncle was quick to take advantage of the opportunities provided by the West to enhance the family fortune; his wealth is said to have increased greatly during the Russo-Japanese War, when he was lucky enough to be the head of a district in Manchuria where taxes were being collected on horses transshipped from Mongolia for sale to the belligerents. The family fortune had already grown shortly before this time, when a British firm in Beijing supplied Chen's uncle with the capital to set up an exclusive soybean purchasing center in his district; the soybeans purchased under this monopolistic arrangement were in turn sold to the British company in Beijing for a fixed price. The Chen family fortune suffered a small disaster in 1913 when a British company set up a second soybean purchasing center in the same district, destroying the monopoly the uncle had had over the price in the area and making it impossible for him to deliver the beans to Beijing at the price promised.[16]

Of course none of these details about Chen's uncle found its way into his autobiography. It is understandable that Chen, who recorded his life story while he was in jail for his Communist and Trotskyist activities, would not want the facts

[14] Ibid. Also, "Chen Xifan xiansheng zhuan" [A biography of Mr. Chen Xifan], excerpted from the *Huaining District Gazette* in *Chen Duxiu yanjiu cankao ziliao*, vol. 1, pp. 62–63.

[15] Ibid.

[16] Chen Songnian, "Zaifang Chen Songnian tanhua jilu." Also Chen Songnian, "Guanyu jiachan xingbai de huiyi."

about the family business to be known to his readers. More-over, the traditional Confucian bias against mercantile activities might have made Chen even more reluctant to discuss his uncle's dealings. It is nonetheless interesting to continue to speculate on the extent of the influence of this family background upon Chen. For example, every comprador, while admiring the techniques of his Western partner, also resented the way he was being used and felt that if he were freed of governmental restraints and imperialist oppression, he could manage all the affairs single-handedly at a better profit for himself and his family. Chen Duxiu, throughout much of the first forty years of his life, reflected this belief, insisting that tremendous rewards awaited the Chinese if they could adopt Western methods without the restraining influence of either their autocratic government or imperialism.

But Chen also reacted against much of what he was exposed to in his family surroundings. Throughout his life he complained about how the Chinese traditional culture encouraged officials to enhance their own family fortune rather than think of the public benefit. He particularly denounced those Chinese who allowed themselves to be tools of foreign business interests.

STUDENT OF TRADITION

More important than Chen's family background on the formation of his later character was the cultural and intellectual milieu to which he was exposed at an early age. As Chen relates in his autobiography, he was immersed in the Confucian classics while he was young. He never mentions the specific schools of Han or Song learning that he studied, but he does state that very early in life he became bored with the official Eight-Legged essay style and preferred to read the *Zhaoming wenxuan*, a sixth-century collection of parallel verse containing many obscure characters. Chen's study of these characters hints at an early interest in the ideas of the *kaozheng*, or evidential research movement, whose proponents had undermined much of the orthodox neo-Confucian Song

learning school. He also mentions reading the works of Yuan
Mei, the eccentric eighteenth-century poet, who was an eloquent advocate of women's rights, particularly of women's
literature, a critic of the examination system, and a proponent
of writing that freely expressed emotion. By mentioning these
topics, Chen was signaling to his Chinese readers his early
identification with iconoclastic elements within Chinese tradition. He does not explain his interest in these works in any
great detail, but he does attempt to excuse his later success
in the civil service examination by implying that his knowledge
of obscure characters confused the ignorant examiners.

In reality, Chen, like many of those who had begun to
experiment with traditional iconoclastic ideas, was also an apt
student of the official culture—which may account for the
vehemence with which he opposed it later. Chen passed his
xiucai, or the first level of the Confucian civil service examination, in 1896 at the precocious age of 17, ranking as the
number-one candidate in his district.[17] He was not as successful at the imperial examination in 1897, when he sat for
his *juren*, or the second level of the civil service exam, an event
described vividly in his autobiography.

To compete in this higher-level examination Chen traveled
with his brother, Chen Mengji, his brother's tutor, and several
other students to Nanjing, where the biennial test was held.
Chen was the only member of his group who had not com-
peted in the previous provincial examinations, and as he approached the Nanjing city wall for the first time, riding on
the back of a donkey, his heart soared. The gigantic phoenix
gate on the outside of the city was considerably bigger than
were the city gates of his hometown in Anqing, and he imagined that the buildings and the street markets of the city would
be dazzlingly beautiful. But he was disappointed; the city was
as dirty and run-down as the provincial capital he had left
behind in Anhui. "The levelness and width of the big streets
in the northern section were heavenly compared with those
of Anqing's . . . nevertheless, the buildings were just as small

[17] Chen Duxiu, *Shian zizhuan*, p. 34.

and cracked as Anqing's. The slums in the northern part of town matched Anqing's just like a brother. Nanjing's special character was only that it was big. ...."[18]

If the city was not exactly as Chen may have envisioned it, the often crude behavior of Chen's fellow students was even more of an eye-opener. Under the tension of waiting for the exams and in the companionship of the moment, many of the students indulged in constant whoring and pranks. The merchants and shopkeepers of the city had no way to protect their shops against thefts or their daughters against seduction by these exalted members of the "intelligentsia."

Any affront would stir the candidates up into a melee. Passing students, whether they knew the others or not, would rush to help. The merchants knew that the real reason that the candidates came forward was not to help in the battle but to steal as much as they could in the confusion. Even if they were informed of the theft by the merchant, the officials couldn't do anything about the many and influential candidates.[19]

Fortunately, the opportunities afforded by the congregation of so many young students were not purely libidinal but intellectual as well, allowing for the exchange of new ideas and attitudes. Because they allowed large numbers of young members of the gentry class to assemble for several months at a time, the examinations had traditionally served as sounding boards for the gentry class.[20] The 1897 exam in which Chen participated was politically a very significant one, coming as it did on the heels of China's humiliating defeat by Japan under the terms of the Treaty of Shimonoseki signed in April of 1895. Reform groups of examination candidates under the leadership of Kang Youwei and other liberal gentry leaders had already begun to petition the capital for changes in the

[18] Chen Duxiu, *Shian zizhuan*, p. 37.
[19] Ibid., p. 39.
[20] Kang Youwei, for instance, first came to the attention of the central government in 1895 when he got over a thousand signatures on a petition against the Treaty of Shimonoseki.

traditional Chinese political system. The movement, which was then right on the verge of its short-lived political success known as the Hundred Days of Reform, was centered in the main coastal and Yangzi River towns. Consequently, Nanjing was a hotbed of reformist organizations and newspapers.[21] One can imagine Chen, alienated by the crudities of the older students and the new living conditions to which he was exposed, eagerly listening to discussions of Western concepts and devouring news of the foreign world.

When it finally came time for the examination, an event far more grueling than Chen had imagined even in his most dreary moments, these new ideas took on added significance for Chen. Short of stature and frequently sickly, the eighteen-year-old boy wearily lugged "an examination basket, books, writing materials, food and provisions, the cooking stove, and an oil cloth" through the mob of students into the narrow little stalls where the candidates lived during the nine days of testing. Terrified and nearly overwhelmed by the crowd, Chen was saved from being crushed only through the aid of his elder brother. Inside, where he would have to sleep sitting on the board that was to be his writing table, cobwebs and soot covered the place so liberally that it was difficult to sweep it clean. In the hot summer air, the cooking stoves of the students "turned the long passageway into a fire alley." For Chen, who knew nothing about cooking, there was nothing to eat "but half-cooked, or overcooked, or globbed noodles" during the nine days of the three examinations.[22] Even worse was the fate of the other students. Since there were no toilets, the students merely used any available empty room to relieve themselves. When the rooms were reassigned during the second examination, some were forced "to endure a terrible stink for three days."[23]

Conditioned by the iconoclastic authors he had been read-

[21] See H. B. Morse, *The International Relations of the Chinese Empire*, vol. 3, pp. 128–33.

[22] Chen Duxiu, *Shian zizhuan*, pp. 41–42; (translation adapted from Kagan, *Chen Duxiu's Autobiography*, pp. 313–14).

[23] Ibid.

ing on his own, Chen now found the system unbearable. He began to "question the whole phenomenon of selecting men of talent by the examination system. It was just like an animal exhibition of monkeys and bears performing every few years."[24]

In this negative mood (Chen may have been further discouraged because he failed his *juren* examination, though he never states so explicitly in his autobiography), Chen Duxiu was attracted to a new kind of iconoclasm, the writings of the reformers Kang Youwei and Liang Qichao in publications such as *Chinese Progress (Shihwu bao)*, which he now discovered. Later Chen was to relate on several occasions that it was only after reading the works of Kang Youwei that he learned for the first time that not everyone who studied Western learning was a "slave to the foreign devil."[25] For Kang showed Chen that Western learning could be as respectable as the iconoclastic Chinese studies he had coveted earlier.

Heady with these ideas, Chen resolved to join the reformist group of Kang Youwei and Liang Qichao. He collected some of his ideas of this period in a pamphlet he published in Anqing shortly after returning from the 1897 examination. Entitled *An Account of the Topography of the Yangzi River (Yangzi jiang xingshi lunlue)*, the article is a detailed geography of the Yangzi "based on old travel books as well as the descriptions of foreigners."[26] The pamphlet details the points at which the Yangzi could and should be defended to protect the area from foreign incursion. It discusses where military units should be stationed, how guns should be positioned, and the kinds of naval vessels that could come up the river.

The book is at first glance a surprising document, quite unlike all of Chen Duxiu's later writings. But members of the

[24] Ibid., p. 42; Kagan, *Chen Duxiu's Autobiography*, p. 314.

[25] Chen Duxiu, "Bo Kang Youwei zhi zongtong zongli shu" [Refuting Kang Youwei's petition to the President and the Premier], *Xin Qingnian [New Youth]*, vol. 2, no. 2 (Oct. 1, 1916). See also "Kongzi zhidao yu xiandai shenghuo" [The Confucian way and present-day Life], *Xin Qingnian*, vol. 2, no. 4 (Dec. 1, 1916).

[26] Chen Duxiu, *Yangzi jiang xingshi lunlue [An account of the topography of the Yangzi River]* (Anqing, 1897; reprinted in *Chen Duxiu yanjiu cankao ziliao*), pp. 169–80.

school of Han learning, such as the early nineteenth-century scholar and founder of the Guangzhou naval academy Ruan Yuan, had long been interested in problems of naval defense and geography.[27] Having learned about the growing foreign invasion of the country as well as about Western ideas during his stay in Nanjing, Chen was naturally interested in foreign accounts of China as well as the writings of those Chinese who had already begun to make studies of practical ways of defending and arming the country. Couched in very polite terms, the document shows evidence of Chen's later stylistic brilliance and his already virulent nationalism. The piece ends by calling on the government to take action "to avoid the ruin of our nation" and imploring the people to "care about the fate of our country."[28]

Perhaps these words—so mild in retrospect but clearly identifying Chen as part of the movement for reform that swept the youthful gentry examination candidates—created the shock felt among the local gentry of this town when Chen became a member of the Kang-Liang group. Chen says nothing about the reaction of his own family.[29] It may be that his uncle, who was then probably beginning his dealings with his British partners, thought that it would not hurt the boy to learn about the practical techniques of the West. It is more likely that the uncle, while not discouraging Chen from learning more about the West, also persuaded him to abandon temporarily his reform efforts and pursue his examination studies. Although in his autobiography Chen claims to have broken off his examination studies after sitting for his *juren* examination in Nanjing,[30] in fact after 1897 he followed his uncle to Manchuria, where the latter personally undertook to tutor Chen.[31] Chen was therefore not in Anhui in 1898 when Kang and his followers succeeded in coming to power temporarily in the ill-fated Hundred Days of Reform.

[27] Elman, *From Philosophy to Philology.*
[28] Chen Duxiu, *Yangzi jiang xingshi lunlue.*
[29] Chen Duxiu, *Shian zizhuan.*
[30] Ibid.
[31] Chen Songnian, "Fangwen Chen Songnian tanhua jilu."

COMING OF AGE

Certainly Chen's reformist activities did not do too much harm to his reputation. In 1896 or 1897 his uncle was able to arrange a high-status marriage for him to a woman named Gao Xiaomen, whose father, a former classmate of Chen's uncle, was the military prefect of Anqing and even wealthier and more powerful than the uncle.[32] The marriage was not a particularly happy one. Chen's wife was a very traditional woman who rarely set foot outside her house and had little sympathy for Chen's radical ideas—the opposite, incidentally, of her younger, college-educated, Western-dressed half-sister, with whom Chen would later have a long-lasting liaison.[33] In 1902, when Chen wanted to go to Japan to study for the first time, his wife refused to part with some of her gold bracelets to finance his trip.[34]

These experiences with his wife may have confirmed for Chen the value of education for women, although this idea was not new. Education for women had been proposed by many former iconoclastic Chinese writers such as the poet Yuan Mei,[35] whose writings had interested Chen during his examination studies.[36] The famous sixteenth-century philosopher Li Zhi had argued that widows should have the privilege to remarry and that women should have the right to choose their own marital partners.[37] And one of the most vociferous advocates of women's rights was the early eighteenth-century Anhui novelist Wu Jingzi.[38] In more modern times, Kang Youwei found justification for his ideas on women from both

[32] Ma Qirong and San Yijiao, "Guanyu Chen Duxiu yinqin de xie qingkuang" [A few circumstances according to Chen Duxiu's relatives], draft of a series of interviews conducted in August 1980 in Beijing.
[33] "Chen Duxiu de sanwei furen" [Chen Duxiu's three wives], in Chen Duxiu yanjiu cankao ziliao, vol. 1, p. 94.
[34] Zhang Dong et al., "Chen Duxiu jiashi gaolue," p. 194.
[35] Arthur Waley, Yuan Mei: Eighteenth Century Chinese Poet, Stanford, 1957. Also Paul Ropp, Dissent in Early Modern China (Ann Arbor, 1981), esp. chap. 4.
[36] Chen Duxiu, Shian zizhuan.
[37] Ropp, Dissent, esp. chap. 4.
[38] Ibid., esp. pts. 2 and 3.

traditional and Western sources.[39] The topic is an excellent example of how ideas to which Chen was exposed early merged with Western notions to reinforce his own personal experiences—in this case the difficulties he encountered in his marriage.

Chen would soon learn more about both Chinese and Western iconoclastic values. In 1899 he returned from Manchuria to Anqing to attend the funeral of his natural mother.[40] It is said that Chen then went to Hangzhou, near Shanghai, in 1900[41] (another source claims, however, that Chen may instead have returned to Manchuria, staying there until 1902)[42] to become a student at the Chiushi Academy, the first institution to teach Western as well as traditional subjects in the southern Yangzi Valley region.[43] The radical scholar Zhang Binglin had taught at the school before Chen arrived, and his influence still lingered. The academy's emphasis on iconoclastic interpretations of Chinese tradition as well as on Western ideas proved to be a combination of tremendous appeal to Chen Duxiu. His decision to attend this school also meant

[39] Lawrence Thompson, "Ta-t'ung Shu and the Communist Manifesto," in *Jung-pang Lo, K'ang Yu-wei: A Biography and A Symposium* (Tucson, 1967).

[40] Chen Duxiu, "Shuai" [An expression of my grief], *Jiayin zazhi*, vol. 1, no. 5 (May 10, 1915).

[41] Most writers on Chen Duxiu's life have claimed that he entered the Chiushi Academy in 1897 or 1898. This is apparently based on a statement in Julie Lien-ying How's dissertation to the effect that Chen entered the Chiushi Academy after he failed his examination; see Julie Lien-ying How, "The Development of Ch'en Tu-hsiu's Thought, 1915–1938" (Master's thesis, Columbia Univ., 1949), p. 42. This does not agree with what Chen Duxiu mentioned of his own activities in the poem "Shuai," ibid. Moreover, the revolutionary tide at this school with which Chen Duxiu usually is associated did not begin until 1901. See Mary Backus Rankin, *Early Chinese Revolutionaries: Radical Intellectuals in Shanghai and Chekiang, 1902–1911*, pp. 140–43.

[42] Li Fanqun, ed., "Chen Duxiu nianbiao buzheng" [A correction of Chen Duxiu's yearly chronology], in *Chen Duxiu yanjiu cankao ziliao*, vol. 1, p. 225. Working off the same material that I have already quoted, the author of this work has decided that Chen Duxiu went to Hangzhou in 1897 and then the following year joined his uncle in Manchuria.

[43] See note 41.

a final break with his examination studies. While at the school, Chen is said to have enrolled in a naval architecture program, probably to continue the studies that had led to the publication of his 1897 pamphlet, "An Account of the Topography of the Yangzi River."[44]

The Chiushi Academy became one of the centers of the new Chinese student culture. The name *chiushi* (search for the truth) was a familiar slogan of the *kaozheng* movement and the school was evidently established in the tradition of the radical *kaozheng* academies that had flourished in the area during the eighteenth century. The sense of distinctiveness that had been felt by the students in these schools was now enhanced by the new Western learning to which the Chiushi students were exposed, as well as by the feeling that China was confronting an urgent crisis. The students at the school were immersed in a situation in which they lived together in areas separated from their families and much of the outside world, where they engaged in a learning process emphasizing that certain age levels were related to certain degrees of academic achievement, and where they studied a cultural pattern and set of ideas totally dissimilar to those of their tradition. As a result of these new experiences and living patterns, Chinese students began to develop a feeling of separateness from their society as well as a conception of youth as a special phase of social development.[45] Since the ideas they were studying were those which supposedly contained answers to the myriad of problems confronting China, many of these youth developed a particular sense of mission about their role within Chinese society as well as a feeling of hostility—sometimes even rebelliousness—toward the ideas and traditions of their elders.

In 1901 several of the students and teachers at the Chiushi Academy were expelled after being involved in a minor but highly celebrated confrontation with the Qing government over the insertion of an antigovernment phrase in an essay

[44] Chen Duxiu, *Yangzi jiang xingshi lunlue.*
[45] Chow Tse-tsung, *The May Fourth Movement*, p. 96. Also see Marion Levy, *The Family Revolution in Modern China*, p. 90.

circulated among the students and faculty.[46] Chen is rumored to have been among those forced to flee the school after speaking out about the incident.[47] According to some sources, Chen went first to Nanjing, where Zhang Shizhao was running a kind of underground revolutionary dormitory. Chen was certainly in Nanjing in 1901–1902, for it was there that he was to become acquainted with his lifelong friend and sometime benefactor, Wang Mengzou.[48] By the end of 1902, Chen was in Japan, where he and other former participants in the Chiushi Academy helped establish the Youth Society (Qingnian hui), the first avowedly revolutionary organization among Chinese students in Japan.[49]

In Japan even more than at Chiushi, the Chinese students nurtured a sense of themselves as different from the rest of their society. Far from home, suddenly confronted with the necessity of thinking of themselves in nationalist terms as a result of the alien, often hostile, environment in which they were living, the Chinese students naturally began to develop a distinct culture and life style. This was reinforced by the Japanese students with whom the young Chinese then came into contact, for the Japanese students were themselves

[46] For an account of this see Rankin, *Early Chinese Revolutionaries*, p. 142.

[47] See Chow, *May Fourth Movement*, p. 42. This may have been based on He Zhiyu, "Duxiu zhuzuo nianbiao" [A chronology of Chen Duxiu], in *Duxiu Congshu Qizhong [Seven works by Duxiu]*, vol. 1 (Shanghai, 1948), p. 2. He mentions Chen fleeing in 1901 after giving an anti-Manchu speech and then meeting up with Zhang Shizhao. He, however, is referring to Chen's flight from Anhui following the dissolution of the Anhui Patriotic Society in 1903. His date here was off by two years.

[48] Wang Mengzou, "Dongya jianshi" [A brief history of the East Asian Publishing House], in *Anhui gemingshi yanjiu ziliao*, vol. 1, p. 10.

[49] Feng Ziyou, *Geming yishi [Anecdotes of the Chinese revolution]*, vol. 1, pp. 151–54; vol. 3, pp. 67–70. Zhang Shizhao, "Shu huangdi hun" [Comments on the spirit of the yellow emperor], in Zhongguo renmin zhengzhi xieshang huiyi chuanguo weiyuan hui wenshi ziliao yanjiu weiyuan hui (Committee on written materials of the national committee of the Chinese people's political consultive conference), ed., *Xinhai geming huiyi lu [A record of remembrances of the 1911 revolution]*, vol. 1, p. 130. See also Chun-tu Hsueh, *Huang Hsing and the Chinese Revolution*, p. 8.

undergoing a period of cultural change. Most important, the Chinese students' sense of distinctness was buttressed by the earthshaking (to them) ideas then being studied in Japan. The turn-of-the-century liberal democratic and scientific concepts they studied told the students in Spencerian terms that change was inevitable and that progress would come to those who threw off the fetters of family, superstition, and political repression and allowed the emergence of their individual potential—a potential that youth in general and Chinese youth in particular under these heady circumstances tended to value very highly. Under the influence of these notions and the new cultural norms and dress to which they were exposed, Chinese youth now attempted to mold themselves into the embodiment of this emancipation from traditional norms and habits. The sense of self-importance and rebellion that had always been present in the Ming and Qing academies and even earlier, and had caused the traditional examination-time madness described vividly by Chen in his autobiography, could now express itself as part of a full-fledged student culture.

The name of the student group Chen Duxiu helped form in Japan, the Youth Society, reflected the youths' new feeling about themselves as a special group capable of revitalizing their country.[50] The name was taken from that of another political association of youth who had played an important role in the transformation of their country. This was the Young Italy society organized by the leader of the Italian unification movement, Giuseppe Mazzini. The Chinese students greatly admired Mazzini as a promoter of national independence and leader of youthful revolutionaries. Besides Chen Duxiu, the Youth Society's members included many of the famous early nationalist leaders, such as Zhang Ji, Su Manshu, and Feng Ziyou.

Members of the Youth Society became especially concerned about Russian activities in the Manchurian provinces, an area of interest to the Chen family. In April 1903 most of the group formed a student volunteer army, which rather superciliously

[50] Ibid.

offered its services to the Qing government to help fight the
Russians, demonstrating not only their nationalist sentiments
but also their condescending attitude toward their government's capabilities.

Chen Duxiu departed from Japan shortly after this army
was formed (it was subsequently disbanded by the Qing government), expelled for his part in a frequently cited episode.
Chen and several of his fellow students had broken into the
office of the government agent appointed to watch over Hubei
student affairs in Japan. The man had made himself especially
unpopular with his attempts to regulate the activities of all
the Chinese students in Japan; the students also felt that he
had been guilty of sexual improprieties. To punish the agent,
Zhang Ji and Zou Rong held the man down, while Chen
Duxiu manned scissors and cut off the man's queue, which
was later hung in the Chinese student union.[51]

This incident created a sensation among the radical students
in Japan and caused a diplomatic uproar that ended in the
expulsion of Chen Duxiu and his cohorts.[52] Zou Rong and
Zhang Ji went off to Shanghai, where Zou Rong made the
acquaintance of the activist scholar Zhang Binglin and became
involved in the radical student newspaper, the Subao. When
this paper ran afoul of the authorities in mid-1903, Zhang
and Zou were imprisoned, and Zou Rong eventually died in
jail. Chen Duxiu was not directly involved in the Subao incident. After leaving Japan, he returned to his native Anhui,
where in the space of a few short months he helped establish
a small revolutionary library, which later grew into the basis
for the Anhui provincial library. He also participated in the
Youth Determination Study Society (Qingnian lizhi xuehui),[53]
an organization of like-minded political reformists, and then
helped form the first major Anhui revolutionary group, the

[51] Zhang Shizhao, "Shu huangdi hun," p. 229.
[52] Ibid.
[53] Li Fanqun, "Chen Duxiu nianbiao buzhong," p. 226. See also Ren Jian-
shu, Wu Xinzhong, and Zhang Tongmo, "Chen Duxiu he Anhui suhua bao"
[Chen Duxiu and the Anhui Vernacular Journal], in Dangshi ziliao [Materials
on party history], vol. 1, pp. 69–78.

Anhui Patriotic Society (Anhui aiguo hui), to organize his fellow students in mobilizing sentiment in his native province against the Russian usurpation of Manchuria.[54] The zeal that Chen and these other students demonstrated in all of their activities stemmed from their sense of themselves as part of a special group that would replace the scholar-gentry class. This sentiment was expressed vividly in an article published by Chinese students in Japan. In the *Hubei Student World (Hubei xuesheng jie)*, Li Shuceng maintained that the students occupied a unique position between the corrupt unchangeable officials on the top and the uncultured common people on the bottom. The officials, he insisted, because of their tendency to jockey for power, were naturally inclined to yield to the foreigners. The job of the student intellectuals was therefore to bypass the officials and to lead the people, teaching the commoners about the skills and democratic institutions of the West.[55] In forming his Anhui Patriotic Society, Chen manifested what was to become his lifelong belief that the principal actors within the society should no longer be the scholar-gentry but the new student stratum.

THE ANHUI PATRIOTIC SOCIETY

Chen based the Anhui Patriotic Society in his native town of Anqing in 1903, shortly after the provincial capital had been made into a treaty port under the terms of the Sino-British trade agreement of 1902.[56] The organization was composed primarily of students from the three major institutions of higher learning in the province, the Anhui Upper Level School, the Military Preparatory Academy, and the Tong-

[54] "Anhui aiguohui zhi chengjiu" [The establishment of the Anhui Patriotic Society], *Subao*, May 25, 1903, pp. 1–2.
[55] Li Shucheng, "Xuesheng zhi jingzheng" [Student struggle], *Hubei xuesheng jie [Hubei Student World]* 2:9.
[56] For a discussion of the effects of this, see Anhui kexue fen yuan lishi yanjiu shi jindaishi zu diaocha [The investigative branch for modern history in the Anhui Scientific Institute's Department of Historical Research], "Wuhu dichu de xinhai geming" [The 1911 Revolution in the Wuhu area], *Anhui shixue tongsu [The Anhui Historical Studies Bulletin]*, 14 (Dec. 1959):1.

cheng Public School.[57] Chen's new group was able to take advantage of both the nationalist sentiment aroused by the imperialist incursions into his native province and the newly developed political consciousness of the youth in Anhui—feelings similar to those he had already observed among the Chinese students in Hangzhou, Nanjing, and Tokyo.

Chen clearly saw the student members of his society as a group that would assume the role of leading the masses. The constitution that he helped write for the Anhui Patriotic Society announced that "because the foreign calamity is daily growing worse, the society seeks to unite the masses into an organization that will develop patriotic thought and stir up a martial spirit, so people will grab their weapons to protect their country and restore our basic national sovereignty."[58] This proclamation was followed by a series of prohibitions. Individual freedom that "interfered with the national welfare" would not be permitted, but at the same time members were warned against "blindly hating all foreigners" in the pursuit of that welfare. Furthermore, members were forbidden "all vices such as smoking cigarettes, visiting prostitutes, and gambling."[59] Instead, a rigorous physical and moral regimen was prescribed. Those who joined the society had to exercise daily, in regular physical education classes if possible but otherwise in self-organized groups; anyone missing more than three exercise sessions was to be expelled from the organization.

This concern with moral rectitude and physical vigor, which has been a common element of many youth groups throughout the world, was especially prevalent among the early (and later) Chinese student revolutionary groups. Exercise groups were particularly widespread. In March 1903 the Patriotic School in Shanghai (founded by Cai Yuanpei and closely associated with the *Subao*) established a physical-education society that it hoped would spread throughout the country; one month after the start of this program, Chen affiliated his Anhui Pa-

[57] "Anhui aiguohui zhi chengjiu," pp. 1–2.

[58] "Anhui aiguohui nizhang" [Proposed constitution of the Anhui Patriotic Society], *Subao*, June 7, 1903.

[59] Ibid.

triotic Society with the school.[60] Since physical strength and vitality are prime characteristics of youth, it is not surprising that the students involved in the early Chinese youth movement stressed the need for physical activity; one would imagine they had felt extraordinarily frustrated by the years of solely mental efforts necessary for the study of their Confucian classics. They felt this was especially important since one of China's prime problems at that time was the obvious physical weakness of the nation's military. Chen remained convinced throughout his life that physical well-being was the cure to many of the ills of Chinese society. It was a concern he was to share with Mao Zedong, whose first published article was an essay on the virtues of exercise, selected by Chen in 1917 for the pages of New Youth.[61]

All this huffing and puffing by Anhui Patriotic Society members to get into shape was directed to the opposition of a secret treaty that had just been signed between the Chinese and Russian governments, giving the Russians considerable economic and political power in Manchuria.[62] "If our government allows this treaty," Chen Duxiu maintained in an emotional speech to an overflow crowd at the organizational meeting of the Anhui Patriotic Society, "every nation will moisten its lips and help itself to a part of China,"[63] and in the end China will not have "one foot or inch of clean land."[64] Chen was particularly adamant in his denunciation of this treaty because he had personally seen the Russian occupation of Manchuria in the wake of the Boxer Rebellion. And, as he related to his audience in graphic detail, he had also observed firsthand the brutality of the Russian troops and officials in Manchuria toward the Chinese population, as well as the

[60] Chen Youji (Chen Duxiu), "Anhui aiguohui yanshuo" [Lecture to the Anhui Patriotic Society], Subao, May 26, 1903, p. 2. See also "Anhui aiguohui zhi chengjiu."

[61] Ershibahua (Mao Zedong), "Tiyu zhi yanjiu" [A study of athletics], Xin Qingnian [New Youth], vol. 3, no. 2 (April 1, 1917).

[62] Chen Youji (Chen Duxiu), "Anhui aiguohui yanshuo." See also "Anhui aiguohui zhi chengjiu."

[63] Chen Youji (Chen Duxiu), "Anhui aiguohui yanshuo."

[64] "Anhui aiguohui zhi chengjiu."

subservience of the Qing government officials (perhaps including his uncle) in this area toward the Russians. Chen, like almost all Chinese revolutionaries and reformers, felt that if the Chinese people were to stand a chance of defeating the Russians, they would have to unite. "When we go to war with our Russian enemies, we must be united. If there is one person not willing to fight to the death against the Russians, then none of us can be considered manly."[65]

Chen was not overly optimistic that this united struggle on the part of the Chinese people would occur. Chen deplored, as he would throughout his life, what he considered to be the backward, self-serving traditions of the Chinese people. "The Chinese people," he feared, "do not know how to struggle for glory or against insults. They seek to live dishonorably in the world, willingly receiving the extermination of their country (*mieguo*) and their own enslavement."[66] Reversing Western stereotypes of "oriental" imperviousness to death in the defense of honor, Chen maintained that the "foreigners' character is such that they will struggle for glory or against insult, lightly regarding matters of life and death. They prefer to die for their nation rather than live as slaves."[67] The Chinese, however, "only know how to covet life and fear death. Even when they are insulted, they are afraid to show any opposition."[68]

Comments like these earned Chen a reputation for gloomy words; years later Li Dazhao was to complain about the "fog of pessimism" that hung over the writings of Chen and many other intellectuals in the wake of the failure of the 1913 revolution.[69] It is true that such pessimism pervaded Chen's writings not only after 1913 but well before 1911—no doubt in part a result of his disillusionment with the traditional Chinese elite. But since Chen also had hope for the new youth organ-

[65] Chen Youji (Chen Duxiu), "Anhui aiguohui yanshuo."
[66] Ibid.
[67] Ibid.
[68] Ibid.
[69] Li Dazhao, "Yanshi xin yu zijue xin" [Pessimism and self-consciousness], *Jiayin zazhi*, vol. 1, no. 9 (Aug. 10, 1915).

izations such as the Anhui Patriotic Society, he was actually not as pessimistic as he sometimes sounded. What Li did not realize is that these statements of criticism were in part rhetorical—designed to spur Chen's audience into action by taunting them so that they would not depend on their government and its officials but act for themselves. In the speech just quoted, Chen made this very clear by following up his negative remarks with a question. "Alas, are we Chinese really like this? Or is it that other countries are only boasting . . . ? We should take the responsibility of struggling to the death to protect our land."[70]

Another explanation for the harshness of Chen's language can be found in the "moral passion" he displayed throughout his life in his vehement attacks on traditional leaders and ideas. Ironically, in his autobiography Chen criticized the strict moralism of his grandfather, his first Confucian teacher, and implied that it was a result of the Confucian tradition.[71] Chen of course was not aware that he displayed a similarly strict moralism; in fact he criticized himself for being too weak. But the concern for moral rectitude that is part of the Confucian tradition has often led to a fear of moral weakness among Confucians. It has been suggested that Liang Shuming, fourteen years younger than Chen, was testing his moral rectitude when he publicly remonstrated with Mao Zedong in 1953.[72] In Chinese tradition, a sense of moral rectitude is so closely associated with Confucianism that Mao Zedong's teacher, Yang Changji, a Kantian scholar who was a friend of Chen Duxiu and a writer for *New Youth*, was, in spite of his very antitraditional ideas, popularly known among his students as the "Confucianist" precisely "because of his stern regard for morality";[73] the description could also be used in that context for Chen Duxiu himself.

[70] Chen Youji (Chen Duxiu), "Anhui aiguohui yanshuo."

[71] Chen Duxiu, *Shian zizhuan*.

[72] Guy S. Alito, *The Last Confucian: Liang Shu-ming and the Chinese Dilemma of Modernity*, esp. the first chapter.

[73] Frederick Wakeman, Jr., *History and Will: Philosophical Perspectives of Mao Tse-tung's Thought*, p. 157.

Thus this "moral passion" of Chen's was no doubt at least in part a result of the lingering influence of the Confucian culture in which Chen had been immersed prior to 1897. As Thomas Metzger has pointed out, "for Confucians, man in his ordinary condition has available to him a power which the Judeo-Christian tradition reserves for God."[74] This meant that man has the ability to utilize his "unique moral energy with complete objectivity, to achieve a society free of the distortions of self-interest."[75] Such a viewpoint put a tremendous amount of pressure on the individual to ensure that his actions were correctly motivated. This Confucian belief in the power of moral thinking assumed that if an individual's actions, or at least the actions of a small determined minority, were benevolent and sincere, they would have far-reaching effects. Consequently, the doctrine placed a premium on moral behavior.

One further explanation of the moral passion Chen displayed can be found in the nature of the youth groups with which he was involved. Youth is a time when one is particularly concerned with "fidelity,"[76] and one can imagine that this concern was greatly magnified among the Confucian-influenced Chinese youth groups with which Chen was associated. Thus his moralistic message proved attractive to his youthful audiences, accustomed as they were to the traditional categories of Confucian thought.

In the speech mentioned above, Chen aimed most of his venom at those who "talk about loyalty and filial piety and criticize others as rebels."

When there is a national crisis, they will not work for the public good. Their only thought is to put their money into foreign banks. The plan that they embrace is to sell out to the enemy to protect themselves. . . . If these na-

[74] Thomas Metzger, *Escape from Predicament: Neo-Confucianism and China's Evolving Political Culture*, p. 38.

[75] Ibid.

[76] Erik Erikson, "Youth: Fidelity and Diversity," in Erik Erikson, ed., *The Challenge of Youth*, pp. 1–27.

tional traitors and rebels are not slain our country will
be lost.[77]

Chen felt nearly as much disdain for those indifferent on-
lookers who "only care about themselves and their families
and are unconcerned about national affairs, considering the
order and prosperity of the nation to be solely the government's responsibility."[78] What these people did not understand, Chen Duxiu explained, was the relationship between
their own affairs and those of the nation. And finally Chen
looked down on "the intellectuals who seem totally to understand the problem, but who do not really understand. . . .
The things this type of person says may seem very true, but
they cannot be implemented."[79] Chen Duxiu was well aware
of the tendency of some thinkers to make the mistake of seeing
things from only a theoretical point of view. Though sometimes guilty of the fault himself, Chen, even in his most intellectual writings, constantly cautioned against it. He insisted
on the necessity of practicality and direct empirical knowledge—a heritage, perhaps, of his uncle's cold, hard world of
horse-trading with the Russians and soybean buying with the
British.

Indeed, the position of Chen's family was in many ways
similar to that of the student audience Chen hoped to arouse
with his speech. Both groups were newly arisen, still somewhat
alienated from the traditional gentry and yet identified with
their presumptions and privileges. In this situation, Chen, like
the writer in the *Hubei Student World* quoted earlier,[80] tended
to assume a special relationship with the masses; Chen felt
his student audience had a duty to awaken the masses to the
dangers confronting China.

Though Chen had roasted the Chinese upper crust earlier
in his speech, he had great hope for "those deceived rustics
who do not know about the oppressive treaty with the Rus-

[77] Chen Youji (Chen Duxiu), "Anhui aiguohui yanshuo."
[78] Ibid.
[79] Ibid.
[80] See note 42.

sians or the [threatened] division of their country and so have
no basis on which to develop ideas of patriotism. The despised
humble peasants of the countryside are all in this category,"
and, Chen stated, they "encompass eighty or ninety percent
of the people."[81] Chen was never to have the simple populist
belief that the poor and humble were naturally good. He
agreed, though, with those who felt that the largest problem
was simply that the Chinese masses were "lacking patriotic
sentiment,"[82] energetically insisting that this problem could
be solved by prodding the masses into expressing their "natural spirit."[83] Unfortunately, he lamented, the masses were at
that point near death, and unless they were stirred to fight
they would perish.

Chen believed that the small group of people who had responded to his message could develop a new relationship with
the masses. As he put it: "We must get rid of our usual selfish
opinions and strive to uphold the goal of patriotism and union
with the masses [hequn]."[84] To this end, Chen divided his new
organization into two parts, a lecturing society and a newspaper, to disseminate this information among the commoners.

Chen did not immediately achieve all of these goals, but he
did stir his listeners into action. Right after the meeting at
which he spoke, a group of students from the Anhui Academy
who had attended the speech confronted their school super-
intendent, demanding a change in restrictive school regula-
tions and an increased emphasis on physical education classes
so that the students could prepare themselves physically to
fight the Russians. They also asked to be allowed to telegram
a petition to the higher governmental authorities to urge them
to take whatever action was necessary to block the treaty with
the Russians.[85]

[81] Chen Youji (Chen Duxiu), "Anhui aiguohui yanshuo."
[82] Ibid.
[83] Ibid.
[84] Ibid.
[85] "Anhui daxuetang zuzhi xuesheng jue qingxing" [The circumstances of
Anhui Higher School's hindering of students involved in expelling the Rus-
sians], Subao, May 29, 1903, p. 2. See also "Anhui shengcheng daxuetang

The results in Anhui were similar to those of the student demonstrations in Shanghai and Tokyo. Nearly a week of altercations between the students and the educational authorities ended with the dismissal of several students and the withdrawal of several others.[86] The provincial officials issued a warrant for the arrest of Chen Duxiu for having instigated the disturbances and prohibited any further public speeches in the area.[87] Chen Duxiu, however, was forewarned about the order for his arrest and managed to leave town before he could be apprehended.[88] But before departing, Chen provoked similar incidents at other schools throughout the area.[89]

Though Chen had to flee, his experiences with the Anhui Patriotic Society helped him to develop his concept of youth—particularly those gentry youth who had not become part of the scholar-official class—as a moral group that should assume leadership of society. Moreover, Chen learned how contagious the student culture he had earlier imbibed in Tokyo had now become. Living together in their dormitories away from home, Chinese students in Anhui had begun to form groups and ideas similar to those of the Chinese students in Tokyo.

THE YOUTH CULTURE

From Anhui, Chen journeyed to Shanghai, where he joined the staff of the *China National Gazette (Guomin riri bao)*. This paper was the successor to the famous *Subao* on which Zhang Binglin and Zou Rong as well as Zhang Shizhao had

di yici chengtu zhi yuanyin" [The reasons for the first conflict at the Anhui Higher School in the Anhui capital], *Subao*, May 26, 1903, pp. 2–3.

[86] Ibid. Also, "Zaiji anqing daxuetang wubei xuetang tongcheng xuetang chengtu shi" [Another account of the conflict at Anqing's Upper Level School, the Military Preparatory Academy, and the Tongcheng Academy], *Subao*, May 30, 1903, p. 2.

[87] "Anhui daxuetang zuzhi," "Anhui shengcheng daxuetang," and "Zaiji anqing daxuetang."

[88] "Anhui shengcheng daxuetang."

[89] "Zaiji anqing daxuetang."

worked.[90] Before its demise, the *Subao* had printed accounts of Chen Duxiu's Anhui Patriotic Society. When a successor to this paper was established by Zhang Shizhao, it was natural for him to invite Chen Duxiu to work on it.

Like its predecessor, the *China National Gazette* appealed to the new generation of students, addressing them as the natural leaders of Chinese society. Although the *China National Gazette* did not maintain the strident tone and feistiness on current issues that characterized the *Subao*, the paper did mount a radical attack on the cultural and intellectual foundations of traditional Chinese civilization, similar to the assault Chen Duxiu was to launch eight years later in the pages of the culturally radical but seemingly politically moderate *New Youth*. The *China National Gazette* seethed with the moralism of these radical youths who were sure that their education had provided them with an understanding of society their elders did not possess. Article after article in the magazine emphasized the necessity of historical progress and nationalism and contained characterizations of the Chinese people, family, culture, and government as constituting a slave society. The denunciations of the culture and morals of the scholar-gentry class in particular were similar in tone and content to many of the writings of the later New Culture movement.[91]

[90] Zhang Shizhao, "Subao an shimo jixu" [A complete narration of the *Subao* case], in Chai Degeng et al., comps., *Xinhai geming [The revolution of 1911]*, vol. 1, pp. 388–89. Zhang Shizhao, "Yu Huang Keqiang xiangjiao shimo" [The complete account of my acquaintance with Huang Xing], in *Xinhai geming*, vol. 2, pp. 338–50. Feng Ziyou, *Zhonghua minguo kaiguo qian geming shi [A history of the revolution prior to the founding of the Republic of China]*, pp. 139–42; idem, *Geming yishi [Anecdotes of the Chinese Revolution]*, vol. 1, p. 125; vol. 2, pp. 84–85. Liu Yazi, "Ji Chen Zhongfu xiansheng guanyu Su Manshu de tanhua" [A talk with Chen Duxiu concerning his remembrances of Su Manshu], in Liu Wuji, *Su Manshu nianpu ji qida [A yearly record of Su Manshu and other items]*, p. 284. Feng Ziyou, *Zhongguo geming yundong ershiliunian zuzhi shi [Twenty-six years' organizational history of the Chinese revolutionary movement]*, p. 76.

[91] Examples of some of these articles in the *Guomin riri bao* are "Daotong ban" [The handling of the orthodoxy of precepts], vol. 2, no. 33, pp. 1–7; "Zhen nuli" [An exhortation to slaves], vol. 1, no. 1, pp. 6–26; "Nuli yu xu" [A preface to slave jail], vol. 1, no. 4, pp. 15–18.

Unfortunately, the articles in the short-lived *China National Gazette* were not signed, so Chen's specific contributions cannot be identified; but at least one article, "Admonition to Youth" (Zhen xiaonian), has a title and content that foreshadow "Call to Youth" (Qinggao qingnian), the famous lead article, signed by Chen, in *New Youth* (originally called *Youth Magazine*).[92] Both pieces equate the position of youth with that of the nation, the *China National Gazette* article claiming: "If the youth's position is venerable and serious, the nation's position is venerable and serious. When the youth's position is humble, the nation's position is humble."[93] The two articles associate youth with a vigorous and fresh condition of mind but express the fear that it is all too easy for young people to lose their "youthful qualities." The *China National Gazette* piece even closes by warning, in a tone that would be very typical of *New Youth*, that one should not bear "the foul air brought into human circles by Chan (or Zen) Buddhism and Confucius. If we are not to grow old and not to die we must whip up our creative spirit and encourage it to expand into the limitless heaven and earth."[94]

Years later, in founding *New Youth*, Chen insisted that the purpose of his magazine was to train a new generation to uphold and develop its culture.[95] Youth, he maintained, could bring vitality and growth to a society, but only if the young obtained a "self-awareness" of their responsibility and willingness "to struggle . . . to exert one's intellect, discard resolutely the old and the rotten, regard them as enemies and as

[92] "Zhen xiaonian" [Admonition to youth], *Guomin riribao*, vol. 1, no. 4, pp. 13–15. Chen Duxiu, "Qinggao qingnian" [Call to youth], *Qingnian zazhi*, vol. 1, no. 1 (Sept. 15, 1915). Zheng Xuejia has pinpointed several articles in the *China National Gazette* that he thinks may have been written by Chen. See "Ban *Xin qingnian* qian Chen Duxiu shenghuo de pianduan" [A slice of Chen Duxiu's life before his editing of *New Youth*], in *Zhonggong xingwang shi* [A history of the rise and fall of the Chinese Communist Party], app. 4, pp. 764–84.
[93] "Zhen xiaonian."
[94] Ibid.
[95] Chen Duxiu, "Reply to Wang Yuangong," *Qingnian zazhi* [Youth Magazine], vol. 1, no. 1 (Sept. 13, 1915).

a flood or savage beasts, keep away from their neighborhood and refuse to be contaminated by their poisonous germs. . . ."[96] This insistence on maintaining the purity of spirit of the young— similar to the mandate that the Confucian gentleman is supposed to remain pure of heart in order to serve as a moral example for others—was the major element in Chen's own faith in youth as a new group of leaders for Chinese society.

A celebration of youth characterizes many radical movements, whose members typically are young and who consider the qualities of spontaneity and daring necessary for revolutionary activity. Indeed, the figure of the "ideal youth," which has been a standard character in popular myth, has tended to replace the yeoman and untutored peasant as a cult personality in modern revolutionary ideology.[97] In China, it is clear, this emphasis on youth was a reaction to the value the scholar-gentry had placed on age and unchanging sobriety. The written record shows that in the early part of this century, Chen Duxiu was the originator of the idea that the fate of the Chinese nation depended on the way its youth were treated.

As Chen's ideas on youth were crystallizing, he was becoming totally immersed in the new student culture in Shanghai. Here the life style of the students seemed to exemplify the liberation from family and tradition that was necessary to bring about development and growth in all of China. Among those working on the *China National Gazette* with Chen Duxiu in the spring and summer of 1903 were Zhang Ji and Su Manshu, with whom he had been associated in the Youth Society in Japan, as well as Zhang Shizhao, who had been the editor of the original *Subao*.[98] Chen Duxiu and several other

[96] Chen Duxiu, "Qinggao qingnian." This translation borrows heavily from Chow Tse-tsung, *May Fourth Movement*, p. 46.

[97] Philip Abrams, "Rites de Passage: The Conflict of Generations in Industrial Society," *Journal of Contemporary History*, 5 (1970):178.

[98] Zhang Shizhao, "Subao an shimo jixu" [A complete narration of the *Subao* case], in *Xinhai geming [The Revolution of 1911]*, comp. Chai Degeng, 1:388–89. Yan Duhou, "Xinhai geming shiqi shanghai xinwenjie dongtai" [Developments in Shanghai newspaper circles around the time of the 1911 revolution], *Xinhai geming huiyi lu* 4:78. Zhang Shizhao, "Shuangping ji" [A record of both sides of the chess board], *Jiayin zazhi*, vol. 1, no. 4 (Oct.

members of the editorial staff shared communal living facilities, and revolutionary comrades from different areas continually drifted in and out of their house. Years later, Zhang
Shizhao, who, as mentioned earlier, ran a revolutionary dormitory in Nanjing around 1902 where Chen Duxiu may have
hidden for a short time, recalled that he, Chen, and He Meishi,
another roommate who was a former student at the Shanghai
Patriotic School, would often spend their nights proofreading
copy for the next morning's paper.[99]

During work hours Chen Duxiu and his friends crowded
into tiny, poorly lit lofts, which were so narrow that Chen
later described himself and He Meishi as being literally knee-
to-knee while writing and propagandizing.[100] During their
leisure they frequented bars and sought the company of dance-
hall girls, often overindulging in wine, food, and sex.[101] Su
Manshu, who moved in with Chen Duxiu for a while, was
supposed to have been particularly renowned for his con-
sumption of food and cigars, habits that may have helped
hasten his early demise.[102] The eccentric Su, who had gone
through the motions of joining a Buddhist holy order a few
years earlier in order to avoid an arranged marriage, would

11, 1914). Zhang Shizhao, "Shu huangdi hun" [Comments on the spirit of
the yellow emperor], in *Xinhai geming huiyi lu*, 1:212–304. Feng Ziyou,
Geming yishi [Fragments of revolutionary history], 1:195–96. Chen Duxiu,
"Ji Chen Zhongfu guanyu Su Manshu de tanhua" [Transcripts of a discussion
with Chen Zhongfu concerning Su Manshu], in Liu Yazi, *Su Manshu nianpu
ji qida [A yearly record of Su Manshu and other items]*, p. 284.

[99] Zhang Shizhao, "Shuangping ji."

[100] Chen Duxiu, "Yemeng wangyou He Meishi jue er fuci" [A night dream
about my lost friend He Meishi and then awakening and committing it to
verse], *Jingzhong ribao [The Alarm Bell Daily]*, May 7, 1904.

[101] *Jingzhong ribao*, Aug. 30, 1904, p. 4, and Jan. 1, 1905, p. 4.

[102] Henry McAleavy, *Su Man-shu: A Sino-Japanese Genius*, p. 49. Leo Ou-
fan Lee, *The Romantic Generation of Modern Chinese Writers*, pp. 58–59.
Su Manshu, "Yu mojun shu" [A letter to a certain gentleman], in *Manshu
dashi jinian ji*, p. 60. Also see "Yu Yechu cang Liu Yazi Zhu Shaopin shu"
[Letter from Yu Yechu to Liu Yazi and Zhu Shaopin], in ibid., p. 58. Liu
Wu-chi, *Su Man-shu*, p. 126. Liu Yazi, "Su heshang zatan" [Miscellaneous
remarks on the monk Su] in *Manshu chuanji [Collected works of Su Manshu]*,
vol. 5, p. 217.

insist, according to Chen, on wearing his monk's habit on their visits to dance halls, something that apparently came as quite a shock to some of the other patrons.[103]

Chen Duxiu's own appetite for women was also renowned, and in his later years this was a constant topic of gossip among his friends and a source of much malicious propaganda by the right-wing press.[104] In one interview reported to the right-wing papers in the 1920s, Gao Junman, Chen's wife's younger sister and his paramour in his earlier years, was asked how many women she thought Chen Duxiu had slept with.[105] Her answer was that it had to be a lot, for when she last had seen him ten years ago he had already been intimate with several hundred and bragged that he had had women from every province except Gansu. As a poetess and adherent of the new literature, Gao Junman herself may be assumed to have participated in this bohemian culture. The lives of the women radicals were similar to those of the men. They also frequently went out drinking and sometimes indulged in extra- and pre-marital affairs.[106]

Still, women participants in this revolutionary life style were few and far between. The famous martyr Qiu Jin and Gao Junman were part of a small minority within this Chinese youth culture. Unlike the men, the women did not have the option of returning to their families and becoming traditional wives when their financial resources were depleted or they desired a breather from the new life style. The women who participated in this culture found themselves completely cut off from the rest of Chinese society. Gao Junman, for instance, after separating from Chen in the early 1920s, died in poverty and squalor, abandoned by the family that still gave support to Chen, even though he had become a Communist.

---

[103] Chen Duxiu, "Ji Chen Zhongfu guanyu Su Manshu de tanhua," pp. 279–86.

[104] Li Eng, *Hongse wutai* [The red stage], p. 125. Zhou Zouran, *Zhitang huixiang lu* [Remembrances of Zhitang], p. 181.

[105] Kang Ming, "Huidao Chen Duxiu furen" [Meeting Chen Duxiu's wife], *Shehui xinwen* [Societal Mercury], vol. 1, no. 3, p. 59.

[106] See, for instance, *Jingzhong ribao*, July 26, 1904, p. 4.

On the other hand, the behavior of Chen and his associates was part of a tradition familiar to most and tolerated by many educated Chinese. In the past, iconoclastic Chinese, such as Chen, had often preached sexual equality and spent their time in the company of dancing girls, sipping wine and writing poetry while leaving their traditional wives at home. Indeed, Chen and his associates often modeled themselves as much on traditional profligates like Yuan Mei (although they might have objected to any analogy between their lives and that of Yuan Mei, whose homosexual exploits were notorious) as on Western bohemians. While copying Western ideas, Chen and his associates still viewed themselves within the Chinese iconoclastic tradition.

The association of traditional and Western ideas is seen clearly in Chen's relationship with Su Manshu, with whom he now became fast friends. Su Manshu had spent much of his youth in Japan, where he was born, and his Chinese was apparently quite poor. As a result, Chen Duxiu began to instruct Su in the writing of traditional Chinese poetry as well as French and English.[107] Either Su was an exceptional student or Chen an exceedingly gifted teacher, for Su Manshu soon began to contribute poems to the *China National Gazette* in the literary style that he was to make famous. In addition to writing traditional verse, Chen Duxiu and Su Manshu began the first Chinese translation of Victor Hugo's novel *Les Misérables*, apparently more because of the appeal of his romantic style to their revolutionary tempers than because they felt his ideas to be particularly meaningful.[108]

The novel began to run serially in the *China National Gazette*. But the paper, beset by internal squabbling and pressure from the Qing government, folded in early October after only three months of operation, before the final installments of their translation could be published. A few days later, Su Manshu suddenly left town, taking with him thirty dollars of

[107] Chen Duxiu, "Ji Chen Zhongfu guanyu Su Manshu de tanhua," p. 34.
[108] Liu Wu-chi, *Su Man-shu*, p. 34.

Zhang Shizhao's money[109]—an action typical of Su's unpredictable and highly unorthodox character—and it was left to Chen Duxiu to finish the last two chapters of the book.[110]

CALL TO ARMS

In their attempted translation of *Les Misérables*, Chen Duxiu and Su Manshu in fact only loosely translated book 2, section 1 of the original text. They added to the book their own story of a young revolutionary hero who attempts but fails to carry out the assassination of Napoléon in order to prevent him from assuming the emperorship. Chen Duxiu's fascination with assassination as a political weapon went beyond literary fantasy. In early 1904, after a trip to Anqing to prepare for the publication of a new vernacular paper, as will be discussed in the following chapter, Chen returned to Shanghai at the invitation of Zhang Shizhao to join a secret assassination squad.[111] The group was organized by the Hunanese anarchist, Yang Yulin, as well as Zhang Binglin's son-in-law, Gong Baochuan. Yang and Zhang had both been associated with the Youth Society that Chen Duxiu had helped found in Tokyo little more than a year before. Other members of the Shanghai Assassination Corps included Cai Yuanpei, his young brother, Cai Yuankang, Wang Xiaoxu, Zhong Xianchang, and He Haiqiao.[112]

[109] Ibid. The original title as it appeared in the *China National Gazette* was "Grieved Society" (Can shehui). Chen Duxiu changed the title when he published it as a book. In later years another character was added to the title, and the translation of the book now in use in China is "Deeply Grieved World" (Beican shijie). Chen later claimed that his name was originally supposed to be only on the introduction and not on the cover of the translation, but the publisher added it to the cover without his knowledge.

[110] See "Ji Chen Zhongfu guanyu Su Manshu de tanhua," p. 284. Also Huang Mingqi, *Su Manshu pingzhuan* [A critical biography of Su Manshu]. Yang Honglie, "Su Manshu zhuan" [A biography of Su Manshu], in Liu Yazi, *Manshu chuanji*, vol. 4, p. 200.

[111] Chen Duxiu, "Cai Zimin xiansheng cheshi houganyan" [Words on Cai Yuanpei's death], in *Shian zizhuan*, p. 123. See also note 108.

[112] Lu Manyan, *Shixian bianji [Another record of contemporary worthies]*, vol. 1, pp. 2–3. Sun Dezhong, *Cai Yuanpei xiansheng yiwen leichao [A topical*

Chen did not continue to be directly associated with the assassination society when, after a few months of training, the group moved to formalize its role and developed into the Restoration Society (Guangfu hui), an organization that, under the leadership of Cai Yuanpei, became one of the major revolutionary groups in the Lower Yangzi Valley.[113] Chen chose instead, in a manner that was to become typical for him, to return to Anhui to carry out his own independent revolutionary work, which had already begun with the formation of the *Anhui Common Speech Journal.*

During the time Chen was associated with the assassination society, the group studied bomb and weapons making and trained in calisthenics and paramilitary techniques. Presumably, the members also studied Russian anarchist and nihilist writings, which were gaining popularity among the Chinese students via Japanese sources. Yang Yulin was fascinated with these Russian groups and organized the assassination society in an attempt to imitate them. There was an element of identity with the "enemy of their enemies" that was partly responsible for the fascination of Chen and his friends with the Russian radicals. Moreover, like some of the Russians they imitated, student members of the assassination society had a naive populist belief that the problems besetting Chinese society resulted from the actions of a few evil governmental officials and that the elimination of the latter would instantly improve the condition of the former. This would be in accord with the Confucian notion that individual morality can affect the characteristics of the society.

Certainly, members of the assassination society believed

---

selection of Cai Yuanpei's writings], p. 584. Cai Yuanpei, *Cai Yuanpei zishu* [Cai Yuanpei's autobiography], p. 21. For other discussions of the Assassination Corps, see Rankin, *Early Chinese Revolutionaries*, pp. 103–4. Also "Yang Dusheng zhuan" [Biography of Yang Dusheng], in *Geming xianlie zhuanji* [Biographies of revolutionary martyrs]. Shi Diemin, "Ji Guangfu hui ersan shi" [Recollections of two or three things about the Restoration Society], *Xinhai geming huiyilu*, 4:131–34. Li Shiyue, "Lun Guangfu hui" [On the Restoration Society], in *Xinhai geming yanjiu hui lunji* [Collection of research on the 1911 Revolution], pp. 68–69.

[113] Ibid.

that their dramatic example would cause others to follow them. Chen's friend and student Wu Yue maintained that the people's spirit could be aroused only by the actions of the brave.[114] Convinced that history was in their favor, it was easy for Chen and his associates to believe that if they acted sincerely and decisively, all they needed to do was eliminate a few officials on the top and seize a few key points, and then the people would rise, the government would crumble, and the gates through which historical progress would march into China would be flung open by a new Chinese leadership.

Besides his participation in the assassination society, Chen manifested his commitment to moral violent action in one of the few poems he signed and published in the pages of the *China National Gazette*, lamenting that his friend Wang Xiyan, who before his death had worked with Chen in the Anhui Patriotic Society, had not been able to die like a hero "on the battlefield" and stressing that "Anhui needs men who will speak for a new unified political system."[115] In another poem published at the same time, "Writing for the Hunting Picture of General Saigo Nanshu," Chen used Confucian terms to call for immediate action to rectify that which offends one's "good heart" and asserted that in life "a man should only take up his sword and not consider whether he will succeed or fail."[116]

These calls for action on the part of Chen and his compatriots were attempts to imitate what they believed to be the example of European, especially Russian, anarchists and nihilists. But they also saw themselves in terms of "older precedents in Chinese history and literature."[117] Feeling themselves possessed by a Confucian "moral presence," they combed the history books to find heroic examples from the past. At

[114] Wu Yue, "Zixu" [Personal introduction], in Feng Ziyou, *Geming yishi*, vol. 3, pp. 199–202.

[115] Chen Duxiu (Youji), "Ku Wang Xiyan" [Crying over Wang Xiyan], *Guomin riri bao*, August 8, 1903, p. 13.

[116] Chen Duxiu, "Ti Xixiang nanzhou youlie tu" [Writing for the hunting picture of General Saigo Nanshu], *Guomin riri bao*, August 17, 1903, p. 16.

[117] Edward S. Krebs, "Assassination in the Republican Revolutionary Movement," *Ch'ing-shih wen-t'i*, Dec. 1981, p. 60.

this time, Chen saw no contradiction between iconoclastic Chinese ideas and new Western ones. Chen's exact commitments—besides a desire to preserve the territorial integrity of the Chinese nation and to reestablish a strong moral government that had the involvement of his countrymen—are still unclear. To the extent that Chen had a definite political identity at this time, it was as a part of the counterculture that had emerged among student rebels in China in the early 1900s.

This counterculture owed much to the iconoclasm of traditional Chinese sources: the feminist proposals of Wu Jingzi, Li Zhi, and Yuan Mei; the unconventional life styles exemplified in the Qing by Yuan Mei but already part of Chinese culture since at least the period of the so-called Seven Sages of the Bamboo Grove in the third century at the end of the Han dynasty; the scholarly critiques of neo-Confucian thought by members of the *kaozheng* school; and finally, the calls for further participation in the political system by the newly risen official class of the Jiangnan area. Still, it was the shock of the invasion of China by the forces of Western imperialism and the Western ideas that flooded into China in their wake that suddenly made this traditional iconoclasm attractive. When the traditional examination system was abolished in 1905 and the old alternative was eliminated, conventional behavior and ideas lost much of their appeal and the attraction of the new culture became even greater. Concerned about the division within and encroachments upon their country, many of these youth felt an unquenchable desire to prove themselves by redeeming their country through action. By 1904 or 1905, Chen Duxiu had developed a clear sense of youth as crusaders with a special mission within Chinese society.

As Chen and Trotsky entered their twenty-fifth years, their two societies and their individual activities stood in marked contrast to one another. Trotsky had matured in a society with a longstanding revolutionary tradition and an already burgeoning proletariat. The son of a highly successful Jewish farmer, Trotsky was far more removed from the Russian aristocracy, whose presumptions his family had begun to imitate, than was Chen from the upper-level Chinese scholar-gentry. An alienated youth, Trotsky naturally gravitated into revolutionary circles. There, no one needed to be told the czar was bad and should be overthrown or that foreign imperialism presented a danger to his society. Rather, Trotsky almost immediately began to grapple with the problem of socialism. After a short flirtation with the *narodniki*, or populist movement, he became a Marxist. By 1904 he had become a major national leader of the party and had already spent two years in czarist prisons and two more in Siberian exile. A year later, in 1905, Trotsky helped organize the Petersburg Soviet and became the leader of the aborted revolution of that year. The iconoclastic tradition with which Trotsky had to identify in his country was that of a socialist revolution. Chen's revolutionary accomplishments were no less than Trotsky's at this time, but they tend not to stand out as much in a world that has heard much of the Petersburg Soviet but little of the Anhui Patriotic Society.

Chen was one of a small group who had begun to question some of the traditional assumptions of its society and started to develop a new cultural tradition. By 1905 Chen had developed the idea that Chinese youth had the sincerity and purity necessary to liberate society from the corruption and constraints imposed by their elders and to develop the potential of the Chinese people, which had reached such great heights in the past. Chen felt that China, propelled by its youth, could enter the twentieth century once again powerful and prosperous.

CHAPTER THREE

REVOLUTIONARY TEACHER
IN ANHUI

As Chen matured, he advanced from his role of student activist to that of intellectual leader and political instructor. Chen exercised his growing influence in two major ways: one, as a teacher involved directly with his students; and two, for a much broader audience, as a writer, editor, and journal founder. Both of these roles reflect the paradox of Chen Duxiu's modus operandi: though he espoused increasingly radical views, he did so from the most traditional of vehicles, capitalizing whenever necessary on the time-honored authority of the scholar over his disciples.

Although he was later to be known as a Westernizer who supposedly sought to eradicate all aspects of Chinese tradition, Chen at this time saw certain traditional ideas as perfectly compatible with Western values. Indeed, Chen felt that the Chinese nation again would become strong only when China restored its original *guocui*, or national essence. What he hoped to eliminate were the vulgarisms that Chinese rulers had allowed to creep into Chinese society; he felt these distortions prevented China from obtaining the wealth and dignity of the West.

THE *Anhui Common Speech Journal*

As early as 1903, when he began the Anhui Patriotic Society, Chen had had the idea of founding a newspaper that would help student activists in awakening the commoners to the problems and traditions of their country directly—in the vernacular.[1] Although the Anhui Patriotic Society had been dis-

[1] Chen Duxiu, "Anhui aiguohui yanshuo."

solved quickly by the Qing government, the idea of establishing a newspaper in Anqing had remained with Chen Duxiu. He set to work to accomplish this task when he returned from Shanghai to Anqing in early 1904. Between February 15, 1904 and August 1, 1905, Chen established, edited, and wrote for the *Anhui Common Speech Journal (Anhui suhua bao)*, the first vernacular paper in Anhui and one of the earliest in China.

The *Anhui Common Speech Journal* was first written in Anqing and then dispatched to Wuhu, where it was published and distributed by the Science Book Company. The Science Book Company was founded by Wang Mengzou, who later headed the East Asia Book Company and became a frequent benefactor of Chen Duxiu. After a few issues Chen moved the editorial department to Wuhu as well, so that he could receive help with his paper from Wang Mengzou and the workers at the book company. Chen lived in a room above the company office, subsisting on two meals of gruel a day supplied to him by Wang and editing the *Anhui Common Speech Journal* in his room.[2] With Wang he helped develop the book company into a convenient conduit for dispensing revolutionary propaganda and maintaining contact with outlying student revolutionary cells; company haulers frequently traveled back and forth to Shanghai for supplies, and company salesmen plied a route that took them through many little towns in southern Anhui every six or seven days, bringing to the schools along the way the newest books, magazines, and newspapers.[3] Chen and his comrades thereby developed a network of radical youth throughout the province.

With an opening run of one thousand copies (the same circulation as the early issues of *New Youth*), the *Anhui Common Speech Journal* gradually increased its print run to more than three thousand copies per edition by the time of its closing, allegedly making it the most widely read vernacular jour-

[2] Gao Yuhan, "Rushu qianhou" [Before and after entering Sichuan], *Minsheng yu tongyi [People's livelihood and unification]*, July 20, 1946, as quoted in Zheng Xuejia, *Zhonggong*, vol. 2, p. 770.

[3] Yu Yimi, ed., *Wuhu xianzhi [Wuhu District Gazette]*, 1919.

nal in China.[4] Its influence has been attested to by the famous educator Cai Yuampei, who years later recalled the "unforgettable impression" made on him by Chen Duxiu as a result of the daring *Anhui Common Speech Journal*.[5]

In this journal Chen began to assume the role he was to exercise throughout the rest of his life—that of "Mandarin" teacher whose duty it was to spread the new ideas to the masses. In beginning this paper, Chen complained: "People go through life without understanding any scholarship or knowing anything about reality." Instead they "are happy to lie around in their houses, chasing their wives and concubines, and eating delicious foods." But, he continues, in order to protect "life and family" it is necessary to know about the world. Chen explained how writings in the vernacular language would "make it easy for the *xiucai* (first-level degree holder) who never goes out to know something about the world" and for teachers, businessmen, and even women and children to increase their "shallow knowledge."[6] To perform this task, Chen included information on a diverse assortment of topics: early Chinese history; Western educational methods and science; new military techniques and weaponry; and explanations of the way in which the imperialist powers were gobbling up China's precious mining preserves and violating Chinese sovereignty.

But the most important lesson Chen sought to impress upon his readers was that of the unique identity of the Chinese nation. Chen hoped his readers would see beyond life inside their homes and realize they were part of a Chinese nation. Chen's mentor Zhang Binglin, writing in the *People's Paper (Min Bao)* in 1906, argued that people should "cherish the

---

[4] Shen Ji, "Chen Duxiu he Anhui suhua bao" [Chen Duxiu and the *Anhui Common Speech Journal*], in *Anhui gemingshi yanjiu ziliao*, vol. 1, pp. 18–19.

[5] Cai Yuanpei, "Preface," to *Xin qingnian [New Youth]* 1 (1935 reprint).

[6] Sanai (Chen Duxiu), "Kaiban anhui suhuabao deyuan" [Reasons for publishing the *Anhui Common Speech Journal*], *Anhui suhua bao*, hereafter *AHSHB* 1 (Feb. 1, 1904). Sanai was the pen name used by Chen Duxiu in all of his *AHSHB* writings.

history of the Chinese race."[7] It was a similar kind of thinking that two years earlier had led Chen in the pages of the *Anhui Common Speech Journal* to complain that although everyone can say "we are Chinese," few know anything about "Chinese history."[8] Chen made this comment in a column that he inaugurated on "Great Events in Chinese History." In this column, Chen reflected the influence of Zhang Binglin. In earlier writings, Zhang had attempted to trace the biological and cultural origins of the Chinese, showing their descent from the legendary Yellow Ancestor, or Huang Di.[9] As Charlotte Furth has shown, Zhang's work lacked a "specifically biological definition of race."[10] Zhang was primarily concerned with the inheritance of cultural identity. Barbarian groups, according to Zhang, had become Chinese and Chinese had become barbarians when they abandoned their cultural heritage.[11] Chen, however, emphasized the tribal nature of the Chinese people. He traced the origins of the Han people to present-day Xinjiang, showing how they gradually expanded into what is today central and south China. As they did they came into conflict with the Miao people; led by Huang Di, they defeated these people. Here Chen differed from Zhang by stressing that Huang Di is the spiritual, not biological, ancestor of the Chinese people and that he is revered because he saved the Chinese people from being "expelled from China" or becoming "slaves of the Miao."[12]

Like Zhang, Chen obviously felt that the heroes of the past are also part of China's "national essence." But Chen believed in the biological existence of a Chinese race. He stressed that

[7] Zhang Binglin, "Yanshuo lu" [A record of a speech], *Minbao [People's Paper]* 6:10–11.

[8] Sanai (Chen Duxiu), "Zhongguo lidai de dashi" [Great events of Chinese history], "Kaiguo yuanliu" [The origin and development of the nation], *AHSHB* 3 (April 1, 1904).

[9] Zhang Binglin, *Qiushu [Book of raillery]*.

[10] Charlotte Furth, "The Sage as Rebel: The Inner World of Chang Pinglin," in Furth, ed., *The Limits of Change*, p. 135.

[11] Ibid., pp. 133–34.

[12] Sanai, "Zhongguo lidai de dashi," "Han Miao jiaozheng" [The Han Miao disputes], *AHSHB* 4 (April 15, 1904).

because Huang Di defeated the Miao, "our ancestors have lived perpetually in this good China." Following his discussion of the further defeat of the Miao by the great Sage King Yu, Chen emphasized that the story of China is that of a single people, not a "mixed race."[13]

Chen's insistence on the biological purity of the Han people is surprising in one who was later to become the founder of the Chinese Communist party. But even as a Communist, Chen was to insist that the revolution's most important goal was to be the material well-being of the Chinese people. In the *Anhui Common Speech Journal*, Chen's identification with the physical existence of his people led him to insist that a nation "must have a definite land," "definite people," and "a definite society."[14] The ownership and control by the Chinese people, and only the Chinese people, over their land were the people's hereditary rights. But these rights were being threatened by foreign invasion. Chen pointed out to his countrymen how foreign invasion violated China's "people, land, and sovereignty," resulting in a "lost nation" and radically affecting the lives of the people.[15] In making this statement, Chen emphasized that the preservation of the nation was not the same as the preservation of a dynasty. He therefore took pains to instruct his countrymen that "changing of dynasties" would not result in "losing the nation" as long as sovereignty continued to be held by the people of that nation.[16] "A nation," he insisted, "is originally that which belonged to all the people."[17] China could once again be a nation, he implied, only when the foreign Manchu rulers who had founded the Qing dynasty were eliminated and the Chinese people again exercised sovereignty over their land.

Chen believed that China's Manchu rulers were allowing the foreign powers to take Chinese territory—hence his par-

---

[13] Sanai, "Zhongguo lidai de dashi," "Dayu zhishui" [The great Yu saves us from the flood), *AHSHB* 5 (May 1, 1904).

[14] Sanai, "Wangguo pian" [Lost country article], *AHSHB* 8 (June 15, 1904).

[15] Ibid.

[16] Ibid.

[17] Ibid.

ticipation in the Shanghai Assassination Corps. To prevent this, Chen sought to alert the people of Anhui to the dangers of this foreign imperialism. Chen especially concentrated on what was happening "in the three northeastern provinces [Manchuria]."[18] Since Chen's own patriotism had been developed largely in response to Russian intervention in this area, he hoped to awaken similar sentiments in his readers by acquainting them with the ongoing story of the foreign penetration of that region.

He also tried to explain to his readers the way the foreign powers were gobbling up commercial and mining resources throughout China. Chen insisted in article after article that China must control its own industry, and he decried the plundering of China's resources by foreigners. Just as he felt the Chinese could regain their sovereignty only when they once again controlled their government, so he also felt that the Chinese people could truly control their land only by retaining power over their own industrial development. One of the first people in China to raise this issue,[19] Chen warned that if the Chinese did not take the initiative to begin to mine and use their own resources for themselves, there would be no way to forbid foreigners to mine in China; once the foreigners were engaged in mining, they would soon have to build railroads to transport the mined goods—railroads that could be used to dispatch troops and transform Anhui into a colony like India. To counter this, Chen urged the formation of the Anhui Mining Company, somewhat naively insisting that if everyone in Anhui contributed fifty cents to the company, there would be enough capital for the Chinese to do their mining for themselves.[20]

Proposals for the formation of Chinese companies to supplant the foreign enterprises which the Chinese government was allowing to come into China were to become increasingly common in the years before the 1911 Revolution. The agi-

[18] Sanai, "Kaiban anhui suhuabao deyuan."
[19] Shen Ji, "Chen Duxiu he Anhui suhua bao," p. 22.
[20] Sanai, "Lun anhui de guangwu" [On mining affairs in Anhui], *AHSHB* 2 (March 15, 1904).

tation for the formation of just such a company in Sichuan in the summer of 1911 was to create the crisis that immediately preceded the outbreak of the Republican revolution. That Chen would make such a proposal at this time would seem to be evidence of his sympathy for those gentry like his uncle who were interested in utilizing the new Western technology to form mercantile enterprises. He saw this as a way of recovering Chinese sovereignty, which he hoped would inspire his fellow countrymen to work to regain the land and rights of their "ancestors."

But Chen felt that China would not be strong enough to protect itself until the Chinese eliminated some of the debilitating customs that had perverted the society. In the *Anhui Common Speech Journal*, as in the later *New Youth*, Chen made the attacks on the Chinese family system the basis of many of his most trenchant articles, hoping to educate his readers about the inequity of the family as it existed in China. This was a familiar theme for many Chinese reformers, including Chen's original mentor, Kang Youwei. Moreover, it was a theme that ran through the writings of many traditional iconoclasts, especially those who, as mentioned earlier, had discussed the oppression of women in Chinese society. Following in this tradition, Chen, in the pages of the *Anhui Common Speech Journal*, denounced the way the family restricted its members' freedom of choice and thus their ultimate happiness.[21]

Chen criticized the Chinese family structure because it was inequitable; he also criticized it because he felt that the family system as it existed in China was responsible for the dearth of patriotic sentiment in the country. Chen intoned again and again that the Chinese "care about their family and do not care about their nation."[22] Chen, in fact, compared the Chinese to the Jews, whose nation, he claimed, perished through neglect because of their total absorption with family.[23] He felt

[21] Sanai, "Wangguo pian," "Wangguo de yuanyin" [The reasons for lost country], *AHSHB* 14 (Sept. 15, 1904).
[22] Ibid.
[23] Ibid.

that by assuming such an attitude, the Chinese were sacrificing their own well-being: he was sure that, without concern for the greater whole, the individual family could not survive.

He was also upset with how the Chinese family reduced women to creatures that men treated "as if they were raising them to produce sons and nothing else."[24] Chen insisted on equality for women, maintaining that "if there were no women, there would be no world."[25] To facilitate this equality of the sexes, Chen advocated freedom of divorce and the right for widows to remarry. Marriages, he felt, should be arranged for the happiness of the couple rather than the convenience of the parents. And he was vehement in his criticisms of the Chinese practice of introducing the bride and groom for the first time on their wedding day, and then allowing friends and family members to use the smallest pretense to suddenly burst in on the couple in their room.[26] Still, Chen stopped short of advocating total freedom of marriage, suggesting that it might cause problems with women with no education. Showing the influence of his foreign education, Chen proposed the Japanese system, whereby the couple would be introduced by their parents but would have to give their consent before the marriage finally could be arranged.[27]

Chen also parroted the pseudoscientific criticism of Western writers of the time who felt Chinese superstitious practices were very harmful to the society. Chen introduced a regular column on "bad customs" in the *Anhui Common Speech Journal*. He particularly censored practices considered to be wasteful to the development of China, such as geomancy, which he felt to be a superstition that prevented the development of China's native mining industry.[28] Although he was very critical of what he considered to be the wasteful worship of Bud-

---

[24] Sanai, "E supian" [Essay on evil customs], article 1, *AHSHB* 3 (April 1, 1904).

[25] Ibid.

[26] Sanai, "E supian," article 2, "Hunyin" [Marriage], *AHSHB* 4 (April 15, 1904).

[27] Sanai, "Wangguo de yuanyin."

[28] Sanai, "E supian," article 3, "Hunyin," *AHSHB* 6 (May 15, 1904).

dhist icons and idols, which he felt was totally at odds with original Buddhist practices, he was careful not to criticize Buddhist ideals per se.[29]   .

Like many other thinkers of the time, Chen at this time declared himself to be a believer in Buddhist doctrines,[30] although he would later denounce the religion in the pages of *New Youth*. His attitude toward Buddhism was similar to his attitude toward other Chinese values at this time; he did not feel the difficulty was with the original tradition but with the way the traditions had been perverted. Although believing in Buddhist doctrine, he criticized superstitious values such as the worship of icons, which had long been the bane of the educated.

VERNACULAR REVOLUTION

By making these criticisms in the vernacular, Chen made sure that his writing reached a larger audience than would something written in the complex literary language. But his use of the vernacular, like many of his efforts at this time, was also an attempt to return to an original national heritage. An editorial in the *Alarm Bell*, a Shanghai publication edited by the future Beijing University president Cai Yuanpei, specifically took note of Chen Duxiu's *Anhui Common Speech Journal*. The editorial suggested that vernacular writings helped to spread cultural awareness throughout the country and to eliminate the separation of speech and writing that developed in China as a result of the differences in dialects in the various regions. As Chen Duxiu would do later in the pages of *New Youth*, the author partially blamed the Confucians for this separation. Ignorant Confucians had unwittingly condemned as vulgar the local colloquialisms that appeared in many of the ancient books, which had used the language of everyday speech. As a result, as Confucian literary views became predominant, the written word moved further away from the

---

[29] Sanai, "E supian," article 4, "Jing pusa" [Honoring the Boddhisattva], *AHSHB* 7 (June 1, 1904).

[30] Ibid.

spoken language and "writing became more and more shallow."[31]

This article provides an important insight into the link between two of the activities (both begun during this period) that seem most contradictory in Chen's life—his passion for etymological research and his leadership of the so-called "vernacular revolution." At first glance, the scholarly essays that Chen wrote throughout his life on the origin of obscure words and characters would seem to be antithetical to his desire to create a new vernacular language based on the spoken word. When asked about this by a nephew during an interview from his prison cell in the 1930s, Chen insisted that his etymological research was necessary in order to establish the original sounds of the words and create the basis for a true vernacular language which would lend itself to being written with roman characters.[32]

This statement is indicative of the curious origin of Chen's iconoclasm. Desiring to romanize Chinese speech to make it similar to Western languages, he felt he could do so only by discovering the "lost past" of the Chinese vernacular. A similar concern for a "lost past" had been the central focus of traditional iconoclasts during the Qing dynasty from the early *kaozheng* leaders to Kang Youwei. Chen's mentor Zhang Binglin insisted that China's national language and literature were part of the Chinese national essence and believed that "in changing language, we must make words flow properly from their origins."[33] To be sure, Chen's interest in the use of the vernacular was sparked by his stay in Japan, where he was introduced to popular publications easily accessible to the general public. He also became aware of the use of vernacular writings in the West. But it is clear that Chen was attracted

---

[31] "Lun baihua bao yu zhongguo qiantu zhi guanxi" [On the relationship between the vernacular papers and China's future road], *Jingzhong ribao [Alarm Bell Daily]*, April 5, 1904.

[32] Pu Qingquan, "Wo so zhidao de Chen Duxiu" [The Chen Duxiu that I knew), in *Wenshi ziliao xuanji [Materials on literature and history]*, no. 71, p. 52.

[33] Quoted in Furth, "The Sage as Rebel," p. 127.

to these foreign ideas because of his earlier interest in iconoclastic Chinese concepts; Chen's interest in vernacular reform began with the ideas of philological research of his early Chinese compatriots.

In accord with this traditional iconoclasm, Chen, like the unknown editorial writer in the *Alarm Bell* quoted earlier (Chen sometimes contributed to this journal and was very closely associated with it) looked to iconoclastic sources within the Chinese tradition. In a radical break with traditional literary analysis later echoed by many of the New Culture writers, the anonymous author of the *Alarm Bell* article not only saw the Chinese vernacular novels as superior to the Confucian literature but looked to them as the "first pointer to vernacular newspapers, histories, and biographies."[34] The author attacked the Confucianists for not realizing this and falsely taking it as a sign that "the culture is daily declining." Showing the influence of Western revolutionary doctrines, the writer concluded by noting that "China in the present must pass through a stage of establishing the vernacular."[35]

In attempting to return to a vernacular tradition that supposedly had been abandoned by the Confucianists, the anonymous author mentioned above was not rejecting the Chinese past. Instead, while endeavoring to help China along the same path that the West had taken, he was also recalling a tradition in which the culture of the Chinese elite and masses had been united, as he imagined was the case in the contemporary West. Within even orthodox Confucian circles, the reform and simplification of literary writing was a recurrent countertheme; in modern times, this standard had been borne largely by the so-called Tongcheng faction. In his early years Chen Duxiu, in addition to his association with Zhang Binglin and other Han learning people, was also closely identified with this faction (largely as a result of family connections),[36] whose name was taken from the Tongcheng district of Chen's native Anhui.

[34] "Lun baihua bao yu zhongguo qiantu zhi guanxi."
[35] Ibid.
[36] Chen's father previously taught in Tongcheng, and Chen's family was associated with several prominent Tongcheng adherents. See the discussion at the end of this chapter.

Even as he labored to restore what he considered the traditions of the past, Chen moved beyond the desire of Tongcheng adherents to unify the style and intent of Chinese writing, to an embracement of what was previously considered to be the vulgar popular prose fiction of the masses. By doing so, Chen had hit on the formula that was to make his writings popular and accessible to a generation of young Chinese.

Over fifteen years later Chen Duxiu introduced the Chinese vernacular novel to a mass audience by editing the first punctuated versions of such classics as *Dream of the Red Chamber* and *The Scholars*.[37] In the *Anhui Common Speech Journal*, Chen Duxiu pioneered in the publication of short stories and even plays in the vernacular. Chen wrote a short novel himself, *Black Paradise (Hei tianguo)*, a love story about a Russian revolutionary sent to Siberia.[38] Moved by what he had learned about Western literature, he also tried to form drama troops to reach those who could not read the *Anhui Common Speech Journal*. Calling plays "the world's best educator," Chen insisted that "it is only in China that plays are regarded as vulgar. . . . In the West playwrights are on a par with other men of learning and culture."[39] To be sure, Chen still wanted rules for these new plays so that lewdness and superstition would not be allowed, so that the plays would concentrate instead on the elimination of bad customs.[40] Chen Duxiu's belief that language could introduce cultural change can further be seen in his attempt to do away with differences in speech as well as in writing. He proposed that the various Chinese dialects be replaced by a single national spoken language to be taught in the schools, and he suggested that this would promote national unity and a patriotic spirit.[41]

Chen Duxiu's faith in the suitability of the vernacular for

[37] Chen Duxiu, "Hong loumeng xinxu" [A new preface to *Dream of the Red Chamber*]; idem, "Rulin waishi xinxu" [A new preface to *The Scholars*].

[38] Sanai, "Hei tianguo" [Black paradise], *AHSHB* 11–15 (Aug. 1–Oct. 1, 1904).

[39] Sanai, "Lun xiqu" [On plays], *AHSHB* 11 (Aug. 1, 1904).

[40] Ibid.

[41] Sanai, "Guoyu jiaoyu" [The teaching of Mandarin], *AHSHB* 3 (April 1, 1904).

communicating with China's masses carried through later to his highly influential journal *New Youth* which he converted to the vernacular in 1917. In *New Youth*, Chen was considered radically innovative when he insisted that vernacular writings, being more natural and freely written, were basically superior to those written in the literary language. Few were then aware that Chen had adhered to this same principle in a journal he had edited a decade earlier. Similarly, few were aware that his attempts to unify China's spoken language had also been his goal for over a decade, and that it was to remain his goal for the rest of his life, even as he occasionally dabbled in what many took to be his somewhat eccentric and quite traditional philological research.

THE USE OF TRADITION

When Chen began his highly influential journal *Youth*, later *New Youth*, in 1915, many of the themes he emphasized in this publication that were assumed to be so novel were those that he had already written about earlier in the pages of the *Anhui Common Speech Journal*. Indeed, it is hard to write about the *Anhui Common Speech Journal* without thinking about this later publication.

In spite of the many similarities between the *Anhui Common Speech Journal* and *New Youth*, especially the importance of the two publications in the promotion of vernacular writing, there were also many differences among them. The first and most obvious was that *New Youth* was a far more sophisticated publication. By 1915, the year *New Youth* was established, Chen and his associates had obtained much more revolutionary experience and exposure to Western ideas than in 1905. Moreover, *New Youth* was written in Shanghai and then Beijing—areas which even in 1905 were much more cosmopolitan than Anhui. An illustration of these differences can be found in the reminiscences of one of Chen Duxiu's assistants on the *Anhui Common Speech Journal*, who suggested that even though he was relatively liberal for the time, he opposed as too radical Chen's calls in the paper for liberalization of marriage and for family planning, because he feared an official crackdown on the paper.[42] Another example of the backwardness of Anhui in 1904–1905 can be seen from the fact that when the *Anhui Common Speech Journal* pleaded for more reader contributions on Western science and industry, there were no takers.[43]

A more fundamental difference between *New Youth* and the *Anhui Common Speech Journal* is that by 1915 Chen was interested in a much more thorough transformation of traditional Chinese values than he had been before 1911. Though *New Youth* would occasionally cull positive examples from the Chinese past to support its acerbic comments about the present, it was generally much more hostile to the traditional culture than was the *Anhui Common Speech Journal*. Conversely, the *Anhui Common Speech Journal*, though studded with critical remarks about Confucianism and scathing in its denunciations of evil customs and superstitions, continually cited examples of heroism from the Chinese past.[44] Chen's initial reaction to Western ideas was through the eyes of the Chinese iconoclasts he had studied as a youth.

Although much of the discussion so far has emphasized the influence on Chen of the school of Han learning as well as of Kang Youwei and his associates, Chen had also been exposed to other traditional influences. An example of a different kind of influence can be seen in an article Chen wrote in the *Anhui Common Speech Journal* on the progressiveness of the system of education of the great Ming dynasty neo-Confucian philosopher Wang Yangming.[45] Wang's idealistic brand of neo-Confucianism, with its emphasis on self-cultivation, was

[42] Shen Ji, "Chen Duxiu he Anhui suhua bao," p. 18.

[43] "Guanggao" [Announcement], *AHSHB* 12 (Aug. 1, 1904).

[44] See the regular column of the *AHSHB*, "Zhongguo lidai de dashi" [Great events of past Chinese dynasties] and the more or less regular feature on military affairs, especially the two columns entitled "Zhongguo binghun lu" [A record of Chinese martial heroes] in issues 8 and 9 (Sept. 15 and Oct. 1, 1904).

[45] Sanai, "Wang Yangming xiansheng xunmeng dayi dejie" [An explanation of Wang Yangming's opinion on enlightening the youth], *AHSHB* 14 and 16 (Sept. 15 and Oct. 1, 1904).

generally condemned by the followers of the school of Han learning who felt Wang had helped introduce Buddhist doctrines into Confucian thought. But Chen cites Wang's ideas favorably, especially in his use of songs to encourage the "liveliness" of children and for the attention that Wang paid to the need to strengthen the body as well as the mind of his pupils. Chen felt the schools of his own day wrongfully used the opposite approach. He considered Wang's educational policies similar to those employed in the West and felt that they would help promote national strength by "following the original purpose and natural disposition of the mind" so as to develop independent students.[46]

Western imperialism initially awakened in Chen a sense of nationalistic pride in Chinese traditions. Although Chen wanted China to adopt the positive features he saw in Japan and the West, he still felt that Chinese tradition, particularly the traditions of the ancient past, could provide guidelines for solving the problems of the present. Just as he favored an education that could bring out the natural strength of Chinese students, so he hoped the original strength of the Chinese people could be fostered by a return to their national essence. Then the Chinese people would act again in the tradition of the great sage King Yu. In his article on Wang Yangming's system of education, Chen praised King Yu for having solved the problem of the floods. Chen felt the way Yu took advantage of the "natural flow" by working with nature in handling the waters is similar to what Wang Yangming (and Western educators) hoped to do with their students' "natural disposition of the mind."[47]

THE REBEL: TEACHER AND WARRIOR

This same attachment to certain traditional values and institutions that characterized Chen Duxiu's writings in the *Anhui Common Speech Journal* can be seen in the political and

[46] Ibid.
[47] Ibid.

intellectual activities in which he became involved while still editing the paper. Though the schools and revolutionary organizations in which Chen participated at this time were aimed at changing tradition, they were nevertheless based on the very conventional ties that Chen and his colleagues had made among the elite and on the age-old respect that students showed for their teachers. Typical of these organizations that used traditional structures for achieving untraditional goals was the Anhui Public School in Wuhu, where Chen Duxiu accepted a position in the summer of 1904, when he moved the *Anhui Common Speech Journal* to that town.

The Anhui Public School was established by a group of radicals under the direction of Li Guangjiung, one of the best-known students of Wu Rulun, an educational reformer in the late Qing dynasty. The radicals set up shop in Wuhu because of its strategic position within the Yangzi River Valley, from which they hoped to gain control of the central Yangzi and access to Nanjing, the old southern capital.[48] Perhaps even more important was that Li Guangjiung, whose earlier efforts to begin a school in Changsha in connection with the student revolutionary leaders Huang Xing and Zhang Ji had met with persecution, could take advantage in Wuhu of the protection of the powerful Li Hongzhang family. In his time Li Hongzhang had been China's most powerful viceroy; his son, Li Jingmei, was the titular head of the school.

The Li family contributed much to the institution's funding.[49] Chen's selection for the position as a special lecturer at the Anhui Public School may also have resulted from the rumored connections between his family and that of Li Hongzhang: Chen's father-in-law was a noted army official asso-

[48] "Zhonghua minguo zhiqian Anhui yu geming dangren zhi huodong" [The movement of the revolutionary party in Anhui before the founding of the Republic], in *Zhonghua minguo kaiguo wushinian wenxian*, vol. 12, sec. 1, p. 184. Also see Yu Yimi, *Wuhu xianzhi.*

[49] Feng Xu, "Zai wuhu ban xuetang" [The establishment of revolutionary schools in Wuhu], manuscript from the Anhui Historical Society; see especially the preface to this work. This association was also confirmed to me in an interview with Jin Weixi, Taipei, 1975.

ciated with Li Hongzhang's military; the *Anhui Common Speech Journal* spearheaded the successful movement to recover the Tongshan mining rights from the British and return them to a provincial company to be run by the Anhui gentry, a movement with which the Lis were also closely connected;[50] and in 1908 Chen's family capped their wealth by building a huge housing complex on land in Anqing, adjoining property owned by the Li Hongzhang family, often a sign of close connections in traditional Chinese society.[51]

Some of the best-known radical and intellectual lights in China were associated with the Anhui Public School, including the radical scholar Liu Shipei, the writer Su Manshu, and the first revolutionary governor of Anhui, Bo Wenwei. While at the school, Liu helped to recruit for the Restoration Society, furnishing the society head, Cai Yuanpei, with a list of the names of over a hundred new members in one message alone in 1905.[52] Others helped work for Sun Yatsen's revolutionary group, the Revolutionary Alliance (Tongmeng hui), an organization that Chen pointedly refused to join, scorning it as being composed mostly of the scions of high officials. In refusing to join this national revolutionary group, which had the allegiance of most of the radical students of the time, Chen displayed the preference for the sort of independent organization that could be controlled by him personally that was to characterize him throughout his life. For in this distinguished company it was Chen Duxiu who was to organize the area's most powerful revolutionary organization—the Warrior Yue Society (Yuewang hui)—a group that, though short-lived, was to be extraordinarily influential in its activities.

Chen's teaching and editing had given him great influence

---

[50] Record of the British Foreign Office, ME 2963, F.O. 371/18–19, letter of October 10, 1906. See also ME 2989 (1907). The British dispatches constantly complained that "Lord Li" (Li Jingfang), who was supposed to be helping the British obtain mining rights in Anhui, was actually on the side of the rebels.

[51] "Chen Jiawen tan Chen Duxiu," *Chen Duxiu yanjiu ziliao*, p. 92.

[52] "Wuhu dichu de xinhai geming," *Anhui shixue tongsu [The Anhui Historical Studies Bulletin]*, Dec. 1959.

among Anhui student radicals. In forming the Warrior Yue Society, he took advantage of his standing among his readers and students as a respected intellectual figure; later, as he was beginning formation of the Chinese Communist party, his editorship of *New Youth* and his position as dean of the Faculty of Arts and Letters at Beijing University served the same purpose. The influence Chen exercised through the *Anhui Common Speech Journal* can be seen by British reaction to the paper. The British put pressure on the Qing government to close the paper, finally succeeding in early 1905. (The Chinese government may incidentally also have been worried by the leading role of the paper in the anti-American boycott of 1905.)[53] The British consul in Anqing wrote to his government about the movement Chen was organizing, complaining that "the young are in strong ascendency and seem to be exerting a strong influence on the Mandarinate."[54] Still British efforts did not prevent Chen from expanding his influence over the student youth of Anhui. By 1906, he had taken on two new jobs—one as a teacher at the Wan Jiang Middle School (Wanjiang zhongxue)[55] and the other as director of educational matters at the Official Weizhou Elementary Accelerated Teachers' School (Gongli Weizhou chuji sucheng shifang xuetang).[56]

In effect then, Chen, while belaboring the traditional Chinese family, was to take advantage of traditional relationships to form his own revolutionary organization and exert his own revolutionary appeal; the customary role and authority of the teacher in Chinese society was much like that of the parent. Chen, who himself came from a family of teachers, used this

[53] Fang Zhiwu, "Fang Zhiwu huiyi 'Suhua bao' shi yi shou" [A poem about Fang Zhiwu's remembrances of the *Common Speech Journal*], in *Anhui geming yanjiu ziliao*, vol. 1. See also H. B. Taylor to U. M. Martin, July 26, 1907, enclosed in a report of Hankow consul U. M. Martin Jan. 29, 1907, U.S. Dept. of State, General Records, Record Group 59, Numerical F.C. no. 8019/2–3. Also see E. Satow in letter dated March 7, 1906, ME 2970, F.O. 371/25–6.

[54] Quoted from Sir Charles Dudgeon, ME 29633, F.O. 371.

[55] Feng Xu, "Zai Wuhu ban geming xuetang."

[56] Ibid.

authority to form his students into a small, tightly knit group like a family—a pattern Chen was to repeat throughout his life.

It is not coincidental that Chen named the group he formed with these students the Warrior Yue Society. The group was named in honor of the Song patriot Yue Fei, who stemmed the Jurched invasion of China in the twelfth century and was eventually martyred for his efforts by a peace faction in the capital when he recalcitrantly continued to insist on attempting to recover the lost Chinese territories in the northern part of the country. In the *Anhui Common Speech Journal*, Chen had honored the heroes of China's past. In writing about these heroic figures, Chen had shown his adherence to Zhang Binglin's ideas that these great men of the past were part of China's national essence, which if restored could revive the Chinese nation. Zhang had particularly singled out Yue Fei as deserving of emulation because he "employed southern troops to defeat the barbarians."[57] In accord with this idea, Chen requested from members of the Warrior Yue Society the heroic actions that had been exhibited by the great figures of the Chinese past. Still acting on the convictions that had motivated his participation in the Shanghai Assassination Corps the year before, Chen asked his followers to risk their lives to awaken the Chinese people with their example.

Like the Restoration Society and other groups operating at this time, the Warrior Yue Society was a small, conspiratorial organization that relied upon assassinations and infiltration of the armed forces to achieve its aims and used secret oaths and ceremonies as well as coded writings to conceal its plans.[58]

[57] Zhang Binglin, "Yanshuo lu," p. 12.

[58] Wang Yugao, "Bo Wenwei zhuan" [A biography of Bo Wenwei], *Anhui wenxian*, vol. 1, no. 4, pp. 2–8. Also, Sun Zhuanyuan, "Xinhai geming qian Anhui wenjiaojie de geming huodong" [The revolutionary cultural movement in Anhui before the 1911 Revolution], *Zhonghua minguo wushinian wenxian*, vol. 2, pp. 384–85. Chang Hengfang, "Ji Anhui yuewang hui" [Remembrances of the Anhui Warrior Yue Society], *Xinhai geming huiyi lu* 4:431–37. Also, Chen Zifeng, "Bo Liewu xiansheng geming tanhua gao" [An outline of a discussion with Bo Wenwei], 1941. Guomindang Historical Archives, Taiwan. Chang Hengfang, "Shi lieshi jingwu zhuan" [A biography of the

Despite its limited size, its activities were extremely widespread.

Formed mainly from a small group of Chen Duxiu's students and fellow staff members, the group soon gained adherents from among those living in areas where the *Anhui Common Speech Journal* circulated. Two fellow teachers, Bo Wenwei and Chang Hengfang, were Chen's chief lieutenants, and the three men used their school vacations for travel into the northern part of the province to expand their organization. Bo and Chang were northerners and were able to gain military contacts in these areas. Chen may have been able to use his connections with his father-in-law, an important northern military man, to increase his own influence. As a result, Chen was able to make contact with people such as Sun Yuyun, who later was to become the first revolutionary governor of Anhui and then a turncoat to the cause and a supporter of Yuan Shikai's efforts to dampen revolutionary reforms.[59] With these contacts, the Warrior Yue Society expanded to the point where it became desirable for Chang Hengfang to move to Anqing, where he became the head of a separate chapter of the society. Chen Duxiu, as overall chairman of the organization, remained in Wuhu, directing the local branch and coordinating policy for the operations of the society as a whole.[60]

The society became best known for the action of one of its members, Wu Yue, a former student of Chen Duxiu. In Beijing in September 1905, Wu attempted to assassinate the five members of an imperial mission slated to depart for an inspection tour of governmental institutions in Europe. Wu planned his attack in conjunction with Chen Duxiu and other members of the Warrior Yue Society in Chen's rooms above the Science

---

martyred Shi Jingwu], *Anhui wenxian*, vol. 4, no. 5 (1937), pp. 3–4. Also, "Bo Wenwei shilue." [A brief account of the events of Bo Wenwei's life], *Anhui wenxian*, vol. 1, no. 4 (Jan. 1948). Shen Ji, "Xinhai geming shiqi de yuewang hui [The Warrior Yue Society of the time of the 1911 Revolution]," *Lishi yanjiu [Historical Research]* 10 (1979):36–45.

[59] Shen Ji, "Xinhai geming shiqi." Also, Chang Hengfang, "Ji Anhui yuewang hui." Also, Sun Zhuanyuan, "Xinhai geming qian Anhui."

[60] Ibid.

Book Company in Wuhu;[61] some evidence suggests that Wu may even have built the bomb in the house of Chen Duxiu's stepfather in Manchuria.[62] As it happened, the bomb Wu had intended for the five imperial commissioners blew up in his own hands before he could carry out his attempt, but the highly celebrated event provided impetus for the revolutionary cause. Moreover, Wu's posthumous writings served to popularize his elitist ideas and assassination methods.[63]

Wu's racist testament held that the only way to create revolution was to kill Manchus, and he called for the use of assassination to "build the people's morale and promote the spirit of bravery."[64] The ideas in this document, particularly the emphasis on bravery, are extensions of the notions extolled by Chen in the pages of the *Anhui Common Speech Journal* and are indications of the success of Chen's teaching to the members of his group. Following Wu's failure, the members of the Warrior Yue Society were involved in a whole series of assassination plots and military schemes throughout late 1905 and early 1906. The secondary organizations formed by Warrior Yue Society members to carry out their plots provide an interesting picture of the dazzling organizational strategy of Chen Duxiu and his fellow revolutionaries. In Wuhu, Bo Wenwei, Liu Shihpei, and Li Guangjiung formed a Yellow Race School that specialized in teaching assassination methods.[65] Around the same time, Shi Jingwu, an Anhui man who was to become a martyr to the movement when he was arrested by the Qing authorities in early 1911, established a branch of the organization in northern Anhui. In order to disguise the activities of this group while recruiting further

    [61] Ibid. Also Guan Peng, "Anhui geming jilue" [A remembrance of the Anhui revolution], in *Zhonghua minguo kaiguo wushinian wenxian* 2:253–57. Also "Wu Yue," in *Anqing shihua [A historical discussion of Anqing]*, pp. 78–79.
    [62] Interview with Lin Maosheng, Beijing, 1981.
    [63] Mary Backus Rankin, *Early Chinese Revolutionaries*, pp. 39–40, 107–8.
    [64] Wu Yue, "Zixu" [Personal introduction], in Feng Ziyou, *Geming yishi*, vol. 3, pp. 199–202.
    [65] Chen Zifeng, "Bo Liewu xiansheng geming tanhua gao." Also, Wang Yugao, "Bo Wenwei zhuan." See also Shen Ji, "Xinhai geming shiqi."

members to the cause, Shi was authorized by Chen to establish two new cover organizations, the Chinese Race Society (Hua zu hui) and the Comforting Heart Group (Wei xin hui).[66] The pronunciation of the Chinese characters of this latter group is very similar to that of the Reform Society (Wei xin hui), another suborganization of the Warrior Yue Society formed in Anqing to assist in the recruitment of the new army soldiers from the Third Battalion stationed there.[67]

Meanwhile, Bo Wenwei, a graduate of the Anhui Military Academy, managed to receive a commission in the Thirty-third Regiment (Biao sui) in Nanjing.[68] As the head of the Warrior Yue Society in that area, Bo was involved in the attempts by Sun Yuyun (whom Bo was later to succeed as governor of Anhui) to assassinate the infamous Qing dynasty governor-general Duan Fang, whose rule made life so difficult for the revolutionaries. Bo assisted Sun with explosives and tranportation expenses. But when the plot failed and Sun was jailed, Bo had to flee the area.[69]

By mid-1906, as a result of the growing number of revolutionary plots of the Warrior Yue Society, pressure on the organization had begun to intensify.[70] And in 1907, after Xu

[66] Shen Ji, "Xinhai geming shiqi." Chang Hengfang, "Shi lieshi jingwu zhuan," pp. 3–4.

[67] Shen Ji, "Xinhai geming shiqi." Also, Chang Hengfang, "Ji Anhui yue-wang hui."

[68] Shen Ji, "Xinhai geming shiqi." Also, Chen Zifeng, "Bo Liewu xiansheng geming tanhua gao." Also, Wang Yugao, "Bo Wenwei zhuan," pp. 92–94.

[69] Ibid.

[70] In the summer of 1906, Chen Duxiu and Su Manshu made a trip to Japan, perhaps to escape the intense government crackdown that ensued after Sun Yuyun's arrest or perhaps to seek new recruits for the Warrior Yue Society among the Chinese students in the Japanese military academies. Although Chen apparently enrolled in some courses at this time, by the fall he and Su were back in Anhui, where they were joined by their former Shanghai roommate, Zhang Shizhao. It has been suggested that it was at this time that Chen participated in a brief effort to found another radical paper in Anhui, the *Anhui Vernacular Journal (Anhui baihua bao)*; but this is impossible, since that paper was not published before early 1908, when Chen Duxiu was in Japan.

The Anhui Public School eventually was divided into two parts, one a middle school and the other a teachers' college. The teachers' college grew

Xilin's assassination of Enming,[71] the governor of Anhui, a
general crackdown on revolutionaries in the area forced Chen,
Liu, and most of the other leading revolutionaries to flee the
area. Chen fled from Wuhu to Japan, where he remained for
the next two years.[72] He did not go to France during this
period, as some have claimed.[73]

The popular story of Chen's alleged visit to France during
this period seems to have arisen from a misreading of a Japanese source which discusses the visit to France by Chen Duxiu's two eldest sons.[74] Since in his *New Youth* period Chen

---

into the Wuhu Women's Teachers' College, while the middle school became
the Anhui Provincial Number Two Agricultural School. See Anhui kexue
. . . , "Wuhu dichu de xinhai geming." Also, "Su Manshu yu Liu San shu"
[A letter from Su Manshu to Liu San], July 1906, in *Su Manshu chuanji [The
complete works of Su Manshu]*, vol. 1, p. 331. Liu Yazi, "Manshu he wo de
guanxi" [My relation with Su Manshu], in Liu Yazi, ed., *Manshu chuanji*,
vol. 5. He Zhiyou, "Duxiu zhuzuo nian biao," p. 2. Chen Chunsheng, "Anhui
zhi geming wenhua yundong," p. 35. Zhi Youru, *Chen Duxiu nianpu [Yearly
chronology of Chen Duxiu]*, p. 14. See also, "Li Guangjiung xiansheng shilue."

[71] Xu was a fellow member of the Restoration Society. His assassination
plot has usually been assumed to have been carried out without the knowledge
or cooperation of any of the other radical leaders in the area, including Chen
Duxiu. (See Rankin, *Early Chinese Revolutionaries*, pp. 179–81.) In my
interviews with Chinese historians in 1981, many of them expressed the belief
that Xu was connected with Chen's Warrior Yue Society, though they admitted that no evidence proving this conclusively had as yet been found.
Anyone connected with Xu in this plot would have attempted to destroy all
evidence of their involvement.

[72] Anhui kexue . . . , "Wuhu dichu de xinhai geming," and "Ji Anhui yuewang hui."

[73] See, for instance, Chow Tse-tsung, *The May Fourth Movement*, p. 42.
See also Howard Boorman, ed., *Biographical Dictionary of Republican China*,
1:241.

[74] See Nakajima Nagafumi, *Chin Dokushu Ninpu Chohen skoku [A first
draft of a yearly chronology of Chen Duxiu]*, Kyoto Sangyo Daigaku Ronshu
[Kyoto Industrial University Papers], no. 3, Gaikokugo to Bunka Keiretsu
[Foreign language and culture series], vol. 2, no. 1 (March 1972), p. 174.
Thomas Kuo makes a similar point, although he was unable to confirm Chen's
stay in Japan during this period; see Kuo, *Ch'en Tu-hsiu*, p. 35, no. 3. Some
of the controversy over this issue is ridiculous, particularly the dispute as to
whether or not Chen knew French. Since he frequently used French sources,
there is no reason to believe that Chen did not understand the language.

was known, somewhat misleadingly, as an ardent Francophile, it apparently was assumed that Chen himself had gone
to France and that the visit had to have been during this period,
when his activities were not well known. But Chen's presence
in Japan from 1907 to 1909 (in 1909 he returned to China
for his brother's funeral) is confirmed by the recollection and
correspondence of several of his friends from this time.[75]
Moreover, none of the Chinese students who were in France
prior to 1911 had any memory of Chen's presence,[76] nor did
the Chinese Educational Ministry list Chen's name among this
small group of students.[77] The simple explanation for this was
that Chen Duxiu was in Japan during this period, concerned
with the national studies movement and apparently closely
associated with Zhang Binglin, Liu Shipei, and other scholars
from the *National Essence Journal (Guocui xuebao)*.[78] Chen

Chen could have learned French either during his studies at the Chiushi
Academy, where he is alleged to have studied French and English, or later
during one of his stays in Japan. During his sojourn in that country in 1914,
Chen seems to have made a concerted effort to learn about the West.

[75] Chen Duxiu, "Shu ai." This must have occurred after the beginning of
the year. In a letter written in early 1909, Su Manshu mentioned that Chen
was still living in Japan. Wen Gongzhi, ed., *Manshu dashi chuanji* [*The
collected works of the Reverend Manshu*], p. 178.

[76] Su Manshu, "Su Manshu yu Liu San shu" [A letter from Su Manshu to
Liu San], 1909, in *Su Manshu chuanji*, p. C21. Sun Bocun remembers seeing
Chen and the Minbao people together in 1907–1908, as quoted in Nakajima,
Chin Dokushu, 2:165–66. In a discussion with Liu Yazi concerning Su Man-
shu, Chen mentioned talking with Su about Liu Shipei's falling out with
Zhang Binglin when the two lived in Japan in 1908–1909; see "Ji Chen
Zhongfu guanyu Su Manshu de tanhua." See also Kuo, *Ch'en Tu-hsiu*, p.
35. Also, Zhi Yuru, *Chen Duxiu nianpu*, pp. 16–17. Moreover, during this
period Chen joined with Zhang Binglin, Su Manshu, and others in forming
the Asian Study Society and in making plans for a Sanskrit Library.

[77] Archives of the Ministry of Education of the Republic of China (now
stored in Taiwan).

[78] Chen wrote an article for the *National Essence Journal*; see "Shuowen
yin shen yixiao" [The speaking and writing inferred from the Yili and the
Xiaojing], *Guocui xuebao (National Essence Journal)* 6 and 7 (1910). This
was published by Liu Shipei in 1910 after he had defected from the revolutionary cause and supported the Qing dynasty. Chen was one of the very
few revolutionaries who continued to remain in touch with Liu after this
time.

wrote his first published philological article for the *National Essence Journal* at this time.

NATIONAL ESSENCE

In Japan, Chen continued his philological studies of the origins of Chinese words and pursued an interest in Buddhism. Although these two studies seem somewhat antithetical, they clearly have a similar root—a desire to find a Chinese national essence that would provide a basis for restoring the vitality and courage of the Chinese nation. In discussing Wang Yangming's theory of education, Chen had mentioned the need for education to bring out a person's "natural disposition," a goal he considered analogous to that of a ruler—in this case Yu—working successfully with his nation. The influence here of Chan or Zen Buddhist ideas (condemned in the earlier article "Admonition to Youth" in the *China National Gazette* mentioned in the previous chapter) is apparent and may have been one of the bases for Chen's interest in Buddhist doctrine.

In the *Anhui Common Speech Journal*, Chen had acknowledged that he was a Buddhist, a belief he had in common with Zhang Binglin and Su Manshu, who saw Buddhism as a possible alternative to Confucianism as the source of China's traditions.[79] Chen, Su Manshu, Gui Bohua, and Zhang Binglin even became involved in a project to start a Sanskrit library of Buddhist works in 1909, but the project fell through for lack of funds.[80] Chen himself seems to have begun the study of Sanskrit at this time, as did Zhang Binglin and other members of their group.[81] And a short time later, at least one of Su's references to Chen uses the respectful *jushi* after his name, a term commonly reserved for members of the Buddhist lay

[79] Michael Gasster, *Chinese Intellectuals and the Revolution of 1911*, pp. 197–200.

[80] Liu Wu-chi, *Su Man-shu*, p. 61.

[81] Nakajima, *Chin Dokushu*, 2:175.

priesthood.[82] It is extremely unlikely that this was meant to be taken literally, especially since Chen began in 1910 to live openly with Gao Junman, his wife's younger sister, with whom he had two children.[83] Rather, it is a sign of his great interest in Buddhism, one reflected not only in his poems but also in his later interpretations of certain Western philosophical concepts.

Since Buddhism is not originally a Chinese doctrine, it would seem strange that Chen would be interested in this religion as a possible source of national inspiration for China. But Chen's primary allegiance was to a national essence which sought the physical preservation of the Chinese people. In turning to Buddhism, Chen was turning to a source that would explain how to revitalize personal and national vigor; he was also seeking common roots with other Asian countries he hoped would unite with China to defeat foreign imperialism. In March 1908 Chen, along with Zhang Binglin, Zhang Ji, Liu Shipei, Su Manshu, and others, formed an Asian Cousins Society "in order to oppose imperialism and protect the allied nationalities."[84] The society suggested the use of the various traditional religions and philosophies of Asia to combat the "false doctrines" of the West. Moreover, it was opened to "all Asian people, except those promoting invasion of other countries," regardless of whether they were "nationalists, republicans, socialists, or anarchists"; it was predicated on the assumption that when a revolution occurred in one Asian nation, the people from the other nations would support it.[85]

Chen's interest in the biological and territorial preservation

[82] Chen Duxiu, "Ti Su Shanran tianwan tianshi" [Verse preface to Su Manshu's Sanskrit dictionary], *Tianyi bao*, Sept. 1, 1907.

[83] Anqing shi lishi xuehui, "Chen Duxiu jiashi gaolue," in *Chen Duxiu yanjiu cankao ziliao*, pp. 192–193. Also, Li Fanqun, "Chen Duxiu nianbiao buzheng," in ibid., p. 227. When Chen returned to Anqing with Gao Zhunman, he did not dare to move into the family compound with her but rented rooms on the other side of town; see Chen Songnian, "Zaifang Chen Songnian tanhua jilu," p. 10.

[84] Zhang Taiyan, *Zhang Taiyan nianpu zhangpian [A Yearly Chronology of Zhang Taiyan]*, pp. 243–44.

[85] Ibid.

of the Chinese people made him very selective in his choice
of what parts of Chinese tradition he hoped to salvage. Although his interest in the Asian Cousins Society was to be a
temporary phenomenon, it shows how Chen's biological nationalism could lead to a pan-Asianism similar to his later
internationalism.

Chen's intellectual ambivalence toward Chinese tradition
at this time paralleled a similar ambivalence in his personal
life and in his style of political action. Though he denounced
the traditional Chinese family as a great evil to the Chinese
nation, Chen's own relations with his large patriarchal family
remained strong. In spite of the shock he gave his family at
this time by beginning his liaison with his wife's younger half-
sister, traditionally this did not prevent Chen from simultaneously continuing to have relations with his wife (Chen's
youngest son, Chen Songnian, was born to his legal spouse
in 1912).[86] Nor did Chen prevent his wife and children from
moving into the sumptuous new quarters erected by his uncle
in Anqing—quarters described by several relatives as resembling those in the famous picture of feudal Chinese family
life, "Dream of the Red Chamber."[87] Moreover, it was Chen
Duxiu, an excellent calligrapher, who wrote the characters
for the newly constructed ancestral temple.[88]

Chen also took advantage of his family's position in carrying out his radical activities. It was no doubt because he
was the scion of a wealthy family that he was able to edit a
radical newspaper in Anhui. In addition, his espousal of the
development of Anhui's industrial resources by an Anhui company certainly represented the interests of at least a considerable portion of the Anhui gentry, probably especially those
already interested in commerce, such as his stepfather and the
Li Hongzhang family, with whom his stepfather may have
been associated.

[86] Li Fanqun, "Chen Duxiu nianbiao buzheng," p. 227.
[87] Ma Qirong and San Yijiao, "Guanyu Chen Duxiu yinqi de xie qingkuang." (This was based on an interview in Beijing with a former wife of
one of Chen Duxiu's sons who lived in the house for a while.)
[88] Chen Xiawen, "Chen Xiawen tan Chen Duxiu," p. 93.

Upper Versus Lower Gentry

There would seem to be a considerable amount of hypocrisy on Chen's part if one is to believe the report that at about the same time he used his connections to further his revolutionary activities, he refused to join the Revolutionary Alliance (Tongmenghui) organized in 1905 by Sun Yatsen—although almost all of the other members of the Warrior Yue Society joined it. Chen's reasons for refusing to join the Revolutionary Alliance were his objections to what he considered to be the Alliance's excessive nationalism,[89] and his condescending dismissal of its members as the sons of high officials.[90]

One explanation for this seeming duplicity is that in fact Chen was not simultaneously reaping benefits from the same group of people he was denouncing. Rather, he was responding very differently to two different groups—between which there were, in Chen's mind, vast distinctions. These two groups were the upper and lower strata of the scholar-official class. While the upper stratum of the scholar-official group served as a nonspecialized class that was more concerned with humanistic problems and moral dilemmas than with technical solutions to social, economic, military, or even scientific difficulties, the actual running of Chinese society was often left to those legions of clerks, landlords, merchants, and others who were part of the scholar-official group but not part of its upper stratum.

Chen and his family, as previously mentioned, tended to sympathize with the active, pragmatic lower level of the scholar-official group. Despite the fact that at the end of the Qing dynasty, *juren* like Chen's uncle and others managed to move up to the highest reaches of power, these people did not necessarily identify with this stratum. (This is true particularly for Chen Duxiu, whose family did not move into their very large new quarters until he was already grown.) Chen was able to take advantage of the resentment between these two

---

[89] Lin Maosheng, "Dui Chen Duxiu pinjia de jige wenti" [Several problems in evaluating Chen Duxiu], in Hu Hua, ed., *Zhongguo xiandai shijiao*.

[90] Draft of an interview with Chen Yunshan, Beijing, 1979.

groups in his early revolutionary activities, for in Anhui these conflicts were particularly severe and of a regional as well as a class nature. Throughout the Qing, the upper level of the scholar-gentry class in Anhui had been concentrated in a few large clans in the south-central part of the province, especially the rich districts of Taihu, Tongcheng, and Huaining. It is therefore understandable that the *Anhui Common Speech Journal* did not circulate very well among the citizens of Wuhu, in south-central Anhui, where it was published.[91] Rather, the journal's circulation was highest in the area where the lower level of the scholar-gentry was most concentrated—in the northern and southern areas of the province, particularly Huizhou, Luzhou, and Yingzhou.[92]

Luzhou, now Hefei, located in central Anhui, was the hometown of Li Hongzhang, one of the first organizers of this lower stratum of gentry, and the prime area of recruitment for the officers of Li's Huai Army.[93] Although many from Luzhou prospered in the late nineteenth century because of their military connections, they were still not accepted as members of the upper level of the scholar-gentry class and so were bound to resent those south-central gentry who had long dominated the educational system in the province with their monopolistic knowledge of the complex literary language. This was particularly true of those youths who had seen the examination system greatly curtailed shortly before the start-up of the *Anhui Common Speech Journal*, and who felt doubly embittered against those whose position they had coveted and who had now changed the rules on them.

Chen put to use the resentful feelings of these young, lower-stratum gentry in a constructive fashion, harnessing their fury to fight against British incursions into the province, rallying his readers to put a halt to "the plundering of Anhui's mountain mining," and even issuing a special "Warning" cover about the subject in the ninth edition of his journal.[94] Spurred

---

[91] "Anhui suhua bao zhi xiaolu," *Jingzhong ribao*, June 11, 1904.
[92] Ibid.
[93] Stanley Spector, *Li Hung-chang and the Huai Army*, pp. 301–14.
[94] Anhui kexue . . . , "Wuhu dichu de xinhai geming," p. 74.

on by Chen and irked by the dispatch of British mining officials into their province, the gentry, particularly the younger ones in Tongguanshan, near Luzhou, where the British with the acquiescence of the Chinese government were attempting to take over mining rights, demanded the right to form their own company and carry out the mining operations in the province themselves, a familiar scenario in the last years of the Qing dynasty.[95]

Although the lower-stratum gentry of Huizhou, the second area where the *Anhui Common Speech Journal* was widely circulated, would not have been so keenly interested in the Tongguanshan mines, they were very concerned about the effects of the imperialist penetration of their province. Huizhou was well known for its tea and produced many famous trading families, whose sons had frequently excelled at the imperial examinations. The wealth sent back into this otherwise poor area by these merchants had created a strong tradition of scholarship in the region.[96] Nonetheless, the area had not been made into a treaty port and thus was not able to compete in trade or wealth with Wuhu or even Anqing, which became treaty ports after the signing of the Zifu convention. People from the Huizhou locale would therefore also have tended to resent the educational and economic dominance of the south-central areas of the province, particularly its ties to Western trade, at a time when their own status was declining.

Yingzhou, in northern Anhui, the third area where the *Anhui Common Speech Journal* had its strongest circulation, was known for its military men in the late Qing. Like Huizhou and Luzhou, the region had not grasped the reins of the political power of the province, and so the gentry of the area

[95] Record of the British Foreign Office, ME 2963, F.O. 371/18–19, letter of October 20, 1906. See also ME 2989 (1907). The Anhui gentry were aided in this effort by Li Hongzhang's sons. The Li family assumed a dual role in the dispute, attempting at times to mediate on behalf of the British government while still aiding the Anhui gentry, whom Li Hongzhang had first helped organize and whose support his family continued to depend upon.

[96] P'ing-ti Ho, *The Ladder of Success in Imperial China* (New York, 1964), pp. 73–80.

also tended to be concerned with the issues raised by Chen's journal.

These areas had in common the fact that although their elites had mastered specific skills—whether mercantile or military—they had been somewhat deprived of position by the gentry of south-central Anhui. Thus the elites of these outlying areas were likely to view the introduction of Western ideology, which advocated the mastery of just such skills, as a welcome phenomenon that might liberate them from what Thomas Metzger has called the "predicament" of Confucian thought: they believed their morality should resolve social problems yet they were aware that this was not sufficient.[97] Chen's advocacy of the skills and ideas associated with the great material advances of the West appealed to the elite because these skills and ideas might help them out of their predicament while permitting them to remain firmly attached to the tradition in which they had advanced themselves.

GENTRY REVOLUTION IN ANHUI

It is therefore no wonder that many of Chen's ideas were so popular among the Anhui gentry and that some in fact succeeded in being implemented in a very short time. In 1909, after Chen had been forced to flee Anhui, one of the goals for which he had worked was achieved: an all-Chinese mining company was formed to supplant the British efforts in Anhui.[98] Though the people of his province had begun to assert their rights, they did so with the kind of disunity and wavering of which Chen had accused his fellow gentry in his first speech before the Anhui Patriotic Society.

On October 10, 1911, when a minor uprising broke out among a small group of soldiers in the central Yangzi city of Wuhan, the people of Anhui were as unprepared for the collapse of the Qing dynasty as was most of the rest of the country. The activities of revolutionaries such as Chen had

[97] Thomas Metzger, *Escape from Predicament: Neo-Confucianism and China's Evolving Political Culture*, see esp. chap. 3.
[98] Anhui kexue . . . , "Wuhu dichu de xinhai geming."

demoralized the Qing forces, who were fearful that dissent was widespread in their ranks. The gentry, sensing the possibility that local power might fall into their laps, were unwilling to aid the dynasty. In Anhui, which had a large Qing garrison in Anqing, the revolutionary forces were even more uncoordinated than in the rest of the south. The revolution in the province was supported by a series of disparate and uncoordinated local movements, mostly carried out by military power in the areas in which the *Anhui Common Speech Journal* had circulated. Revolutionary governments were formed in the far north of the province, in Luzhou (Hefei), in Wuhu, and in Huizhou.[99] As might have been predicted in this situation, it was not until outside revolutionary troops arrived that the provincial capital at Anqing was finally captured. The province was firmly united under a revolutionary government on November 28, 1911.

The new government was headed by Chen's old revolutionary associate, Sun Yuyun, who promptly made Chen the head of the Anhui provincial secretariat and one of his most trusted advisers.[100] But from the beginning Sun found himself

[99] "Anhui geming jilue," *Xuefeng*, p. 12. Also, "Xinhai geming qian Anhui wenjiao jie de geming huodong."

[100] Ibid. Also Guan Peng, "Anhui geming jishi." Anhui kexue . . . , "Wuhu dichu de xinhai geming." Also Chen Zifeng, "Bo Liewu xiansheng geming tanhua gao." Sun Zhuanyuan, "Anhui geming jilue," p. 11. Chen Zifeng, "Bo Wenwei jiu hen anhui dudu jingguo" [The proceedings in Bo Wenwei's assumption of the Anhui governorship], in *Zhonghua minguo kaiguo wushinian wenxian*, vol. 2, bk. 4, pp. 297–300. Bo's troops entered Anqing on December 1, 1911, three days after Sun Yuyun assumed the governorship with Bo's help and also with the support of a Youth Army formed by Han Yan. After Han was assassinated, Sun, who as a result had been forced to depend increasingly on Bo Wenwei for power, turned against many of his former revolutionary colleagues and went to work for Yuan Shikai, leaving the governorship to Bo Wenwei. It has usually been assumed that Han was killed by an agent of Yuan Shikai, who had a long-standing personal enmity against him. At the time, however, there were several accusations that it was Bo Wenwei who had plotted Han's death so that Bo could personally assume the governorship. This is partially supported by a telegram from that time, sent by Han Yan's Youth Army, defending Han's character from the allegations being spread against him by Bo shortly after Han's death. The Youth

in a weak position, forced to rely on the military might of Bo Wenwei, Chen's former Warrior Yue Society lieutenant. Sun was enticed by Yuan Shikai's offers of an official post at Beijing, and in May he turned against many of his former revolutionary colleagues and allied himself with Yuan.[101] Sun Yuyun's desertion had an electrifying effect on the revolutionary camp. He had been a distinguished member of the Revolutionary Alliance; as a member of Yuan Shikai's camp, Sun defended Yuan's attempts to break up the independent legislative efforts of the revolutionary group headed by Sun Yatsen and Huang Xing at Nanjing, thus helping to destroy the revolutionaries' cohesiveness. Later, Sun Yuyun was one of the most eloquent supporters of Yuan's attempt to restore the monarchy.

Immediately after Sun's resignation, Chen left the government, accepting a position as head of the Anhui Upper Level School, soon to be renamed Anhui University, the most important educational institution in the province.[102] When Bo Wenwei himself moved in to end the chaotic situation in Anhui and assume the governorship directly, Chen returned to his job as head of the secretariat and Bo's most important deputy, working with Bo to ban opium, open skill centers for poor people, and establish a women's school.[103] But they soon found their work hampered by the increasingly autocratic policies

---

Army was eventually dissolved by Bo. See "Nanjing linshi jengfu gongbao" [The proclamations of the Nanjing temporary government], no. 24 (Feb. 28, 1912), as published in *Xinhai geming ziliao [Material on the 1911 revolution]*, p. 197. In either case, it is clear that Chen had aligned himself with Bo Wenwei's outside military force rather than the spontaneous revolutionary elements within the province.

[101] See "Nanjing linshi jengfu gongbao," p. 197.

[102] Chen Zifeng, "Bo Wenwei jiuhen Anhui dudu jingguo." Liu Wu-chi, *Su Man-shu*, p. 98. Wu Xiangxiang claims that Chen became educational commissioner for the whole province at this time; see *Minguo bairen zhuan [Biographies of 100 people of the Republic]*, vol. 3, p. 391. See also He Zhiyou, "Duxiu zhuzuo nian biao," p. 3.

[103] "Jinggao Bo dudu qi ge sheng xingcheng ting" [Telling about Governor Bo Wenwei's administration], *Duli zhoubao [Independence Weekly]*, 10 (Nov. 24, 1912):37.

of Yuan Shikai, who himself had originally risen to power as a member of Li Hongzhang's Huai or Anhui Army.

In 1913 Sun Yatsen made a last-ditch effort to regroup the revolutionary forces of the south and overthrow the growing autocratic power of Yuan Shikai. Bo Wenwei joined the rebels (according to some sources, mainly on Chen's urging),[104] but few of the gentry of the province were willing to support him, and the new revolution in Anhui, as elsewhere, was quickly defeated. When Yuan Shikai appointed a new governor from his own ranks, Chen resigned, fleeing with Bo to Japan and barely escaping death and imprisonment when he was captured en route by forces loyal to Yuan and held for a short while.[105] Before it became apparent that he was to be released through the intercession of friends, Chen had the opportunity to play the part of the hero he claimed his country now needed; he faced down his captors and stated: "If you have decided to shoot me, then be quick about it."[106]

Chen left a letter with the new government, complaining that "an old disease has again arisen," and that "bureaucratic government has resurfaced, and that cannot be tolerated for one day."[107] This old disease was now particularly odious because it was fed by many of the young northern military officers who had worked with Chen in the Warrior Yue Society and had close military connections with Yuan Shikai. It was also supported by people such as Li Guangjiung, Chen's old ally from the Anhui Public School.[108]

Many of those with whom Chen Duxiu had been associated prior to 1911 had cooperated with him as long as he espoused ideas that reinforced their own particularistic interests. Having obtained power, these former allies apparently felt no commitment to the democratic reforms they had earlier ad-

[104] Fu Sinian, "Chen Duxiu an" [The Chen Duxiu case], in Chen Dongxiao, *Chen Duxiu pinglun [Commentaries on Chen Duxiu]*, p. 3.

[105] Gao Yuhan, "Rushu qianhou" [Before and after entering Suzhou], as quoted in Zheng Xuejia, *Zhonggong xingwang shi*, vol. 2, p. 783.

[106] Ibid.

[107] *Minli bao [People's Stand]*, reprint, July 8, 1913, p. 7785.

[108] Ibid.

vocated, which Chen had seen as a way of restoring strength and vitality to the Chinese nation. Rather, they quickly began to promote the same traditional ideas about authority and family as had the Qing government. But Chen, who was particularly concerned with sincerity and the necessity of undertaking moral action, felt these reforms had to be implemented and was especially galled by the hypocrisy of his former allies. A new government was not enough. Chen continued to believe that a social reorganization was necessary if China was to meet the challenge of imperialism. As he had warned in his speech before the Anhui Patriotic Society, the Chinese gentry were again willing to "indifferently look on" as their country was destroyed and the Chinese people became impoverished.[109]

When things did not work out as Chen had hoped and the new gentry proved no more interested in fundamental change in Chinese society than their predecessors had been, he realized it was necessary to look further for solutions. After 1911 Chen came to believe that a thorough change of China was not possible by a revolution that simply eliminated the upper-level officials and did not solve the basic problems of the Chinese people. Indeed, Chen saw that the elimination of the upper level of officialdom merely caused those officials below them to bicker over the spoils with the same greed and lack of concern for the greater whole that had characterized the big officials and their families. The victors were not interested in the changes Chen felt were necessary to save China from imperialism.

In a poem written by Chen after the revolution began to fall apart, he chronicled the history of his failure. He suggested that China had been turned upside down by the forces trampling over her. Admitting that he had searched among the traditions of the past for the solution to China's problems, he confessed that the old heroes like "Yu" and "Huang Di" could

[109] See Chen's speech before the Anhui Patriotic Society as described in chapter 1.

not provide a solution to the problems of the present.[110] Rather than helping to save the nation—China's real national essence—tradition was once again being used by the new power holders to preserve and protect their position. The old family structure still remained, and Yuan Shikai was once again turning to foreign countries for loans and aid. China was more disunified than before, and the nation's "sovereignty" was slipping from the hands of its people. The traditional ideals no longer worked. The next year Chen again went to Japan to study Western ideas. When he returned, it was to attempt to teach this new learning to the one group that had not failed him—the youth.

[110] Chen Duxiu, "Yeyu guangge da Shen Er" [Evening rain wild singing reply to Shen Er], *Jiayin zazhi*, vol. 1, no. 7 (Oct. 7, 1915).

1. Chen Duxiu in traditional garb, probably taken while he was teaching at Beijing University. (*Zhongbao yuekan [China News Monthly]*, July 1980, issue 7)

2. Chen Duxiu in Western garb, probably taken around the time of his imprisonment. The photo was supplied courtesy of the Hoover Institute at Stanford University. The picture originally appeared in *Shian Zizhuan* (Taipei, 1968).

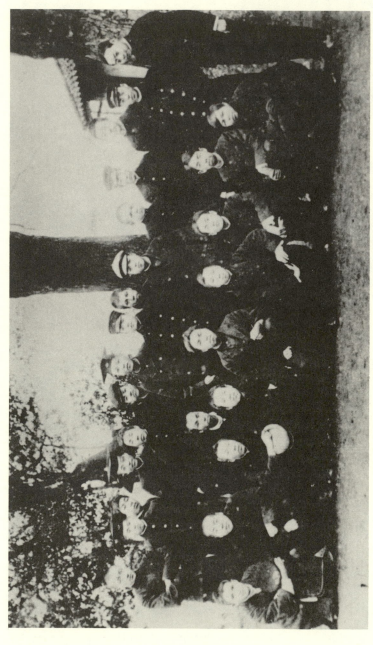

3. Tokyo Youth Society (1903). Chen Duxiu is in the front row, fifth from the left. (Guomindang Historical Archives, Taiwan)

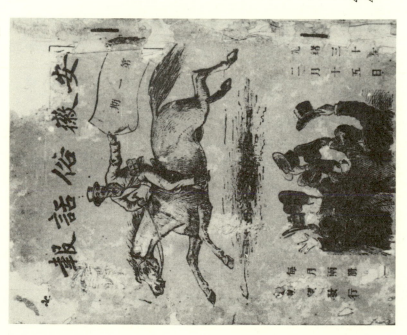

4. The cover plate of the first issue of the *Anhui Common Speech Journal.*

5. A cartoon from the *Anhui Common Speech Journal*, purporting that during the occupation of Tianjin by foreign troops during the Boxer Rebellion, "shameless Chinese" carried signs saying they were "people who surrendered to their new lord." But even they had to "eat the sword."

6. A cartoon from the *Anhui Common Speech Journal* making fun of the reactions of "useless scholars without a fart's worth of value" to the foreign invasion of the capital in the wake of the Boxer Rebellion.

CHAPTER FOUR

THE POLITICS OF CULTURE

The failure of the 1911 Revolution left Chen Duxiu and many other would-be revolutionaries dazed and confused. Chen was disappointed that his scholarly and revolutionary efforts to restore the great traditions of China's past had ended with the resurrection of depotism. Distraught, Chen temporarily thought of retiring from the fray. In a poem published in 1915, he remarked that although at one time he had "heaven-ascending ambitions," now he was content just "fluttering about the rivers and seas," avoiding the clamor of the cities. In this same poem he went on to compare his lonely path to that of Wang Zijin, the son of the Zhou dynasty ruler, Zhou Lin, who was demoted to commoner because he remonstrated with his father over the harshness of his government; afterward Wang paid no attention to political affairs but quietly played his flute in the mountains every day, eventually turning into a kind of Daoist immortal.[1]

In a long poem, "Distant Travels," Chen Duxiu disdains the struggle between weak and strong that goes on in the world, suggesting that one should not care if people "praise or defame you," for what matters is not riches or the writings of intellectuals but only the drinking of wine.[2] Chen Duxiu's friend Su Manshu, who turned to opium to forget his sorrows in the wake of the failure of the 1911 Revolution, summed up the times in his autobiographical story, *Tale of a Broken Hairpin (Suizan ji)*:

[1] Chen Duxiu, "Yonghe" [In praise of the crane], *Jiayin zazhi*, vol. 1, no. 3 (Oct. 8, 1919).

[2] Chen Duxiu, "Yuanyu" (Distant Travel), *Jiayin zazhi*, vol. 1, no. 7 (Oct. 7, 1915).

"Presently, the times and customs have changed, girls grow up and compete with one another in wasting money and making themselves beautiful with hearts drunk on liberty. In reality, they use the name of liberty to commit misdeeds, just like boys borrow the idea of patriotism to plan for their own position and salary. These independent girls and patriotic scholars are not even as good as those men and women who hawk their wares in the streets."[3]

In spite of this feeling of despair and betrayal, Chen Duxiu soon returned to the front line of political and intellectual life, creating between 1915 and 1922 what became known as the New Culture or May Fourth movement, to galvanize the radical youth of Chinese society into an unprecedented and inexorable transformation of the old order. It was by appealing to the youth of China that Chen Duxiu was to exercise such an immense influence over Chinese history for the next decade of his life.

Chen led this movement by attacking the traditional ideology which cloaked those who rose to power after 1911. Having inadvertently helped to establish these people in the government, Chen still hoped to continue the process of political and social transformation that had begun in China around the turn of the century. Chen, who himself had once tried to resurrect traditional ideas in order to strengthen China, now called for China to build a new order, not to restore the old one. But even as Chen called for a new content to Chinese society and government, demanding that the "old wine" be poured out and "new wine" be used to replace it, he continued to use the "old bottles." The message was different but the packaging was still familiar to his readers. Chen had first been drawn to Western ideas because of his interest in traditional Chinese iconoclastic notions, and traditional Chinese iconoclastic concepts continued to influence his understanding of

[3] Su Manshu, "Suizan ji" [Tale of a broken hairpin], in *Su Manshu chuanji,* p. A31.

Western ideas, helping him to make these ideas more palatable to his audience.

DEAN OF THE NEW CULTURE

The appeal of this old-style packaging and new-style message can be seen by the influence of Chen's activities during this period. Between 1915 and 1921, he was the editor of *New Youth*, dean at Beijing University, instigator of the so-called anti-Confucian movements and the vernacular revolution, not to mention founder of the Chinese Communist party. Chen Duxiu was the key figure in one of the most important periods in Chinese history. No one has lauded Chen Duxiu's role during this period more than Mao Zedong himself, who called Chen Duxiu the "commander-in-chief" of the May Fourth period.[4] Since Mao used this phrase in secret speeches during a time when the party was criticizing "the opportunism" of Chen Duxiu most severely, Mao's comments can be seen as private acknowledgment of the tremendous influence that Chen had over Mao and his generation during this period. But Chen's role during the May Fourth period has rarely been given full credit in public. Though his name always appears in any discussion of the May Fourth period and its aftermath, he has usually been upstaged by Hu Shi, Li Dazhao, and a number of other figures.

It was Chen, however, who orchestrated the writings of his friends and induced the audience to read and admire their works. If it had not been for Chen, few would have read the writings of any of his colleagues. He used the appeal of their ideas to further the political and social movement. He was a master of timing who paced his writings and ideas to the changing political events in such a way that they played per-

---

[4] Mao Zedong as quoted in Lin Maosheng, "Guanyu Chen Duxiu yanjiu de yixie wenti" [A few problems in researching Chen Duxiu], in *Zhongguo renmin daxue dangshixi dangshi jinxiuban jianggao* [*An outline of a lecture for a class for advanced studies in party history for the party history department of People's University*], no. 6, Sept. 23, 1980, p. 8. Mao spoke these words in 1945 at the meeting of the Seventh Party Congress.

THE POLITICS OF CULTURE   99

fectly to the new patriotic sentiments and, at the same time, to the traditional biases of the growing Chinese youth movement with which he was so much in sympathy.

The importance of Chen's presentation of these ideas quickly becomes apparent when one realizes that most of his proposed ideas, which created such a sensation among his youthful audience, had already been current in China for at least fifteen or twenty years. The single most important idea held by Chen and other thinkers during the period from 1915 to 1921, often called "China's enlightenment," or for that matter held by almost every other Chinese intellectual influenced by Western ideas since the late nineteenth century, was the desire to see China develop into a strong, independent, and prosperous nation ruled by a government that would be truly representative of the people as a whole, and not of special interests or factions. In 1915, in his famous opening essay in *New Youth*, Chen established the theme for his critique of Chinese society by attacking the "countless unsuccessful and illicit profit-seekers" he saw as destroying China. He repeated this idea throughout the magazine, criticizing the Confucian doctrines for "emphasizing classes"[5] and claiming that the Confucian concern for the family was simply a way of protecting the privileges of the nobility.[6] In launching the literary revolution, which was to occupy such an important role in the New Culture movement, Chen even blasted the classical literature of China's past as that of the "aristocratic few."[7]

Though this rhetoric sounds inflammatory, it was not original; almost all the points had been made countless times before and were similar to ideas being advocated then by other

[5] Chen Duxiu, "Bo Kang Youwei zhi zongtong zongli shu" [Refuting Kang Youwei's petition to the President and Premier], *Xin Qingnian* [*New Youth*] (hereafter *XQN*), vol. 2, no. 2 (Oct. 1, 1916); also see *Duxiu wencun* [*Chen Duxiu's collected writings*] (hereafter *DXWC*), vol. 1, p. 95.

[6] Chen Duxiu, "Kongzi zhi dao yu xiandai shenghuo" [Confucianism and present-day life], *XQN*, vol. 2, no. 4 (Dec. 1, 1916); also in *DXWC*, vol. 1, p. 136.

[7] Chen Duxiu, "Wenxue geming lun" [On the literary revolution], *XQN*, vol. 2, no. 6 (Feb. 1, 1917); also in *DXWC* 1:136.

intellectuals.[8] Even Chen's emphasis on the Darwinian concept of change and his often-repeated calls for the introduction of "Mr. Science and Mr. Democracy," while worded in clever ways in *New Youth*, were ideas that he had presented earlier in the *Anhui Common Speech Journal* and should have been concepts familiar to the intellectuals who read his new publication.

These hackneyed proposals, expounded so many times in the pre-1911 period, were suddenly very popular with the "new youth" of China, partially because of the new political and social situation but also because Chen was a dazzling stylist prepared to talk about a broad range of ideas in an extremely appealing and attractive manner. As Lin Yu-sheng has stated: "In a cultural anomie in which most people were confused and bewildered, Chen's combination of intellectual straightforwardness with moral passion and dogged persistence became highly charismatic."[9] This "moral passion" and "intellectual straightforwardness" that infused Chen Duxiu's writings helped make the Western ideas that he advocated seem novel and yet perfectly understandable to those raised in a traditional Chinese environment. The youth to whom Chen appealed seized on his infusion of moralism into Western ideas because they themselves had been educated in the new Western-style schools with Western ideas. "Moral passion," as discussed in chapter 2, had been particularly characteristic

[8] In the years before 1911, such articles appeared not only in the *Anhui Common Speech Journal*, the *Subao*, and the *China National Gazette*, but also in the *Alarm Bell*, the *New Citizen Magazine (Xinmin congbao)*, and *The Eastern Miscellany (Dongfan zazhi)*. There were also a number of other revolutionary, anarchist, and vernacular papers which expressed similar or often more radical sentiments than that later echoed by *New Youth*. After 1913, the number of new publications was somewhat restrained by the censorship policies of the Yuan government. But even during this time, articles similar to those in *New Youth* appeared in publications such as *Jiayin zazhi* [*The Tiger Magazine*], for which Chen also wrote, and *Da zhonghua* [*The Great China*]. After the death of Yuan Shikai in 1916 and the subsequent loosening of censorship restrictions, the number of publications increased manifold.

[9] Lin Yu-sheng, *The Crisis of Chinese Consciousness: Radical Anti-Traditionalism in the May Fourth Era*, p. 63.

of Confucian writing and was also a special feature of the turn-of-the-century youth groups with which Chen had been associated.

As he had done earlier, Chen again used this "moral passion" to emphasize the role in politics and society that would be played by the elite youth for whom he wrote—a role that the May Fourth youth desired for themselves no less than had the youth of Chen Duxiu's own generation, now near middle age. In his first article in *New Youth*, Chen suggested that the corruption of the old society would be cured only "by one or two smart youths bravely struggling to infuse their knowledge and ability into the people."[10] The idea that the bravery of a few youthful heroes could inspire a society had been one of the key ideas he had advanced in his articles on Chinese history in the pages of the *Anhui Common Speech Journal* and was an idea he had previously used to inspire Wu Yue and other followers in the Warrior Yue Society. After 1915 and particularly after 1917 when *New Youth* moved to Beijing, Chen advanced this argument on a national basis and not just for supporters in Anhui.

More important, after 1915 Chen no longer consciously recalled the bravery of past Chinese heroes in discussing the need for this kind of sincere unselfish action that would inspire others. Rather, Chen now spoke of this action exclusively as imitative of the Western spirit of daring. In his earlier works, for instance his first speech before the Anhui Patriotic Society, Chen had similarly demanded that the Chinese now imitate the Promethean spirit of the West, but he had also seen this spirit as characteristic of the heroes of the Chinese past. Although Chen now called on the people in terms of new and increasingly popular Western ideas, his appeal for sincere moral action that would motivate people was something those raised on Confucian moralistic literature would rarely stop to question.

This moralism was also attractive to many because it was

[10] Chen Duxiu, "Qinggao qingnian" [Call to youth], *Qingnian* (hereafter *QN*), *QN*, vol. 1, no. 1 (Sept. 15, 1915); also in *DXWC*, vol. 1, p. 2.

easy. By implying to the elite that they had the power to instigate change simply by acting morally and resolutely, Chen's writings may also have seemed to steer a safe middle course between the militarism of Yuan Shikai and the violent revolutionism being advocated by Sun Yatsen. Chen began *New Youth* because of his opposition to Yuan Shikai's attempts to restore the monarchy—a political change that must have been particularly galling to Chen because it was drawing a number of prominent intellectuals to its side, including Yan Fu, Kang Youwei, Sun Yuyun, and Liu Shipei, all of whom had at one time or another been allies or models for Chen in the pre-1911 period. Chen may have feared that these figures would exert the same magnetic force on China's new youth that they had once exerted on Chen himself, only this time for undesirable ends. In opposing Yuan Shikai, there were clearly two possibilities: one was the kind of revolution from below under the leadership of a disciplined party being proposed by Sun Yatsen, and the other was to work from within by convincing those gentry and military figures upon whom Yuan depended for support to turn against Yuan. The latter was, in effect, Chen's initial strategy.

This strategy also would appeal to other traditional prejudices. After 1911, Sun Yatsen, although hardly the Lenin of the Chinese revolution, had begun to develop a revolutionary organization based at least in part on modern organizational principles and discipline. While before 1911 radical students had flocked around Sun—in spite of his peasant background and lack of comprehension of Chinese elite society—they bridled at the principles of this new group. Most of these upperclass radicals were more comfortable with political groupings based on personal and often family ties that were legitimized by arcane ideas of culture, history, and moral purpose. This was exactly the kind of revolutionary society Chen had earlier formed in Anhui.

During the period of the New Culture movement, Chen helped lead an opposition to Yuan Shikai based on the old-style alliances rather than Sun Yatsen's new-style organizational practices. Chen had long opposed Sun, refusing to join his Revolutionary Alliance (Tongmenghui) in 1905 and again refusing to join his Revolutionary party (Gemingdang) in 1913 because of the demand that one take a blood oath of fealty to the party leader.[11] Rather, after 1913, Chen was involved in the efforts of his old friend Zhang Shizhao and other members of the European Affairs Research Society to forge a broadly based political movement among the elite in order to force Yuan Shikai to forego his monarchical ambitions. Wu Zhihui has even claimed, no doubt with some hyperbole, that Chen Duxiu was the chief strategist in this effort and the person responsible for the alliance between China's liberal gentry and the relatively conservative Progressive party (Jinbu dang) of Liang Qichao that halted Yuan Shikai's monarchical efforts.[12] Chen's efforts were successful at least in part because they utilized the penchant of the elite for loose political alliances based on personal connections.

In any case, Chen's writings were a repudiation of the strategy of violent uprisings that had been pursued by most revolutionaries since the early 1900s. Having seen the violent approach fail, Chen felt that the revolutionary strategy had to be rethought. People's ideas had to be changed before violence could again be tried. At a time when extremism seems to have been the norm—whether it was that of the military-backed regime of Yuan Shikai or the disciplined Revolutionary party advocated by Sun Yatsen—Chen's insistence that change toward a liberal-democratic social, economic, and political system was necessary and inevitable and that the ideas of principled individuals did make a difference would obviously

[11] Zhiguang, "Chen Duxiu de shengping ji chi zhengzhi zhuzhang" [The life and political views of Chen Duxiu], in Chen Dongxiao, *Chen Duxiu pinglun* [*Commentaries of Chen Duxiu*]. The accusation that Chen Duxiu did not join the Tongmenghui has been questioned, most recently by Richard Kagan. But it has now been substantiated that Chen, like his friend Zhang Shizhao, did in fact refuse to join the Tongmenghui; see chapter 1 of this work. For Kagan's account of these events, see "Ch'en Tu-hsiu's Unfinished Autobiography," *China Quarterly* 50 (April-June 1972):330.

[12] Wu Zhihui, "Zhang Shizhao—Chen Duxiu—Liang Qichao," in *Wu Zhihui xiansheng wencun*, p. 316. Wu claimed that Chen Duxiu functioned as Zhang Shizhao's Zhuge Liang.

be very attractive to the overwhelming majority of the so-called liberal intelligentsia, many of whom had reluctantly accepted the Yuan government.

But while moderate, Chen's writings still used the heroic style that had characterized his pre-1911 exploits. But now rather than calling on his youthful readers to actually risk their lives, he appealed to them to liberate themselves from family traditions and conventions. Chen's youthful audience—unleashed from the restrictions of home life for the first time, disgruntled with the traditions of their parents, worried about the position of their country—desired to liberate themselves from these restraints at least as much as had Chen and his peers a half generation earlier; and Chen now made this liberation seem heroic. The injunctions in "Call to Youth," the first article of his new publication, insist:

1. Be independent, not servile. . . .
2. Be progressive, not conservative. . . .
3. Be aggressive, not retiring. . . .
4. Be cosmopolitan, not isolationist. . . .
5. Be utilitarian, not formalistic. . . .
6. Be scientific, not imaginative.[13]

These articles reinforced the sense of liberation that had begun to pervade Chinese youth in the early part of the twentieth century. Chen Duxiu's youthful and rebellious readers were likely to be particularly sympathetic with the way Chen dwelled on the need for China to eliminate arranged marriages and the bonds of the extended family. Chen's audience was also likely to be flattered by the way Chen coupled his discussion of the abilities and potential of youth with criticisms of his own contemporaries for their abandonment of the values of democracy and science for which they had once struggled. Indeed, the title of Chen's new publication was a reminder to his former revolutionary comrades, now middle-aged turncoats to the Yuan regime, of the values of their youth; this was a warning to his audience that the reforms they had hoped

13 Chen Duxiu, "Chinggao qingnian."

for in the years before 1911 should not be forgotten. Chen repeated this warning in article after article. He called on the intelligentsia not "to retire from the world to keep themselves clean" but to become politically and socially active in helping create the new society.[14] In his early writings Chen had constantly reminded his audience that even their private affairs were affected by the fate of the nation. He lashed out at those who professed unconcern with the affairs of the world. Although Chen had threatened to withdraw from the world himself in the wake of disillusionment with the 1911 Revolution, he now lashed out at this attitude in others.

In a culture in which the tradition of the *junzi*, or moral scholar, was still strong and in which both sides accused the other of moral weakness and inconsistency, these were powerful accusations. As Chen stated in the next issue of *New Youth*: "Strong scholars will not waver; they will work to fill the sea and move mountains so in the future they can see that the educational spirit will one day save the nation and build a new people."[15]

The Politics of the Uncompromising Scholar

The call for "strong scholars [who] will not waiver" recalled the Confucian tradition in which the scholar who does not find acceptance for his ideas refuses to compromise and instead retires to his home to teach or write, an example first set by Confucius himself.[16] Though this type of activity may be considered to be apolitical, it is so only if one accepts a very narrow definition of politics, namely that of direct participation in a governmental movement or political party. Within Chinese society, however, teachers would also often attract a considerable number of followers. The influence of these followers might in some cases result in the recruitment of the

[14] Ibid.

[15] Chen Duxiu, "Jinri zhi jiaoyu fangzhen" [Present-day educational directions], *QN*, vol. 1, no. 2 (Oct. 15, 1915); also *DXWC*, vol. 1, p. 17.

[16] Benjamin Schwartz, "Some Polarities in Confucian Thought," in D. S. Nivison and A. F. Wright, eds., *Confucianism in Action*.

scholar under question to governmental service (or at least the eventual implementation of his ideas by his disciples), a familiar pattern in the lives of many of China's most famous political thinkers. In starting *New Youth*, Chen himself was following in this tradition by seeming to retire from active politics while in fact using his writings and influence to affect future political developments, as seen, for example, by his role in organizing the anti-Yuan coalition.

During a period of great political excitement, Chen consciously avoided any direct involvement in politics for the first six months he edited *New Youth*. Still, he was not a modern scholar supposedly unconcerned with political actions. In traditional fashion, Chen cultivated a group of followers who could develop a new political program by attempting to show them how despotic regimes such as that of Yuan Shikai were eliminated in the West through precisely the kind of liberal values and behavior that he urged on his youthful audience.

In the frequently cited article, "The French and Modern Civilization" (which contributed to the only partially correct idea that Chen was infatuated with French culture and the totally mistaken notion that he lived for a while in France),[17] Chen lauded French culture for nurturing the three ideas fundamental to modern Western society—democracy, evolution, and socialism. Although Western influence in China in 1915 was not as pervasive as it was to become twenty years later, still none of these three theories would have seemed particularly new to Chen's audience of liberal intelligentsia. What gave the article its power and appeal was the fact that Chen postulated that these theories stimulated the West to eliminate the special privileges and authority of the nobles and kings that dominated Western society in the past, and claimed that French devotion to these values would allow the country to triumph over "militaristic" Germany in the world war then raging in Europe.[18]

[17] See, for instance, Howard L. Boorman, *Biographical Dictionary of Republican China*, vol. 1, p. 241. See also Chow Tse-tsung, *The May Fourth Movement*, p. 42a.

[18] Chen Duxiu, "Falanxi ren yu jinshi wenming" [The French and modern civilization], in *DXWC*, vol. 1, pp. 11–15.

This discussion of the French elimination of the privilege and authority of nobles and kings was obviously a slap at Yuan Shikai's attempt to restore the monarchy. For those in the know, the use of French examples was a particularly apt way of criticizing Yuan Shikai. Yuan, like many other Chinese of the time, had been a great admirer of French government, seeing it as a very centralized kind of rule that would put tremendous power in the hands of the president.[19] Indeed, Yuan's American adviser, the former Columbia University professor, Frank Goodnow, who helped provide theoretical justification for Yuan's monarchical bid, was originally hired as an expert on the French constitutional system.[20] Chen was not the only person who used French examples in the effort to discredit Yuan. Dai Jitao, a follower of Sun Yatsen who was also a friend of Chen Duxiu, wrote a similar article.[21] Both men used their discussion of France to rally the liberal intelligentsia against Yuan at a time when many thought this to be impossible. It was this timing that gave Chen's article its impact.

The article's influence was great also because of the seeming mastery that it displayed over foreign ideas and history. Foreign ideas were already regarded as necessary for China. Through this article Chen was showing not only how these ideas could be used to defeat Yuan but how it was he who had mastered them, not those supporting Yuan. Times had changed and Chen Duxiu was particularly sensitive to these changes. In the period before 1911 when Chen had edited the *Anhui Common Speech Journal*, a mastery of traditional scholarship endowed one with great prestige. In this earlier period, foreign ideas were best justified by showing a demonstration of their similarity to traditional concepts. By 1915 it was one's mastery over foreign doctrines that gave one the influence to effect change in people.

Chen's interest in stirring the people to change—rather than actually developing a French-style government—is seen by the

[19] Ernest Young, *The Presidency of Yuan Shih-k'ai*, p. 172.
[20] Ibid.
[21] See Herman Mast, "Tai Chi-t'ao, Sunism and Marxism During the May Fourth Movement in Shanghai," in *Modern Asian Studies*, pp. 232–33.

way Chen was quick to alter his views on France and to instead praise the anti-imperialist manner of the Germans in January 1916, a few months after writing his article lauding French civilization. It has often been noted that Chen, like many other writers of the time, was a very inconsistent thinker;[22] what has not been noted, however, is that the inconsistencies in Chen's thinking were very much attuned to the changing political situation in China. By changing his position on the warring European powers at this time, Chen once again showed his mastery over foreign ideas. In spite of his reputation as a Francophile, in January 1916 Chen suddenly and gleefully predicted a German victory in the war, suggesting that the combined forces of Russia, England, and France were only able to "protect their dying breath and not advance forward."[23] The surge of German victories in late 1915 temporarily aroused Chen Duxiu's hopes that Germany, a newly developed nation, could provide leadership to the colonial peoples of the world.

Seizing on these changes in the international political climate, Chen Duxiu now saw the success of the new German nation as a possible stimulus to the colonial and semicolonial countries of the world in much the same way that he would later view the revolution in backward Russia as a stimulus to revolution in even more backward China. "The Moslem people," he suggested, "are taking inspiration from Germany, and all the countries that made up the old Turkish Federation will take up weapons" and begin the struggle to overthrow the British colonial empire.[24] Li Dazhao and a number of other intellectuals had similar views of Germany at this time,[25] and Chen's attitude was no doubt partially influenced by them.

[22] See Benjamin Schwartz, "Ch'en Tu-hsiu and the Acceptance of the Modern West," *Journal of the History of Ideas*, Jan. 1951, p. 63. See also Lin Yu-sheng, *The Crisis of Chinese Consciousness*, p. 79.

[23] Chen Duxiu, "1916," *QN*, vol. 1, no. 5 (Jan. 15, 1916); also in *DXWC*, vol. 1, p. 42.

[24] Ibid.

[25] Maurice Meisner, *Li Ta-chao and the Origins of Chinese Marxism*, pp. 59–60.

The temporary shift in attitudes on the part of Chen and his friends may have been affected not only by the German victories but by the rumors, which were false, that Germany was discouraging Yuan's monarchical ambitions.[26]

Chen himself soon succumbed to the excitement of the political campaign against Yuan Shikai. In spite of his pledge not to do so,[27] within six months of founding *New Youth*, Chen had become reinvolved in direct political activity. In the spring of 1916, he suspended the publication of *New Youth* to assist Zhang Shizhao in his duties as secretary-general of an anti-Yuan military council established at Zhaoqing, Guangdong. Later Chen assisted Zhang in the organization of the constitutional assembly that convened in Shanghai following Yuan's death and the ascension of Li Yuanhong to the presidency of the Republic.[28] This assembly, about which Chen wrote in his journal, had been formed after the provinces declared themselves independent of Yuan in early 1916.[29] Chen resumed publication of his journal after Li Yuanhong and the assemblymen reached an agreement with Duan Qirui and agreed to meet in Beijing.[30]

A short while later, Chen followed Zhang Shizhao and the other assemblymen to Beijing as the new dean of the School of Arts and Letters at Beijing University. Following his arrival in Beijing in 1917, he joined a group of dissident members of the old Guomindang party who had gathered loosely around Zhang Ji and formed an association known as the Good Friends Society.[31] In 1917, as German military losses mounted, it began to appear that it would be the allies and not Germany that would be in the position to aid China after the war; at the same time it became clear that Germany had actually aided

[26] "Guonei dashi ji" [A record of internal events], *QN*, vol. 1, no. 1 (Sept. 15, 1915).

[27] Ibid.

[28] Wu Zhihui, "Zhang Shizhao—Chen Duxiu—Liang Qichao," p. 316.

[29] "Guonei dashiji," *XQN*, vol. 2, no. 1 (Oct. 1, 1916).

[30] Ibid.

[31] Yang Yuqing, *Zhongguo zhengdang shi* [The history of China's political party], p. 95.

Yuan's monarchical efforts and not opposed them, as had been assumed earlier. Consequently the Good Friends Society decided to campaign against Sun Yatsen's opposition to China's participation in the war against Germany and to support Liang Qichao's attempt to ensure China's entrance into the conflict. Chen again reversed himself and in March 1917 wrote a famous article in *New Youth* in which he argued for this new position.[32]

The question of China's participation in the world war was precisely the kind of political issue with which Chen Duxiu was to become involved throughout his life. At a time when China was engulfed in internal political chaos, Sun Yatsen felt that China must deal with its own internal problems. But Chen, as we have seen, viewed the war as a struggle against imperialism—an issue, he felt consistently, that was the most pressing matter facing China. He therefore supported Liang Qichao's argument that China's entry into the war would help increase her international reputation and consequently the unity of the country. Chen may have been particularly inclined to support China's participation in the war because the issue was also advocated by the government of Duan Qirui (who was from Anhui) with which Chen Duxiu sympathized at the time.[33] But Chen was quick to denounce Duan when it became apparent that the warlord (like Chen's earlier Anhui allies in 1911) wished to use the declaration of war against Germany only to gain power over his rivals. In June 1917, he wrote a bold article in *New Youth* criticizing his former naiveté in desiring to enter the war and calling for increased cooperation between the KMT and Liang Qichao's Progressive party.[34]

At the same time, Chen called for a division of the country that would leave the Beiyang military clique then headed by

[32] Ibid., pp. 91, 95. See also Xiebin, *Minguo zhengdang shi [A political history of the Republican period]*, p. 72. See also Chen Duxiu, "Duide waijiao" [Relations with Germany], *XQN*, vol. 3, no. 1 (March 1, 1917).

[33] Chen Duxiu, "Duide waijiao." See also Chen Duxiu, "Guonei dashi ji," *XQN*, vol. 2, nos. 1 and 2 (Sept. 1 and Oct. 1, 1916). Both these columns were presumably written by Chen Duxiu.

[34] Chen Duxiu, "Shiju zagan."

Duan Qirui in control of the north and allow the Guomindang
to establish a democratic government in the south. This suggestion produced shock waves throughout the Guomindang,
especially among the immediate followers of Sun Yatsen.[35] In
order to implement the proposal, Chen, together with Wang
Zhengting, Chu Pucheng, Hu Hanmin, and others broke away
from Zhang Ji and formed a new political faction.[36]

Chen's participation in these last events is illustrative of the
political influence that he commanded. Chen had obtained his
job in Beijing as dean of the School of Arts and Letters at
least in part as a result of his growing political and intellectual
authority over Chinese activist youth. Cai Yuanpei himself
had accepted the job as chancellor at Beida only after a big
debate within the Guomindang on whether or not he should
cooperate with the corrupt warlord government.[37] In spite of
the fact that Cai came to Beida (the abbreviated way of referring to Beijing University) with a reputation for being above
politics, he clearly supported the reformers at the school. Given
this situation, Cai's selection of Chen for a job which was
second in importance only to that of Cai himself made good
political sense. For Chen, besides being an Anhui person tied
to some of the members of the Duan Qirui government (many
of whose advisers and subordinates had worked with Chen
Duxiu in Anhui and knew his family), was also closely associated with another growing political force in the nation's
capital—Zhang Shizhao. Cai of course knew Chen from their
earlier association together in the assassination squad and had
been an admirer of the *Anhui Common Speech Journal*.[38] Thus
Cai was disposed to be favorable to the suggestions of Shen
Yinmo and Tang Erhe that Chen would be a good youth leader

[35] Zhang Shizhao, "Wu Zhihui—Liang Qichao—Chen Duxiu," *Jiayin
zhoukan*, vol. 1, no. 30 (Feb. 6, 1926), p. 6.

[36] Yang Yuchiung, *Zhongguo zhengdang shi*, p. 95.

[37] This is available from a number of sources. See, for instance, Gao Pingshu, ed., *Cai Yuanpei nianpu*, p. 36.

[38] Shen Yinmo, "Wo he Chen Duxiu" [Chen Duxiu and I], in *Chen Duxiu
yanjiu cankao ziliao*, p. 90. Also Cai Yuanpei, "Duxiu wencun xu" [Preface
to DXWC], in DXWC, 12th edition (1939), pp. i–iii.

and teacher, especially after Cai had read through a few issues of *New Youth* and liked it.[39]

Although Chen Duxiu was picked for the Beida job at least partially because of his political connections, his new post greatly enhanced his influence and following. Prior to 1917 Chen had managed to command a certain following in political and intellectual circles, but it was still a small following. At the start of its existence, *New Youth* could boast of a circulation of only one thousand copies per issue, the same circulation that the *Anhui Common Speech Journal* had had during its first few runs.[40] After his selection as dean of the School of Arts and Letters at Beijing University, the most prestigious intellectual institution in China and one of immense political influence, Chen automatically became one of China's foremost intellectual figures and the circulation of his magazine began to increase dramatically. His words had great impact on China's new radical youth, especially on those who were his students at the university. Moreover, the support that Chen received from his fellow professors at Beijing University, many of whom now wrote for and helped edit *New Youth*, further enhanced his credibility and prestige. When Chen Duxiu in early 1918 added Hu Shi, Chen Yuangtong, Liu Fu, Shen Yinmo, and Li Dazhao—all professors at Beida—to the editorial board of *New Youth*, he was in effect forming them into a political organization, even though the group again pledged itself not to engage in any overt political activity.[41]

Having become disappointed with the Duan Qirui government, Chen and the others felt that it was again necessary to work for more deep-seated changes in the society and not to become involved in everyday political events, which were in any case increasingly corrupt. Moreover, the political situation in 1918, as in 1915, made overt political activity dangerous. Cai Yuanpei's Guomindang sympathies were suspicious to many members of the warlord government that had

[39] Ibid.
[40] Chow Tse-tsung, *The May Fourth Movement*, p. 733.
[41] Hu Shi, "Chen Duxiu yu wenxue geming" [Chen Duxiu and the literary revolution], in Chen Dongxiao, ed., *Chen Duxiu pinglun*, p. 51.

picked him as university chancellor, and his political activities had to be hidden behind a pledge to separate education and government. In addition, Hu Shi and other Western-trained intellectuals on the Beida faculty actually believed that this kind of a separation could be implemented in spite of the chaotic condition of Chinese society. But as might be expected, members of the *New Youth* editorial board found the implementation of this decision as impossible to uphold as the pledge not to engage in political activity that Chen himself had taken upon first establishing the magazine. These intellectuals were drawn into politics by both the traditional Chinese affinity between intellectuals and government and their dissatisfaction with the existing political situation.

By mid-1919, at the time of the May Fourth movement, Chen Duxiu, Hu Shi, and Gao Yihan were all willing to join their students in the streets in protest against the actions of the warlord government. By December of 1919 the entire editorial board of *New Youth* had agreed to join Chen Duxiu in issuing the famous "Manifesto of *New Youth* Magazine," which denounced warlordism, advocated democracy, and declared that "politics is an important aspect of public life."[42] By the early 1920s, as Chen Duxiu became increasingly involved in the organization of the Chinese Communist party, Hu Shi and other liberals, at times joined by Li Dazhao, were to make a series of attempts to influence the various northern warlord regimes to institute what they called "good government."[43]

In taking these actions, Chen's fellow professors, like Chen himself, were working to influence their students, who after 1919 increasingly became a major political force in China. But it was Chen Duxiu, as head of the *New Youth* editorial board and as a prestigious political and intellectual leader, who was able to garner the support of the most important and able of the student leaders. This support was also en-

[42] Benjamin Schwartz, "The Intelligentsia in Communist China: A Tentative Comparison," *Daedalus* (Summer 1960), p. 613.

[43] For a partial discussion of this, see Jerome Grieder, *Hu Shih and the Chinese Renaissance*, chap. 6.

hanced by the dazzling reputation Chen had obtained for himself through his attacks on his political enemies and his bold leadership of the left-leaning Chinese intelligentsia.

Chen Duxiu's influence over the Chinese leftist student intelligentsia was also a consequence of the nature of the Chinese youth movement. Some twenty years ago, Benjamin Schwartz argued that the Chinese New Culture movement intelligentsia had not been as alienated as the prerevolutionary Russian intelligentsia in that most Chinese intellectuals still desired to participate in the society and in the government.[44] Still, in the post-1911 era the position of the Chinese student intelligentsia was precarious. Though the group was highly respected, their living conditions were for the most part oppressed. Many students, without money from their families and with little if any government support, lived a hand-to-mouth existence. After the breakup of the empire in 1911, they had few prospects for future employment in the various warlord governments that then dominated China. Proud of their position as intellectuals and yet unable to take advantage of the new commercial opportunities in Chinese society, they felt particularly resentful of their lowly situation and of those around them who were advancing because of material or mercenary interests.

Members of this group naturally looked forward to a government that would be run by those like themselves who had the new Western knowledge. The issues raised by Chen as part of the New Culture movement reflected the prejudices of many members of the leftist intelligentsia and this student group. In particular, Chen's attack on the Confucian and literary ideals of those older scholars who monopolized the government bureaucracy and thus prevented access to it by the new student graduates was very appealing to his youthful audience. Many of course made such criticisms, but few did it with the authority and prestige of Chen. For Chen Duxiu had led the attacks on Yuan Shikai at a time when most intellectuals still despaired of the possibility of change. His

[44] Schwartz, "Intelligentsia in Communist China."

use of French examples to cast aspersions on Yuan's pretensions, his turn toward Germany when members of the new
student intelligentsia were suddenly interested in that country
as a result of German war victories, and even his short-lived
faith in Duan Qirui (who originally seemed interested in em-
ploying new groups of the student intelligentsia) following
Yuan's death enhanced the students' view of Chen Duxiu as
a scholar and leader. These attacks not only reflected the
students' prejudices but they also put Chen himself in the
position of the bold intellectual leader who stands up against
the forces of immorality in society. Although advocating modern reforms, Chen was in effect appealing to the students as
a traditional *junzi*, or gentleman.

Like the followers of the traditional *junzi*, Chen's student
readers were attracted to his use of an arcane elitist vocabulary
and apparent mastery of the ideals of the new culture, particularly one which was being held in opposition to a social
and political situation they found oppressive. Their view of
Chen as a Mandarin of the new culture is again apparent in
the words of Mao Zedong who, in claiming Chen to be the
"supreme commander" of the May Fourth movement, remarked that even his knowledge of punctuation came from
Chen Duxiu,[45] a reference to the leading role of *New Youth*
in introducing the use of punctuation to Chinese readers. In
a culture in which authority flowed from cultural mastery,
Chen had a flair for constantly awing his young readers with
the wonders of the outside world and making them ready to
follow him politically.

THE DEBATE OVER CONFUCIUS

In a society that was concerned with prestige, Chen had
made *New Youth* the arbiter of political and intellectual fashion for the young radical intelligentsia. Consequently the writ-

[45] Mao Zedong in Lin Maosheng, "Guanyu Chen Duxiu yanjiu de yixie
wenti," p. 8.

ings of Chen and his colleagues took on a special significance
and importance. This then was the background to the two
crusades with which *New Youth* was to be most closely identified and which were to greatly increase its influence—the
anti-Confucian campaign and the vernacular revolution. The
anti-Confucian campaign, mounted in late 1916 in the pages
of *New Youth*, and the closely associated vernacular revolution that was also conducted in the magazine gave the journal
and its chief editor their radical iconoclastic reputation. These
two crusades also helped to boost dramatically the circulation
of *New Youth* from one thousand to sixteen thousand.[46]

If one simply looks at the contents of the articles in *New
Youth* associated with these two crusades without understanding the political background in which they developed, it is
hard to understand why they excited such controversy. Articles criticizing Confucius and Confucianism had been common in the radical press before 1911, as was already shown
in chapter 3, and the idea of reforming China's two-thousand-
year-old literary language had also been broached a number
of times during the same period. To be sure, those ideas were
not looked upon with favor by conservative Mandarins, but
they had not previously excited the kind of controversy that
they did after 1915.

Chen's first articles attacking Confucius stressed that Confucian ideals had been tied to a Confucian form of government
and were incompatible with "a republican constitutional system based on independence, equality, and freedom. . . ."[47]
Later Chen argued against those interested in developing a
Confucian religion in China similar to the state religions of
Western Europe by maintaining that in Europe "religious and
monarchical absolutism, which were related, were abolished
at the same time. . . ."[48] Europe, he insisted, was moving

[46] See note 40.

[47] Chen Duxiu, "Wo ren zuihou zhi juewu" [Our people's most recent
awakening], *XQN*, vol. 1, no. 6 (Feb. 15, 1916); also in *DXWC*, vol. 1, p.
55.

[48] Chen Duxiu, "Bo Kang Youwei zhi zongtong zongli shu," in *DXWC*,
vol. 1, p. 97.

toward a utilitarian belief similar to the original idea of Confucianism.[49] Therefore, rather than regress by developing a Confucian religion, Chen felt that China should develop a society like that of Europe, to be based on an ethic that benefited both the individual and the society; he held that if China could adopt European social and political institutions it could become a creative, enterprising society.

Similar attacks on the idea of establishing a Confucian religion had been made by the *kaozheng* people before and after 1911, and arguments against Yuan which cited the need for China to evolve into a European-style republic also were common. Indeed, most of the themes Chen raised in his own anti-Confucian articles had already been raised in a piece written by his friend Zhang Shizhao in early 1914 in the first issue of his *Tiger Magazine*, in order to combat the arguments of those who were attempting to garner public support for Yuan Shikai's wish to restore the monarchy. Zhang Shizhao attacked an article by Kang Youwei, who had associated himself with Yuan Shikai's monarchical attempts and whose suggestion that Confucian rituals be reinstated as a way of reviving the moral fiber of the country seemed to provide legitimization for Yuan's efforts.[50] Citing the historical analysis of Confucian doctrines that had been carried out by Chen's former mentor Zhang Binglin, then under house arrest by Yuan Shikai, Zhang Shizhao attempted to show that not only was Confucianism not a religion, as Kang Youwei believed, but that actually one of Confucianism's most important tenets was its denial of religion. Thus, rather than establish a Confucian religion, Zhang, as Chen was to do a few years later, proposed the establishment of Christianity as the national religion in order to unify the country.[51]

---

[49] Ibid., pp. 95–97.

[50] Kang Youwei, "Ni zhonghua minguo xianfa zaoan fafan" [Preface to a proposal of a constitution for the Republic of China], *Buren* 3 (April 1913). See also Kang Youwei, "Zhonghua jiuguolun" [On the salvation of China], *Buren* 1 (Feb. 1913).

[51] Zhang Shizhao (Qiutong), "Kongjiao" [Confucianism as a religion], *Jiayin zazhi*, vol. 1, no. 1 (May 1914).

When Zhang Shizhao attacked Confucianism, Zhang Ertian, a former Qing official who was a member of Kang Youwei's Confucian Society and a senior official in the Yuan government's Office for the Compilation of Qing History (Qing
shiguan), merely replied that whatever the actual beliefs of
Confucius, since the majority of the Chinese people believed
in Confucianism the government should remain in accord with
the wishes of Chinese society.[52] Zhang Ertian's reply is interesting as a way of showing how even those who had advocated
Confucian doctrines in the years after 1911 now supported
this position by resorting to Western democratic principles.
But this was the only response Zhang Shizhao's article received. His attack, like those that were launched against Confucius before 1911, did not create the kind of controversy that
would later be sparked by Chen Duxiu's foray into the anti-
Confucian debate.

The reason for this apathy is that before 1916, those attacking Confucius were fighting largely an uphill battle. Although it is true that the Confucian monarchy was ended in
1911, the Yuan government continued to identify itself with
Confucian orthodoxy, particularly after Yuan's attempt to
restore the monarchy in 1914. Thus, prior to 1916 the Confucian establishment, while increasingly defensive about the
attacks on Confucianism, nevertheless felt confident in the
knowledge that they advocated the orthodox doctrine and
that their political power was secure.

After 1916, this situation changed. With the downfall of
Yuan Shikai, the Confucian principles on which he had based
his government were discredited. Yuan's conservative followers soon lost the fight for the passage of a plank for the new
constitution, originally drafted as a result of Yuan Shikai's
influence, calling for education to be based on Confucian ideals.
Most of Chen's anti-Confucian articles were written in opposition to this plank. His viewpoint was thus particularly
popular because his argument that the inevitable thrust of

[52] Zhang Ertian, "Kongjiao" [Confucianism as a religion], letter to the
editor, *Jiayin zazhi*, vol. 1, no. 3 (July 10, 1914).

history was on his side and that a conservative Confucian government should not be established seemed plausible; not only had all governments that had identified themselves with Confucianism been overthrown, but after 1917 Chen, as the dean of an official government institution, seemed to be speaking with official authority. Although not everyone was in full accord with Chen's negative attitude, most of his audience did agree with him that those who were attempting to restore Confucian ideals (and government) were anachronistic; they were aware that history did indeed seem to be going against the conservatives. Like Chen, they were attracted to Western democratic and scientific values and believed that these values were the inevitable wave of the future.

In effect then, Chen used the anti-Confucian debates as a way of destroying the following of Kang Youwei, Yan Fu, Lin Shu, and other so-called conservatives whose admirers since the turn of the century had largely been the young liberal intelligentsia now being drawn to his own cause. In article after article, Chen derided the authority of these figures, remarking repeatedly that although Kang Youwei had once been a respected figure among those interested in Western ideas, he now lacked an understanding of what these ideas meant today.[53] Moreover, it was as a part of the anti-Confucian movement that Chen launched the attacks on the traditional family and society that were so attractive to Chinese youth— implying that it was Kang Youwei and his supporters who were attempting to uphold the authority of these institutions.

Why would Chen Duxiu have felt threatened by the influence of Kang Youwei among the radical youth of the time? Perhaps the major reason is that Kang's reputation as a radical was still overpowering even as late as 1915 despite his recent swing to the right, and Chen feared the power of such a reputation could sway the minds of the same youths he hoped to influence. Even a radical like Mao Zedong was an admirer of Kang Youwei before he began reading *New Youth*. Zheng

[53] See Chen Duxiu, "Bo Kang Youwei zhi zongtong zongli shu"; idem, "Kongzi zhidao yu xiandai shenghuo."

Chaolin, a future Trotskyist associate of Chen's, remarked in an article written in 1946 how the reputation of the "Kang party" both "before and after the 1911 Revolution was as radical as that of the Chinese Communist party after 1925"![54]

This reputation also had political consequences. After 1913, Kang Youwei and the others with whom Chen argued had exercised an important role in garnering support among the elite for the various conservative political powers. Though these conservative forces had suffered a blow with the overthrow of Yuan, they were certainly not defeated; the various warlord powers continued to dominate China for more than a decade after 1916. But the power of the individual warlords was very fragile, and thus they were susceptible, as Yuan had been, to the assaults of Chen Duxiu and his followers. As Chen's attacks on Confucianism began to alienate those who had supported the conservative government, his ideas took on increasing importance in the political struggle that enveloped China after 1917.

The irony of this debate is that it targeted people such as Kang Youwei as the most reactionary elements in Chinese society and as the upholders of the authority of the traditional Chinese family, although in the general political spectrum of the time Kang probably could be considered somewhat to the left. After all, it was Kang who originally had introduced Chen to the Western ideas of progress, science, and democracy that Chen's followers now advocated. And it was Kang who had made the arguments against the traditional family structure that Chen and his generation had found so appealing, although now Chen accused Kang of supporting this structure. These attacks foreshadow a similar tendency within the Chinese Communist movement to accuse supporters who disagree with current policy of siding with the opponents of the regime. The fear behind this was that in a situation of political instability, any weakening of support for a particular position could lead to the upsetting of that position. In this case, Chen's attacks

[54] Tang Lushi (Zheng Chaolin), "Weixin yundong de jieji jichu he jiefang yiyi" [The class basis and liberation intentions in the reform movement], *Jiuzhen [Seeking the Truth]* 3 (July 1, 1946) p. 54.

could be justified somewhat since Kang's support for the idea of Confucian religion did put him into the company of some strange bedfellows.

An example of how the debate over the role of Confucius in Chinese society intruded into the political area can be seen in the events of the summer of 1917, when the troops of the warlord governor of Anhui, Zhang Xun, entered Beijing and at the urging of Kang Youwei temporarily restored the Manchu dynasty. Although the restoration did not last long, Chen thereafter became relentless in his determination to stamp out the influence of Kang Youwei and the Confucian ideas he advocated,[55] hammering away again and again at Confucianism and the debilitating family system that it supported. These attacks continued to attract the youth, who were involved increasingly in their own revolt against the Chinese family system at this time. Zhang Xun's abortive rebellion aroused Chen Duxiu's ire, but it also helped confirm Chen's contention that these old ideas were doomed, thus reinforcing the appeal of his own ideas and his authority among Chinese youth.

Chen's attack on Confucianism as a religion, his attempts to show the relationship between Confucianism and the autocratic structure of the Chinese family, and perhaps even the vindictive hostility with which he confronted Kang Youwei reflected the influence of Zhang Binglin and the school of Han learning. Chen's criticism of Kang Youwei and Confucianism seemed so authoritative because he was able to use the impressive *kaozheng* scholarship that he had studied as a youth to undermine Kang's traditional scholarship. *Kaozheng* scholarship had attacked the authority of neo-Confucian doctrine, particularly the idea of a Confucian religion. When Chen discussed why Confucianism was originally a nonreligious utilitarian doctrine, quite unlike the ideas advocated by Kang Youwei as original Confucianism, he was using *kaozheng* ideas to show the weakness of Kang Youwei's grasp of traditional matters. The traditional iconoclastic ideas Chen had studied

[55] Chen Duxiu, "Fubi yu zunkong" [Restoration and worshipping Confucius], XQN, vol. 3, no. 6 (Aug. 1, 1917).

as a youth thus not only led him to Western ideas but gave him the perspective and background to argue against Confucian religious proposals and the political changes they legitimized. He was one of the few with sufficient knowledge of traditional and Western iconoclastic ideas to be able to make this argument, and his genius lay in his ability to present his ideas with a political timing that gave them an added importance and significance.

THE LITERARY REVOLUTION CONTINUES

In the second crusade Chen Duxiu began against the conservatives—the so-called literary revolution—Chen was able to draw on his knowledge of traditional culture to launch a devastating attack on that culture. In both cases, Chen was to show the continuing influence upon him of Zhang Binglin and the other iconoclastic Confucian teachers with whom he had studied in the pre-1911 period. Perhaps even more than with the anti-Confucian campaign, the literary revolution drew much of its inspiration and impetus from the seemingly conservative ideas of the National Essence group. In both the anti-Confucian movement and the literary revolution, Chen's use of traditional iconoclastic notions made the Western ideas he advocated more compatible to his audience and also enhanced his reputation with his student admirers as a towering intellectual figure worthy of political as well as cultural respect. In both campaigns, Chen advanced his ideas over those of rivals such as Kang Youwei; he also enhanced his political following over those whom he saw as betraying the 1911 Revolution. Using ideas that in many cases he had originally studied with these same political rivals, Chen galvanized a new following. As with the anti-Confucian campaign, the movement for literary reform first created major excitement when it began to take on political as well as cultural significance.

Although Chen had pioneered the use of vernacular writing prior to 1911, the initial articles in *New Youth* were written in a semiclassical style, the language of fashion for the young intelligentsia whom Chen desired to cultivate. Still Chen, who in 1903 had helped with the first translation of *Les Misérables* and in 1904 had written a Russian-style novel, *Black Paradise (Hei tianguo)*, in the pages of the *Anhui Common Speech Journal*, continued to attempt to popularize Western literary ideas. From the start *New Youth* published the translations of famous Western authors.[56] In late 1915, Chen himself wrote a two-part article discussing the literary currents and authors popular in the West.[57] He concluded this article by suggesting that if China were to change, its literature must also reflect this change. This is a sentiment long held by Chen and others interested in the early vernacular movement. The unknown author of an article on the establishment of vernacular journals, quoted in chapter 3, had noted: "China in the present must pass through a stage of establishing the vernacular."[58] Chen had not forgotten this idea after the demise of his first vernacular paper, the *Anhui Common Speech Journal*.

Since in 1915 he hoped to have his new journal evolve into a periodical that would be popular with the so-called *qingnian*, or upper-class youth, he wrote in the lively semivernacular style that had become popular among this group, believing at the time that Chinese would gradually evolve into a more natural and less "classical" form. In a reply to a reader in *New Youth*, Chen pointed out that the stagnant use of obscure terms and imitation of Greek and Roman forms characteristic of Western classicism was similar to the traditional Chinese style in which poets and painters were all expected to imitate the ancients. "The purpose of romanticism," he suggested, "was to give writing more life. Rather than just imitate the

[56] Included in this were stories by Oscar Wilde, Tolstoy, and Turgenev, all of whom adorned the cover of one of the issues of *Youth Magazine*, as well as the French writer Max O'Rell and the Indian poet Rabindranath Tagore, both translated by Chen Duxiu himself. He also printed some of the writings of Irish nationalist poets, including Joseph Plunkett, Thomas MacDonagh, and Patrick Pearse, who were executed by the British in 1916.

[57] "Xiandai ouzhou wenhua shitan" [A discussion of the history of contemporary European literature], *QN*, vol. 1, no. 3 (Nov. 15, 1915) and vol. 1, no. 4 (Dec. 15, 1915).

[58] "Lun baihua bao yu zhongguo qiantu zhi guanxi," *Jingzhong ribao*.

ancients, romantic writing attempts to depict man's condition and describe his spirit."[59] This could be a description of the semivernacular literary form Chen used in the first few issues of his new journal.

But Chen realized that this was not the equivalent of the newest literary style in the West. He wrote that he did not feel that the Chinese were then capable of appreciating the explicit, often ugly details of the naturalist movement—the newest literary trend in the West—and he felt that for the present they should instead be content with romantic thought, later gradually adopting realism and then naturalism.[60] Chen Duxiu did not expect the Chinese to assimilate immediately the latest ideas from the West, for he believed that China had to progress gradually through the same historical stages through which the West had passed.

In accord with this desire for gradual but inevitable change in literature as in all other things, Chen in October 1916 printed a letter to *New Youth* by Hu Shi in which Hu stated his belief, in mild language, that the old idea that "style is more important than content" had resulted in essays with no meaning. To remedy this, he recommended eight steps to make writing more natural and meaningful, the most important of which was: "Do not avoid using colloquialism."[61] An article published in January 1917 written by Hu Shi with Chen's encouragement as a follow-up to his earlier letter, was equally modest in its approach. This piece, entitled "Some Tentative Suggestions for the Reform of Chinese Literature," which is usually considered to have been the starting point of the literary revolution, was largely a reiteration of Hu Shi's earlier eight points. But he now stated his ideas more forcefully, proposing that the vernacular language should be the standard Chinese literary medium, and maintaining that China's passing literary heritage resided in the country's existing but long-neglected vernacular creations.[62]

[59] "Tongxin" [Reply to Zhang Yongyan], QN, vol. 1, no. 6 (Feb. 15, 1916).
[60] Ibid.
[61] Hu Shi, "Tongxin," XQN, vol. 2, no. 2 (Oct. 1, 1916).
[62] Hu Shi, "Wenxue gailiang zhuyi" [Tentative proposals for the improvement of the literature], XQN, vol. 2, no. 5 (Jan. 1, 1917).

THE POLITICS OF CULTURE   125

The controversy did not really begin until the following month when Chen published his boldly headlined article "On the Literary Revolution."[63] Although he obviously was stimulated by some of the issues raised by Hu Shi, his article added a whole new dimension to the vernacular movement by making his call for literary change an attack on the social and cultural ideas of the Chinese gentry who were then monopolizing the government.

Chen Duxiu began by suggesting that "the foundation stone of contemporary Europe . . . is the gift of revolution."[64] Revolution, he said, "means a change from the old to the new, which differs absolutely from what we call the change of dynasties." He continued that the three great principles of the Revolutionary Army were:

(1) To overthrow the painted, powdered, and obsequious literature of the aristocratic few, and to create the plain, simple, and expressive literature of the people;
(2) To overthrow the stereotyped and overly ornamental literature of classicism, and to create the fresh and sincere literature of realism;
(3) To overthrow the pedantic, unintelligible, and obscurantist literature of the hermit and recluse, and to create the plain-speaking and popular literature of society in general.[65]

The responsibility for the worthlessness of present-day literature, he suggested, was that of the Tongcheng and Xijiang factions, whose writings, he felt, dominated the present with their "artificial noble class language."

These types of literature are both causes and effects of our national consciousness of flattery, insincerity, and flagrant disregard of truth and facts. Now that we want political reform, we must regenerate the literature of those who are entrenched in political life. If we do not open

[63] Chen Duxiu, "Wenxue geming lun."
[64] Ibid., p. 135.
[65] Ibid., p. 136. Translation adopted from Chow Tse-tsung, *May Fourth Movement*, pp. 275–76.

our eyes and see the literary tendencies of the world, society, and spirit of the time but instead bury our heads in old books day and night and confine our attention to kings and aristocrats, spiritual fortunes and misfortunes, and in so doing hope to reform literature and politics, it is like binding our four limbs to fight Meng Ben [an ancient strongman].[66]

With these statements, Chen had changed the debate from that of a tentative attempt to undermine the antidemocratic attitudes that were then prevalent among the Chinese elite into an attack that also directly questioned the cultural and intellectual legitimization of specific groups who were supporting the existing political and social system. The Tong-cheng and Xijiang factions Chen mentions were, along with the Changzhou New Text school, the dominant literary forms among the older conservative intellectuals, and those who wrote in these styles were the major supporters of the previous conservative Confucian government.[67] Their adherents had many ties to the bureaucracy and their doctrines were often used to justify the position of the government.

In particular, these factions had dominated Beijing University before and right after 1911.[68] As the intellectual center of China, the school and its faculty controlled access to the official bureaucracy. Writing this piece just as he moved to Beijing to take up his new position as dean of the School of Arts and Letters, Chen Duxiu was challenging the old factions who had previously run the school, many of whom were allied with the same people who had replaced him as head of the Anhui provincial government secretariat following the failure of the so-called 1913 revolution. Now that the dominance of these older factions had been superseded by that of Chen Duxiu and his friends, Chen no longer advocated gradual change but immediate revolution. To be sure, Chen was in-

[66] Ibid., pp. 138–40. Translation adopted from Wm. Theodore deBary, *Sources of Chinese Tradition*, vol. 2, pp. 824–25.

[67] Chow, *May Fourth Movement*, pp. 61–65. Also interview with Lin Yin, Taipei, February, 1975.

[68] Ibid.

sisting on the use of the vernacular form that he and others had been using intermittently for almost fifteen years; but writing from a position of authority at a time when the old culture was under attack, he was also undermining one of the major bastions of power for the conservatives—their control over the literary language. Chen was appealing to the new generation of Chinese youth (many of whom had a rather weak knowledge of the literary language in the first place because of their immersion in the new Western studies) who were worried about their own possibilities for employment and advancement in a bureaucracy that was still not very interested in the Western ideas the students were studying. Chen thus again appealed to the hostility of youth against the values and restraints of the older generation.

Chen's authority to make these attacks on the literary language came not only from his prestigious position but also from his reputation as a master of the language he was attacking. He was able to draw on his *kaozheng* scholarship, which he continued to pursue into the 1920s and 1930s, to make his advocacy of the vernacular seem so convincing. But unlike his writings in the *Anhui Common Speech Journal*, Chen now no longer used traditional ideas to legitimize this change. He now appealed for the use of the vernacular, as he had appealed for the dissolution of the Chinese family and the introduction of ideas of science and democracy, because it would make Chinese society more like that of the West, where similar changes had already been introduced with good results. China, he insisted, had to break decisively with the old ways and the old ideas.

Chen's use of the vernacular considerably hastened the decline of the influence of the representatives of the old order. By changing *New Youth* into a vernacular journal, Chen Duxiu immediately increased its popularity. For not only did the magazine continue to be a highly respected journal—legitimized by the leading intellectual lights of the country—but it was one which was now highly accessible to China's new youth. The more acclimated this new youth became to writings in the vernacular, the more difficult it became for them to read the writings of those of Chen's opponents who still wrote in an obscure literary language. An example of one whose writings were now too difficult for the Chinese youth educated in the new style was Chen's old mentor, Zhang Binglin. Zhang's archaic writing style had been difficult to follow even for members of Chen's generation, and it was almost impossible to do so for those younger than he. To be sure, the vernacular writings now pioneered by Chen Duxiu and Hu Shi were not really all that close to the spoken vernacular language. Although perhaps not quite the "new classical language" that Qu Qiubai once called them, the writings were in a style closely associated with the Western ideas and studies of the educated upper-class *qingnian* for whom Chen wrote and thus could be read easily by this group.

By naming the journal he had begun in 1915 *Youth*, or *La Jeunesse*, the trendy foreign name for the magazine, Chen had signaled his intent to awaken and develop the youth of China. In 1916, when he renamed the journal *New Youth*, he explained that the new title was intended to signify the difference between the "white-faced book worms" of the past who were "sickly and weak of disposition" and the "strong new youth" such as those in European countries, a breed Chen hoped would develop in China. This was the same theme that had been developed earlier in the *China National Gazette*. It signaled a desire to turn away from the culture of the scholar emphasized in traditional exam-oriented Confucianism and instead expounded a return to the militant emphasis on the young and the brave, imbibed by Chen from the anarchist and nationalist writings of the West and the tales of the Chinese past. In changing his publication to one printed in the vernacular—especially a vernacular studded with Western ideas and language—Chen had hit on the formula that would make his journal more attractive and comprehensible to the upper-class youth he hoped to influence.

OUT OF THE IVORY TOWER

As the radical youth began to respond to him, Chen again abandoned his political neutrality. In early 1918, six months after pledging not to become involved in politics, Chen was calling for his youthful followers to take action. The German and Russian revolutionaries, he pointed out (referring to the February revolution in Russia and apparently the German youth movements at the turn of the century that had helped develop Germany into a strong, prosperous state), "were all carried out on the strength of their youth movements." In China, too, "the new youth of the twentieth century" would act forcefully.[69]

This radical political advocacy alarmed many of his compatriots; Chen encountered so much interference from the *New Youth* editorial board that he now was determined to found another magazine. Together with Li Dazhao, Chen began the publication of the *Weekly Critic (Meizhou Pinglun)* in December 1918.[70] In his opening article, Chen still held out hope for help from the West, particularly from President Wilson, to end extraterritoriality and warlord government in China.[71] It was a familiar theme for Chen; Wilson, the former university president, spoke with the moral passion of a new-style Christian *junzi* and Chen looked to him to inspire change in China and in the world. Chen even became optimistic again about the possibility for reform within the Beijing government when Xu Shichang, who was associated with Zhang Shizhao and also seemed to be a scholar and *junzi*,[72] assumed the presidency of China in September 1918.[73] But when the Xu government proved to be no more successful than any of the others in restoring democracy in China, and the Allies failed to come to China's aid, Chen, who had already begun to doubt his earlier conviction that the Chinese elite could be reformed, became disgusted with both Western democracy and Chinese

[69] Chen Duxiu, "Tongxin" [Reply to Gu Kegang], *XQN*, vol. 3, no. 5 (July 1, 1917).

[70] The magazine was finally suppressed by the Beijing government in September 1919.

[71] Chen Duxiu, "Meizhou pinglun fakan zu" [A statement on the publication of the *Weekly Critic*], *Meizhou pinglun [Weekly Critic]* (hereafter *MZPL*) 1 (Dec. 22, 1918).

[72] Li Chien-nung, *The Political History of China*, p. 390.

[73] Chen Duxiu, "Ouzhan hou dongyang minzu zhi juewu."

politics. Instead, he became increasingly attracted to first the February and then the October revolution in Russia as examples of successful movements that could be imitated in China to throw off the kind of political oppression plaguing the country.

The effect of this did not go unnoticed by the conservative and government forces in Beijing, who were aware of the political potential of the authority that Chen retained over Chinese youth. As Chen himself later recalled, he was subjected to continual abuse; among other things he was charged with being unfilial and leading a movement to get the students to rebel against their parents.[74] Examples of this kind of rhetoric against Chen Duxiu were especially prevalent in the *Public Speech Journal (Gongyan bao)*, an organ of the warlord government that frequently printed articles by conservative intellectuals and bureaucrats such as the famous translator and leader of the Tongcheng faction during this period, Lin Shu.[75] Indeed, the writers in the *Public Speech Journal* made it clear that since Cai Yuanpei had become the president of Beijing University, the school had become a center hostile to the old learning and ways. The *Public Speech Journal* writers felt that this threat to them was being organized principally in the School of Arts and Letters by Chen Duxiu who had gathered Hu Shi, Shen Yinmo, and others around him.[76]

Chen counterattacked. On the one hand, he began a campaign against what he called the "three evils" plaguing China— the bureaucrats, the warlords, and the politicians.[77] On the other hand, he suggested the formation of a new political party "based on the people" that would work "to eliminate those

[74] Chen Duxiu, *Shian zizhuan*, p. 24.

[75] See Zheng Xuejia, *Zhonggong xingwang shi [The history of the Rise and Fall of the Chinese Communists]*, vol. 1, pp. 287–90, Taipei, 1970.

[76] "Qing kan beijing xuejie sichao bianyi jian zhi jinchuang" [Please look at the recent circumstances in the changes in the thought tide in Peking's scholarly world], *Gongyan bao*, March 18, 1919, as reprinted in ibid., p. 287.

[77] Chen Duxiu, "Chu sanhai" [Eliminating the three evils], *MZPL* 5 (Jan. 19, 1919); also in *DXWC*, vol. 1, pp. 589–91.

parties without political opinion or good intentions who depend on special power."[78]

In calling for the establishment of a new political party, Chen seemed to be moving toward the strategy of Sun Yatsen, whose actions Chen had seemed to repudiate when he founded *New Youth*. But he still felt that Sun's KMT and also Liang Qichao's Progressive party were too corrupt and decadent to be any good. Still, Chen does not seem to have formed a new party immediately. Instead, as he had done more than a decade earlier in his initial revolutionary activities in Anhui, he began to develop a political following from the teacher-student relationships he had developed, from which were to come many future members of the Chinese Communist party and many of the leaders of the May Fourth movement.[79]

As Chen's following grew, conservative pressure upon him became more intense. In an article that appeared in the *Weekly Critic* in April 1919, Chen complained that several members of the National Purpose party, the group of conservatives opposed to Chen and to the New Culture movement, had begun to spread rumors, suggesting that Chen Duxiu, Hu Shi, and other members of their group were being threatened with expulsion from Beijing University.[80] Chen wrote this article too late to help himself. In March 1919, before his article actually appeared in print, he resigned his deanship at Beijing University in order to stall the interference of the central government in university affairs.[81]

Less than two months later, on May 4, 1919, the May Fourth incident erupted, and Chen soon joined the students

[78] Ibid.

[79] See Chang Kuo-t'ao, *The Rise of the Chinese Communist Party*, vol. 1, pp. 40–43. Chang himself could probably be considered one of the most zealous of Chen's student followers. See also Chow Tse-tsung, *May Fourth Movement*, pp. 187–93. In the meeting of the Seventh Party Congress referred to earlier, Mao remarked that all those "sitting here are students of his [Chen Duxiu]." See note 4 of this chapter.

[80] Chen Duxiu, "Guanyu beijing daxue de yaoyan" [As to the rumors regarding Beijing University], *MZPL* 13 (April 13, 1919).

[81] Thomas Kuo, *Ch'en Tu-hsiu and the Chinese Communist Movement*, p. 61.

in the streets distributing leaflets. On June 11, he was arrested and jailed for this, falsely charged with distributing "bolshevik" propaganda.[82] Because of the great clamor for his release in the newspapers and on the campus of Beijing University, Chen was freed after eighty-three days of confinement. A few months later he was warned by Jiang Monlin (Menglin) that the police were going to rearrest him, and he immediately left Beijing for Shanghai, traveling along back country roads where no one would recognize him.[83] Shortly after arriving in Shanghai, Chen began the formation of the Chinese Communist party.

NEW VOCABULARY, TRADITIONAL STYLE

Before forming the Chinese Communist party, Chen had presented his political ideas within a series of cultural and philosophical arguments. Rather than directly attacking Yuan Shikai, for instance, Chen for the most part had contented himself with attempting to overturn the precepts of those supporting Yuan. To a certain extent, this was a result of the censorship policies of the Yuan government, which made it necessary for Chen to be somewhat circumspect in his political writings.[84] A number of periodicals, including *Tiger Magazine*, on which Chen had worked together with Zhang Shizhao shortly before beginning *New Youth*, were ordered to cease publication by the Yuan regime. Consequently, Chen was very careful to state in the first issue of *New Youth* that the aim of his newly established magazine was solely "to assist and guide the training of the youth" of the country and not to

[82] Zhang Guotao points out that Chen was arrested along with eleven important members of the Peking Student Federation, apparently as part of a conscious effort to break up the burgeoning student movement. Chang Kuo-t'ao, *Rise of Chinese Communist Party*, vol. 1, pp. 65–66.

[83] Jiang Menglin, "Tan zhongguo xin wenyi yundong" [A discussion of the Chinese new literature movement], *Zhuanji wenxue [Biographical literature]* vol. 11, no. 3 (Sept. 1967), pp. 107–8. For some interesting details on this, see "Interview with Hu Shih," in Grieder, *Hu Shih*, p. 184, n. 23.

[84] For a description of these censorship policies, see Chow Tse-tsung, *May Fourth Movement*, p. 43.

criticize the government.[85] But even this frequently-quoted statement followed a very biting and incisive attack on the efforts of those who sought to make Yuan emperor. In fact, the "Internal Events" column of the journal in which the above item appeared was often filled with critical comments about governmental policy. Moreover, much of Chen's discussion of cultural matters contained thinly disguised references to current political matters.

Chen sometimes advocated certain moral and cultural concerns as a way of bringing about political change not simply because he could not address political issues directly and wished to disguise partially his political intent but also because political debate within China was traditionally conducted as scholarly disputations on history and philosophy. The Confucian assumption that governmental policies can be implemented only by an elite who sway others through the force of their example made it incumbent upon individuals to recognize the philosophical consequences of any political situation and to explore them fully in order to ensure that their actions were totally moral and capable of inspiring others. Lin Yu-sheng has suggested that one of the consequences of this belief for Chen Duxiu and his contemporaries was that "the intelligentsia believed in the necessary priority of cultural and intellectual change over social, political and economic changes and not vice versa."[86]

Notwithstanding the imprint that this tradition might have made on the attitudes of the intelligentsia of the May Fourth period such as Chen Duxiu, discussions of political and social theory were still an effective method of arguing for political change among the former members of the Chinese intelligentsia who still occupied many important positions in the government before and after 1911, and whom Chen hoped to draw into an alliance against Yuan Shikai. The highly re-

[85] Chen Duxiu, "Reply to Wang Yuanggong," QN, vol. 1, no. 1 (Sept. 15, 1915).

[86] Lin Yu-sheng, "Radical Iconoclasm in the May Fourth Period and the Failure of Chinese Liberalism," in Benjamin Schwartz, ed., Reflections on the May Fourth Movement, p. 29.

fined content and comparatively modest circulation of *New Youth* may be seen as a reflection of Chen's basic belief that reform would come to China through the actions of the same young student intellectuals with whom he had first engaged in revolutionary activity before 1911 and who, as he had believed earlier, would be responsible for the overthrow of the Qing dynasty. After 1919, Chen turned to a new group—the proletariat—but it was the proletariat under the leadership of the Chinese Communist party. Though Chen no longer had faith in the ability of the elite to reform itself, he did believe that a portion of the youth could detach themselves from their class to help lead the proletariat and develop the Chinese Communist party. But after 1919 he believed this leadership could be achieved only through organization and discipline.

Chen's later espousal of the need for organization and discipline was partially a reaction to the political inadequacy of the following he had created before 1921, which had been attracted to Chen largely because of the traditional Chinese respect for a teacher or moral scholar. In attacking Confucian ideology, Chen utilized the kind of political allegory and philosophical hair splitting that had been part of the traditional Confucian culture, so that he could convince his former colleagues and his youthful followers to change their political program and follow him in a new political movement. But even after he became a Marxist, Chen did not totally abandon this approach. He continued to use a special language. As a Communist, Chen brought to the party certain earlier tendencies to rely on a special language (albeit now a Marxist-Leninist language) to communicate political and social concerns among members of the elite. To this day Chinese Communist debates over political policies tend to be phrased in terms too obtuse to be fully comprehensible to those who are not members of the political and intellectual elite.

During the New Culture movement period, the references to social liberation that ran through Chen's language found a ready appeal in the upper class youth that were his audience. The generation of May Fourth youth, like the young radicals of the pre-1911 era, was involved in a revolt against their traditional family and society. The May Fourth era students, like their forerunners, now found themselves isolated in cities, away from their families, with a lessening of the bonds of parental and social authority. They studied ideas whose content and style were very different from that of the traditional society from which they had sprung and whose message was one of the need for liberation. Moreover, they received this message at a time when the political and social authority of Chinese society was being strained to its uppermost limits. Consequently, the members of the May Fourth generation, which differed from the earlier generation of Chinese youth mainly in its increased size and its further introduction to new and potentially alienating Western ideas, were constantly involved in sexual, social, and political relationships that put them at odds with their background. These new values made them receptive to Chen Duxiu's message that the solution to China's problems lay in the abandonment of Confucian familial norms and the embracement of the ideals of science and democracy that the students were then exploring.

Chen's use of Western ideas and examples in the New Culture movement was clearly as much an attempt to break down the authority of the old society as a real desire to have China look like France or Germany. The example of the West exerted a powerful pull on Chen, one which he hoped to communicate to his readers as a way to help China retain its original sovereignty. But it was the preservation of the Chinese people that was still Chen's most important quest during the New Culture movement period. He was to repeat time after time: "Society is the collective life of individuals. . . . The individual in society is comparable to the cell in the body."[87] The message was clear. If China had to change to preserve itself, if individuals had to be sacrificed, then that change and sacrifice were necesary to retain the Chinese national esssence. Chen's

[87] Chen Duxiu, "Rensheng zhenyi" [The true meaning of life], *XQN*, vol. 4, no. 2 (1918), pp. 92–93; idem, "Jinri zhi jiaoyu fangzhen" [The direction of present-day education], *XQN*, vol. 1, no. 2 (Oct. 15, 1982), *DXWC*, p. 21; idem, "Zisha lun" [On suicide], *XQN*, vol. 7, no. 2 (Jan. 1, 1920), *DXWC*, p. 401.

goals had changed little since the pre-1911 period when he edited the *Anhui Common Speech Journal*. He still wanted to awaken the citizens of China to participate in and work for a government that would have the wealth, technology, and power of the West. What had changed was that Chen no longer felt this could be sanctioned by traditional ideas.

Nevertheless, many of the students Chen influenced, like Chen himself, were in unacknowledged ways still affected by these old values. Believing they were in revolt against their society, the students were attracted to Chen. They liked Chen's apparent understanding of the secrets of Western society that promised to provide alternatives to all that they hated about their own society. The students also appreciated Chen's ability to show the fraudulence of men such as Kang Youwei and Yuan Shikai, who also claimed to understand the new values but insisted that they could be implemented only through the old authority structure.

Because he unwittingly had retained many of the mannerisms and style of the traditional Mandarin, Chen had become the most believable champion of the new Western ideas that were growing popular in China. His moral courage attracted a new student following that was ready to do battle with those who appealed to traditional ideas. This student following became the basis for Chen's new political movement.

CHAPTER FIVE

PARTY FOUNDER
CHEN DUXIU

Without Chen Duxiu it is unlikely that China's Communist party would have developed as quickly or as early as it did. No other Chinese intellectual had the prestige and authority among China's youth that Chen Duxiu had on the eve of the May Fourth movement. His decision to form the Chinese Communist party had an inestimable influence on Chinese youth. Others may have preceded Chen in the study of Marxist thought in China and in taking note of the Bolshevik revolution, but their pursuits would have been hardly worth noting if Chen Duxiu had not formed the party. In the same speech in which Mao Zedong lauded the leading role Chen played in the May Fourth movement, Mao also took note of Chen's efforts in founding the party and helping introduce Marxist thought to China, suggesting to the members of the Seventh Party Congress in 1945 that "all those sitting here are students of his [Chen Duxiu's]."[1]

To understand the history of the development of early Marxist ideas in China, it is therefore necessary to understand the reasons for Chen Duxiu's attraction to Marxism. As we have seen, by 1919 Chen Duxiu was on the verge of forming a new political party that he could use to galvanize his considerable following among the radical Chinese youth and put an end to what he saw as the increasingly corrupt and bankrupt Chinese political world.[2] In Marxism, Chen Duxiu was eventually to believe that he had found an ideology that would allow him to construct the party of the pure and sincere that he had

[1] Mao Zedong as quoted in Lin Maosheng, "Guanyu Chen Duxiu yanjiu de yixie wenti."
[2] See chapter 4.

believed, since the early 1900s, was necessary to restore China's only important national essence—the material well-being and security of the Chinese people. But Marxist ideology would also contribute to transforming Chen's thinking.

Before 1911 Chen had favored the use of violent uprisings and military action, expecting young members of the elite to act in accord with what they felt to be heroic examples of the Chinese past. After 1911 he hoped that Western ideas would stir the elite to gradual reform of the Chinese nation. Neither approach worked. He now firmly believed that Chinese elite society as a whole was tainted by Confucian thought and patriarchal family ties and needed to be eliminated before Chinese society could develop progressively. Chen's allies in this struggle were a select cadre of the young and idealistic. By 1919 and 1920 he was looking for a new plan to execute his dream of an independent, prosperous country. The new plan he discovered was a foreign one that called for a Leninist-style party and a Bolshevik-style revolutionary government.

FOREIGN MODEL

Before 1911, and especially after 1905, Chen had alternated in his admiration for Japan and Russia as examples of countries in revolution. After 1911 he was attracted for a short while to the values of the French revolution and later, for an even shorter period of time, to the model for economic development and anti-imperialist struggle that seemed to characterize Germany. Given this interest in foreign, particularly European, revolution and the fact that beginning in the early 1900s a number of Chinese intellectuals had become cognizant of the similarities between the situations of Russia and China, it is easy to see why Chen and his associates would be very interested in the events occurring in Russia between 1917 and 1918.

The February revolution in particular was noted almost immediately by Chen Duxiu, Li Dazhao, and a number of other Chinese, who viewed it as a foreign revolutionary model of interest to China. In April 1917, Chen praised in writing

the February revolution as a victory of democracy over monarchism and peace over militarism that would herald the elimination of despotism throughout the world, including China.[3]
But considering Chen's emphasis on democracy and peace, it
should not be surprising that the changes in the Russian Revolution in late 1917 and early 1918 did not elicit immediate
positive comment from Chen Duxiu.

Because of their experiences with the abortive 1913 revolution in China, which resulted in the elimination of many of
the reforms that were inaugurated in 1911, most Chinese
radicals were naturally somewhat cautious in their appraisals
of this attempt to carry the Russian Revolution to a new stage.
The immediately positive response of Sun Yatsen and his
Guomindang followers to the Bolshevik Revolution was rather
exceptional; but then, the Guomindang members had all along
distinguished themselves from New Culture movement figures
such as Chen Duxiu by their enthusiasm for radical revolutionary movement.[4] The failure of Chen and most of his colleagues to take notice of the Bolshevik Revolution when it
occurred in October is an example of the naiveté with which
Chen and most of his associates then viewed Marxist ideas.
It was hard for them to understand that the October revolution marked a significant departure from the earlier February revolution. Viewing the situation parochially, they feared
that this new phase of the Russian Revolution would have a
negative effect on the chances for an Allied victory in World
War I, which they expected would restore world peace and
democracy.

It was only after the war ended that Li Dazhao finally com-
mented positively on the Bolshevik Revolution. The famous
article in which Li Dazhao declared his allegiance to the Bolshevik cause, "A Comparison of the French and Russian Revolutions," finally appeared in July 1918. Though it mentions
the socialist and internationalist character that distinguished

[3] Chen Duxiu, "Eluosi geming yu wo guomin zhi juewu" [The Russian
Revolution and our national awakening], XQN, vol. 3, no. 2 (April 1, 1917).
[4] Peng Ming, "Wusi shiqi de Li Dazhao he Chen Duxiu" [Li Dazhao and
Chen Duxiu in the May Fourth period], Lishi yanjiu 6 (1962):52.

the Bolshevik Revolution, this essay was similar in tone to the articles that had appeared about the February revolution, emphasizing that the Russian Revolution heralded a new age for mankind similar to that ushered in by the French Revolution.[5]

Li reacted to Marxism as he, Chen, and other members of the left-leaning Chinese intelligentsia had previously reacted to a number of other new Western ideologies about which they had been enthusiastic: they formed study groups for deeper investigation. Li's Marxist study group was significant for keeping interest alive in the events in the new Soviet Republic among a small group of students, many of whom, such as Luo Jialun, came to believe that a "new tide had arisen in Eastern Europe."[6] This enthusiasm eventually attracted the attention of representatives of the Communist International (Comintern), and Li Dazhao was able to direct them to Chen Duxiu for help in establishing the first Marxist-Leninist party in China, since by now Chen had become captivated by the ideas of the Bolsheviks.

THE SOCIALIST ALTERNATIVE

Chen was attracted to Marxism at a time of general pessimism about Western culture throughout the world because of the horrifying experiences of World War I. Chinese intellectuals were particularly receptive to this pessimism because of their disappointment with the way the Western democracies had rejected Wilsonian idealism at the Versailles Peace Conference, turning China's former colonies in Shandong over to the Japanese. Reacting against what they saw as the hypocrisy of the West, many Chinese thinkers, like many Westerners of the time, began to question the value of progress. The failings of Western culture were broadcast in China most convincingly

---

[5] Li Dazhao, "Fae geming shi bijiaoguan" [A Comparison of the French and Russian revolutions], in Shi Jun, ed., *Zhongguo jindai sixiang shi cankao ziliao jianbian [Source materials for the study of modern China]*, pp. 1201–4.

[6] Luo Jialun, "Jinri zhi shijie xinjie" [The new tide of the present world], *Xinchao [New Tide]*, vol. 1, no. 1 (Jan. 1919).

by Chen's sometime debating partner and former reform-movement leader, Liang Qichao. After a visit to Europe where he witnessed the devastation and demoralization that had occurred as a result of the war, Liang returned to China in 1919 and denounced what he called "the dream of the omnipotence of science."[7] Liang and his associates insisted that the Chinese should respect their own civilization by paying more attention to certain traditional "spiritual values."

This made good sense to many Chinese, appealing as it did to their patriotic pride in their own culture. Chen, who had turned to traditional Chinese values for similar reasons almost a decade earlier and had found them wanting, felt compelled to respond. Although he also was disappointed at the failure of Wilsonian idealism, Chen earlier had made the importance of science one of the focal points of his attacks on Kang Youwei and Kang's disciple, Liang Qichao; he was not willing to allow Liang to disparage Western scientific values. It was in this context that Chen, like many others who were disappointed with Western bourgeois democracy, began to take a second look at the Bolshevik Revolution. In the spring of 1919, Chen mentioned the Bolsheviks for the first time, suggesting that they represented a new historical tide in the world and stood for a new and better morality.[8] He had found a new, nontraditional moral and political model.

These favorable comments on the Bolshevik Revolution were part of Chen's general interest in socialism. The revolution had indeed stirred up a worldwide tide; in its aftermath socialism was studied everywhere. The Chinese received socialist influences during this period as much from the United States and Japan as from the Soviet Union. The period from 1918 to 1921 was not one of a sudden mass conversion to the truths of Marxism-Leninism as has sometimes been implied. Rather, it was a period of experimentation with a wide variety of socialist and anarchist doctrines.

[7] Liang Qichao, "Ouyou xinyinlu" [Impressions of a European journey], *Shishi xinbao [The China Times]*, March 1919.

[8] Chen Duxiu, "Ershi shijie eluosi de geming" [The twentieth century Russian Revolution], *MZPL* 18 (April 18, 1919).

That Chen experimented with an assortment of socialist doctrines before settling on Marxism should not be surprising, for Chen had long expressed an interest in socialism. Anarcho-socialist doctrines had been fervently studied by members of the radical student movement with which Chen had been associated before 1911; an official Chinese Socialist party had been founded in China in 1912, and by 1915, writing in the first edition of *New Youth*, Chen had hailed socialism as one of the three major contributions of French civilization to mankind, the other two being democracy and science.[9] Still, in the initial years of the New Culture movement, Chen, who then believed that even literary change would come slowly to China, maintained in a reply to a reader that there was no point in discussing socialism in China at present since industry had not yet developed to the point where the ideology could be implemented.[10]

Shortly before he wrote this letter in 1917, however, Chen had moved to Beijing and begun the vernacular revolution. As his influence increased, he became more confident about the possibilities for immediate change. By 1919, affected by his disappointment with the failure of Wilsonian democracy, aroused by the general interest in socialism that began to be expressed throughout the world in the wake of the Bolshevik revolution, and emboldened by his own growing confidence in the possibilities for the immediacy of change in China, Chen began once again to consider seriously the possibilities of socialism in China.

Chen was by no means alone in this interest in socialism. Socialism at this time was attracting a considerable following throughout China including such KMT members as Dai Jitao, Sun Yatsen, and Cai Yuanpei, as well as Liang Qichao himself.[11] Another person expressing interest in socialism at this

[9] Chen Duxiu, "Falanxi ren yu jinshi wenming."
[10] Chen Duxiu, "Tongxin" [Correspondence], *XQN*, vol. 2, no. 5 (Jan. 1, 1917).
[11] See Chow Tse-tsung, *The May Fourth Movement*, p. 217. See also Zhang Pengyuan, "Liang Qichao dui shehui zhuyi de renshi qi zhongguo xiandaihua de jianjie" [An understanding of Liang Qichao's recognition of socialism and

time was the warlord, Chen Chiungming.[12] Partially as a result of their mutual interests, Chen Chiungming invited Chen Duxiu to take over the duties of the chairman of the Education Committee for Guangdong.

Few of these people, including Chen Duxiu, understood much about socialism at this time, and their initial interest in socialist doctrines tended to be eclectic and often trendy. During the period from 1919 to 1921, when Chen often is seen moving directly from a belief in Western democracy to a sudden conversion to Marxism, he was actually exploring and alternately supporting a whole series of ideas ranging from the new village movement of the Japanese socialist Mushakoji Soneatsu,[13] a utopian thinker who called for the formation of model villages by followers who would be willing to give up all their private property, to the Christian socialism advocated by the followers of the Korean independence movement.[14] It may seem strange that after rejecting the West, Chen would be willing to turn to Christianity, particularly in the wake of his earlier assertion, in an attack on Kang Youwei, that religion was now outdated; he seems to have been influenced by the idealism of Asian Christian leaders.

Chen had long been searching for the kind of example that would motivate the Chinese people. He had found the revival of historically heroic actions inadequate, and he became disillusioned with the example of "brave scholars who stand firm." Still, Chen did not give up on the Confucian-like idea that the example of a few could motivate many—as a bourgeois democrat, Chen briefly had even hoped to gain from the idealism of Woodrow Wilson. Similarly, Chen's initial interest in socialism also focused less on the ideals of the doctrine than

China's modernization], *Shihuo yuekan [Provisions Monthly]*, vol. 3, no. 19 (Jan. 15, 1974). Zheng Xuejia, *Zhonggong xingwang shi*, pp. 412–46. Chang Kuo-t'ao, *The Rise of the Chinese Communist Party*, vol. 1, p. 108.

[12] Chen Chiungming had such a progressive reputation that even Bertrand Russell compared him quite favorably to Sun Yatsen. See Bertrand Russell, *The Problem of China*, p. 254.

[13] *XQN*, vol. 7, no. 3 (Feb. 1, 1920).

[14] Chen Duxiu [Zhiyan], "Chaoxian duli yundong zhi ganxian" [Feelings about the Korean Independence Movement], *MZPL* 14 (March 23, 1919).

on the idealism of socialist leaders such as Mushakoji Soneatsu. Stirred by the Christian socialism being attempted by
idealistic young Koreans, Chen (as Zhang Shizhao had done
almost five years earlier) began to talk about Jesus and the
effect of his teachings on people.

As late as February 1920, just as he began to commit himself
to Marxism, Chen advocated the adoption of Christianity in
China, saying that Greek and Christian thought were the basis
of modern Western philosophy and what both had in common—and what was lacking in China—was a faith that over-
comes material spirit.[15] Rejecting the notion that Western culture was materialistic and Chinese spiritualistic, Chen claimed
to see in Christianity the kind of purity of intention and ideals
that he had long felt were essential ingredients for motivating
the Chinese people. Because of Christianity, he said, Westerners emphasize beauty, religion, and pure feelings, while
Chinese culture stressed only outer feelings and moral doctrine. Chen had not abandoned his Confucian-influenced stress
on sincerity that had characterized his early activities and
writings; he now professed to see this sincerity in those influenced by Christianity. In typical fashion, Chen may have had
another ulterior motive for his advocacy of Christianity at this
time. In his article, he complains of Christians who "make
use of Christianity for their own purposes," supporting acts
of militarism and imperialism. Such Christians, he concludes,
forget that Christianity was originally the doctrine of the poor
and "attack communism." By thus advocating Christianity,
Chen was not only able to attack the Western imperialist
powers and to cast aspersions on the growing influence of the
so-called Christian warlord Feng Yuxiang, then occupying
much of Hunan, but Chen was also attempting to gain the
goodwill of those interested in Christianity for socialist and
Communist doctrines. But even so his interest in Christianity
was very short-lived.

During this period in his life, Chen continued to experiment
with various ideas. He advocated the Work-and-Learning Mu-

[15] Chang Kuo-t'ao, *Rise of Chinese Communist Party*, pp. 95, 109–10.

tual Assistance Corps (Gongdu huzhu tuan) formed by young Chinese intellectuals in several urban areas as an experiment in a model cooperative society.[16] And shortly before expressing his interest in Christianity, he had even been interested for a short time in John Dewey's guild socialism.[17] Dewey had suggested that grass-roots guild and village organizations could provide a foundation on which political, social, and economic democracy could be built in China, and Chen temporarily found this very attractive. In his earlier study of Chen Duxiu, Benjamin Schwartz has seen this temporary embracement of Dewey's ideas as a detour, "a counterinfluence" that delayed Chen's interest in Marxist doctrines.[18] But Chen's interest in Deweyian socialism should be seen as part of Chen's interest in all socialist doctrines that preceded his embracement of Marxist ideas.

Although during this period Chen seemed to flit from idea to idea in his searches, seeming to espouse a new movement every other day, there was actually a certain consistency in his quest. The various socialist ideologies he briefly championed before turning to Marxism distinguished themselves by their concern with sincere nonself-interested behavior. These doctrines rejected what he now believed to be the crass and destructive materialistic, individualistic society of the capitalist West, which left the poor and the weak trampled in its path. Although Chen had at one time seemed to be an advocate of Western materialism and individualism, he had always felt more comfortable with doctrines that spoke of moralism and social solidarity. Influenced, like other members of the Chinese intelligentsia, by attacks on the so-called failure of Western democratic society conducted by Liang Qichao and others in the postwar period, Chen reacted by not turning back to the traditional Chinese ideologies advocated by Liang that Chen felt had failed in the pre-1911 period; rather, he turned to the

[16] Chen Duxiu even contributed 330 yuan to this project. See Chow Tse-tsung, *May Fourth Movement*, p. 135.

[17] Chen Duxiu, "Shixing minzhi de jichu" [The basis for the realization of democracy], *XQN*, vol. 7, no. 1 (Dec. 1, 1919).

[18] Benjamin Schwartz, *Chinese Communism and the Rise of Mao*, p. 19.

new socialist doctrines that seemed to be addressing this problem. These doctrines appealed to traditional ideas of group harmony and solidarity, emphasizing that by pooling the resources of the society the nation could develop faster and could avoid the cruelty and brutality that Chen felt were already present in growing industrial cities like Shanghai. In a world that seemed to Chen to be crass and hypocritical, these doctrines exuded sincerity and moral commitment—values that he, with his Confucian background, still felt were necessary to motivate the Chinese people.

Chen became obsessed with the way capitalism was transforming China at this time, deploring the greed for money among his friends in Shanghai and complaining that the city was becoming so decadent and money-grubbing that it was beginning to take on the "odor" of a Leeds or Manchester.[19] In contrast to the depressing realities of life observed by Chen in Shanghai, socialist ideals such as those of Dewey, the Work-and-Learning Mutual Assistance Corps, Mushakoji Soneatsu, and the Korean Christian Socialist movement seemed to give Chen hope for the development of China without further impoverishing the lower orders of the society and pitting its members against one another, as had occurred in Western capitalist countries. Socialist ideas also reawakened Chen's concerns regarding the importance of group solidarity. Because these ideologies emphasized the strength of social institutions, they appealed to the many who, like Chen Duxiu prior to 1911, believed in the basic goodness of the Chinese people. Moreover, those who emphasized Western socialist doctrines could continue to believe in the potential of Chinese society while at the same time repudiating the Confucian culture that had become a despised symbol of the parental and social authority that many May Fourth students had rejected. Chen of course was the leader of this later group.

[19] Chen Duxiu, "Shanghai shehui" [Shanghai society], *XQN*, vol. 8, no. 1 (Sept. 1, 1920). Also "Zailun Shanghai shehui," *XQN*, vol. 8, no. 2 (Oct. 1, 1920); and "San lun Shanghai shehui" [A third time on Shanghai society], *XQN*, vol. 8, no. 3 (Nov. 1, 1920).

THE PARTY OF THE ELITE

While others discussed socialist and Marxist ideas in salons and study groups, Chen Duxiu took a drastic new step that would transform radically the politics of Chinese youth, and then of Chinese society as a whole. Chen Duxiu, who had been interested in forming a new political party in China since early 1919, was the first to notice what distinguished the Bolsheviks from the other socialist groups was that they provided the organizational model for the formation of a party that intellectuals like Chen could use to implement socialism in China without having to depend on any existing internal or external political forces. Still, in 1913 Chen had thought that Sun Yatsen's Revolutionary party was too disciplined, and he thus did not become a Bolshevik overnight. His initial idea of the Communist party, like his early ideas about socialism, was very different from those of his Russian counterparts. Unlike Lenin, Chen at first does not seem to have viewed his new party simply as a tool for seizing power; rather, he saw it principally as an organization for building a new society and economy in China.

That Chen's view of the role of the Chinese Communist party was very different from that of Lenin should not be surprising, given the dearth of literature on Leninism that was available in Chinese before 1921. Indeed, the first work on Leninism was not published in China until late 1919.[20] Chen received his ideas of the new Soviet state from a range of sources of varying reliability, including his own imagination. Part of his information came from the representatives of the International who began to appear in China in 1919, but most of it came for several years from other foreigners, such as John Dewey and particulary Bertrand Russell, who lectured in China in early 1920 on the new Soviet state.

Russell was invited to China by Liang Qichao because of Russell's opposition to the Bolshevik experiment in the Soviet Union. Many of his speeches denounced the Russian revolu-

[20] Maurice Meisner, *Li Ta-chao and the Origins of Chinese Marxism*, p. 116.

tion and, to the horror of some of his radical young listeners, he praised certain aspects of Chinese tradition. But, to the satisfaction of people such as Chen Duxiu, Russell also often spoke positively of the Bolsehvik organization. Moreover, his lectures were critical of socialists and anarchists, who believed the masses could organize themselves spontaneously.[21] To be sure, Chen had long doubted that the masses were by themselves capable of change, but his reactions to Russell's observations demonstrate his interest in creating a new political structure to effect change. There was a major transformation in Chen's thinking, for he had always been more suspicious of political structures than most of his contemporaries. Chen's earlier political organizations had relied more on loosely allied groups of individuals loyal to a leader/teacher, as in Confucian tradition, than on a disciplined political organization.

This earlier reluctance to construct a disciplined political organization partially reflected Chen Duxiu's own distrust of governmental institutions, a distrust that many have interpreted as a lack of patriotism; but Chen lacked faith only in Chinese state institutions, not in China. Even Li Dazhao accused Chen of unpatriotic feelings in the well-known exchange between the two future Communist leaders in 1914 in the pages of *Tiger Magazine*.[22] At this time, Chen pessimistically had asserted that he would rather let the country be overrun by foreigners than create a false patriotic state that did nothing to improve the lot of the people; he implicitly criticized those who felt that in the face of the Japanese threat to China posed by the Twenty-one Demands, all Chinese should close ranks with Yuan Shikai to protect China. Chen asserted that those "intellectuals who get angry and desire to raise an army" to drive the foreigners from the country not only lacked self-consciousness but were "laboring in the interests of others."[23]

[21] Chen Duxiu, "Xiaping de wuzhengfu dang" [Lower class anarchism], *XQN*, vol. 9, no. 2 (June 1, 1921).
[22] Li Dazhao, "Yanshixin yu zijuexin" [Pessimism and self-consciousness], *Jiayin zazhi*, vol. 1, no. 8 (Aug. 10, 1915). Chen Duxiu, "Reply" [No title], ibid.
[23] Chen Duxiu, "Reply."

Chen considered this kind of patriotism misguided and dangerous, implying that if the kind of country these people wished to protect did not contribute to the joint welfare of all the Chinese people, then "a nation really has no need to be established."[24]

Li's assertion that these statements created a pessimistic atmosphere seemed to highlight the differences between Li's optimistic faith in the ability of the Chinese people to overcome all obstacles and Chen's gloomy insistence that development and growth must be slow. More important, however, Chen's essay attacking false patriotism underscored the difference between Li's and Chen's attitudes toward state power. Li, who in an earlier essay had suggested that the state was a natural outgrowth of the Chinese people,[25] felt that a state should not be abandoned because it was bad.[26] Chen, however, focused on the welfare of the Chinese people, not just on the strength of the state. As he put it: "A nation's purpose is the protection of the people's power and the seeking to increase the people's happiness and prosperity. If it does not carry out this duty the nation's existence has no special honor. Its death would not be regretted."[27]

This commitment to the Chinese people, and not to their state, had been a major characteristic of Chen's political actions. In his earlier political activity, he had consistently shown a preference for inspirational activities that would directly motivate the masses; his distrust of state organization—indeed of most political organizations—kept him from joining organizations such as the Revolutionary Alliance, the Restoration Society, and the Revolutionary party. He preferred instead to work outside of these large structures with his own cadre of hand-picked leaders who would inspire and educate the masses.

By 1920, however, Chen agreed with Bertrand Russell's

[24] Chen Duxiu, "Aiguoxin yu zijuexin."
[25] Li Dazhao, "Guoqing" [National condition], *Jiayin zazhi*, vol. 1, no. 4 (Nov. 10, 1914).
[26] Li Dazhao, "Yanshixin yu zijuexin."
[27] Chen Duxiu, "Aiguoxin yu zijuexin."

suggestion that the masses needed an organization to direct them and an ideology designed to support this organization.[28] To be sure, Chen Duxiu, as we have seen, had long insisted that the ideas of Chinese intellectuals had to be made more accessible to the masses. He echoed Russell's assertion that people who want to influence the masses must also be prepared to adapt their thinking to that of the people. They cannot, he pointed out, expect the masses to change by preaching elegant thoughts to them; if so, Confucius could have saved the world a long time ago.[29] Chen even agreed with Russell on the need for patriotic thought and began to advocate the emotional kind of patriotic thought that had characterized his political activities and writing before 1911, precisely because it was the kind of thinking that could reach the masses. Chen realized that many "highbrows" who advocated cosmopolitanism would mock this, but it was "appropriate to the low level of Chinese society and not [merely] lofty discussion."[30]

In his own highbrow years just a short time earlier, Chen had denounced "patriotism without self-consciousness" as not conducive to solving China's problems. He implied that the emotional patriotic slogans raised during the 1911 period had prevented the Chinese people from understanding how to exercise sovereignty and had led to a situation where the "animal-like masses could elevate a person above them," an obvious reference to Yuan Shikai's use of patriotic slogans in his rise to power.[31] Even during his *New Youth* period, Chen had of course not been totally immune from using patriotic slogans, but now he discovered how to combine the emotional patriotism of his *Anhui Common Speech Journal* period with the desire for democratic self-awareness that he had tried to promote during his *New Youth* years—the key was the party of dedicated youths described by Russell as necessary to carry

---

[28] Chen Duxiu, "Beishi wushen gaolun" [On being common rather than too lofty], *XQN*, vol. 9, no. 3 (July 1, 1921).
[29] Ibid.
[30] Ibid.
[31] Chen Duxiu, "Aiguoxin yu zijuexin."

out the transformation of China.[32] Patriotism could be used
to organize the masses to support such a group, which eventually could carry out the changes necessary to educate the
Chinese people and transform Chinese society.

Chen had always insisted that patriotism without social
change was of no benefit to the Chinese nation. After the
experiences of the 1911 Revolution, however, Chen, fearing
that the emotional patriotic statements he had once promoted
had spelled disaster for China, bent over backwards to avoid
making the same mistake. But now he felt that emotional
patriotism could help ensure the reform of Chinese society,
and that these ideals could be achieved by a new political
party such as the one Chen had once considered founding
himself. The patriotic values he now advocated helped put
into power an organization of youthful intellectuals—the group
in which Chen had expressed faith since his baptism into
political activity in the early 1900s—who, he expected, would
educate and develop Chinese society. It is true that before
coming into contact with Marxist-Leninist ideas even as interpreted by Russell, Chen had already considered the need
for new political organization. Now, with the new impetus
and influence provided by Bolshevik ideas, Chen began to
advocate organizational discipline. It was this embracement
of Leninist organization that made Chen's espousal of socialism unique from those of his many compatriots.

To be sure, embodied within this notion was some of Chen's
previous faith in the need for bold leaders. But Chen now
tended to emphasize organizational skills as much as good
leadership. Chen quoted Bertrand Russell as saying that "in
the first stage of reform it is necessary to have a group of
people willing to sacrifice their own lives to manage the government, create industry, and carry out new construction."[33]
Chen had long suggested that leaders need to "sacrifice" themselves. Now this "sacrifice" would be not to perform heroic
tasks but to "manage" enterprises.

[32] Chen Duxiu, "Beishi wushen gaolun."
[33] Ibid.

In turning to socialism, Chen had at first hoped to revive the good instincts of the people and reinstate group values and sincere behavior. Now, however, he again concluded that the Chinese people were for the time being incapable of taking this action on their own without a political organization of the sincere to rule for the people. Chen scathingly denounced his fellow countrymen to be

. . . a partly scattered, partly stupid people possessed of narrow-minded individualism with no public spirit who are often thieves and traitors and for a long time have been unable to be patriotic, so there is no point in talking of anything further. . . . Obviously the more people in a nation who will take responsibility the better, but among this kind of irresponsible people with no ability, purpose or knowledge, to give them responsibility is to commit national suicide. In China at this time not only is government by the whole people worthless to talk of but it is a dream.[34]

Like Liang Qichao and other "neo-conservatives" who also claimed to be attracted to the idea of socialism, Chen now felt that the elite must rule the people. But unlike Liang, Chen was interested in discarding all existing social institutions— even those he had experimented with in 1918, 1919, and early 1920. Instead Chen now felt that new organizations and institutions had to be rebuilt by a new party of the elite, a party that, unlike those of the past, emphasized management and organizational skills.

AMBIVALENCE TO STRONG CENTRAL AUTHORITY

Chen now committed himself to new-style institutions that could be used in the transformation of China.

China's governmental revolution in the next couple of years absolutely cannot effect a Western-style democracy. . . . To get to this stage it would be best to undergo

[34] Ibid.

Russian Communist class dictatorship. Because in order to save the nation, make knowledge widespread, develop industry and not be stained with a capitalist taint, Russian methods are the only road.[35]

But Chen did not yet understand what a class dictatorship entailed. Although he was attracted to the example of Lenin in trying to transform the Russian economy, Chen's emphasis was very different from that of the Russian leader. In his initial formation of the Chinese Communist party in 1920, Chen did make some effort to form the party along the general lines of the Russian Communist party as he understood it, creating a general secretary, and a head of propaganda, organization, and so forth. Yet he was very sensitive to the way Sun Yatsen had so completely dominated the Guomindang, and therefore adamantly opposed the position of a strong party chief, instead insisting that the general party secretary be elected by the different committee heads and be responsible to them. This system was exactly like that followed by the Guomindang after the ouster of Sun Yatsen from absolute power in Canton (an action which Chen had backed).[36] The qualifications for membership in Chen's new party would certainly have made Lenin blanch. While government officials were excluded from the party and an effort was made to recruit people who were sympathetic to Marxism and prepared to work actively for the Communist cause, non-Marxist socialists and even anarchists were permitted to participate fully in the party organization.

But Chen and Lenin had bigger differences. Chen was interested in what would happen after the seizure of power, while Lenin concentrated on the process of obtaining power. It did not even occur to Chen to defend the new political organization he was creating in terms of a way to seize power in China. Chen was certain that once he had the proper organization, the power would also be his. Thus he principally

[35] Chen Duxiu, "Zhengzhi gaizao yu zhengdang gaizao" [Governmental and political party change], *XQN*, vol. 9, no. 3 (July 1, 1921).
[36] Chang Kuo-t'ao, *Rise of Chinese Communist Party*, vol. 1, p. 102.

defended his plans for that organization after the seizure of power—namely, the establishment of a dictatorship of the proletariat. He felt that after his party came to power, state power would be necessary at least temporarily to curb bourgeois exploitation and resolve social conflicts.[37]

Chen again defended the dictatorship of the proletariat during a famous debate with a group of Chinese anarchists, which included his two eldest sons. The anarchists opposed the Chinese Communist emphasis on organization and state power. Anarchism was a doctrine to which Chen Duxiu himself had been attracted earlier and which still exerted a tremendous appeal to many Chinese youth. In spite of his new-found interest in the proletariat, Chen was still extremely concerned about the opinions of the Chinese youth, his main constituency. Undoubtedly, Chen also felt a certain psychological tension as a result of his dispute with his own sons (who were part of the generation Chen had been urging to rebel against their parents) over the issue of whether China did or did not need state power to develop.

Chen's concern with anarchists and lack of concern for what troubled his antirevolutionary former peers in Beijing is seen in his relative disinterest in the famous debate between Hu Shi and Li Dazhao on "problems" and "isms," which occurred at the same time as Chen engaged in his own polemic against the anarchists. Hu Shi had fired off a salvo against the new Communist party with his famous article "More Study of Problems, Less Talk of Isms."[38] As has been pointed out elsewhere, "the major thrust of [Hu's] argument was that doctrines advocating all-embracing and fundamental solutions not only were irrelevant but actually hindered finding the real solution of social problems."[39] Li Dazhao replied to Hu's complaints by maintaining that without an ism to focus the people on common goals and directions, there could be no

[37] Chen Duxiu, "Tan zhengzhi" [Talking politics], XQN, vol. 8, no. 1 (Sept. 1, 1920).
[38] Hu Shi, "Duo yanjiu xie wenti, xiao tan xie zhuyi" [More study of problems, less talk of isms], MZPL 31 (July 20, 1919).
[39] Meisner, Li Ta-chao, p. 105.

solution of individual problems. As Maurice Meisner has demonstrated, the real issue at question was whether or not the existing social and political structure was adequate to deal with China's problems or whether a revolution was necessary.[40] But the debate was also significant because it served to show a difference in ideas between Li Dazhao and Chen Duxiu, as well.

Chen joined the debate briefly, making a rather tenuous analogy between the ideas of Hu Shi and those of the so-called revisionist German Social Democrats who supported their government during the war. But it is clear that the issues involved in this argument, which so excited other Chinese intellectuals at the time, were of little interest to Chen.[41] Indeed, of the three great intellectual battles that the Chinese Communists carried out during this early period of their existence—against Liang Qichao's alternate "socialist" proposals, against the anarchists, and over "problems and isms"— the struggle against problems and isms is the only one in which Chen did not lead the Marxist forces. Having come to believe in the necessity of revolution, Chen now felt little need to defend himself to his former comrades from *New Youth* on this matter. He was convinced he was right, and he was relatively unconcerned about the ideas of his middle-aged colleagues, who had no intention of ever joining the Communist party. But Chen was concerned about the ideas of the youthful anarchists, many of whom were or had been party members.

To some extent this difference in concern between the two founders of the Chinese Communist movement reflected the situation of the two men at this time. Li, who had remained in Beijing, was in constant contact and debate with Hu Shi and his colleagues, while Chen, who had been forced to flee to the south, was involved in unending attacks from the left in his attempts to organize the Chinese Communist party. Yet the composition of their enemies was not merely the result of

[40] Ibid., p. 106.
[41] Chen Duxiu, "Tan zhengzhi."

a geographical accident, since many defenders of the status quo could also be found in the south, and there was no shortage of anarchists in Beijing.

As was evident in his earlier debate with Chen Duxiu on patriotism, Li viewed the state as the natural outgrowth of the people. Consequently, he, unlike Chen, felt defensive when faced with arguments that called into question the need for revolutionary actions to overthrow the state; he retorted that the people needed a cataclysmic upheaval and binding theology to unify their consciousness and give them a sense of direction.[42] Chen, on the other hand, had been quite distrustful of the state power before he became a Marxist, viewing political institutions as an unnatural impediment to a society. Now, however, Chen argued that political institutions might indeed be necessary to rebuild China and he defended this position. He did not even bother to argue about the need to overthrow a state that clearly was doing the society no good, nor did he hesitate to accept a totalistic ideology opposing the present political and social system. To be sure, Chen did not believe that the revolutionary process would by itself transform the spirit of the people but only that it would install a new group of leaders capable of inspiring change in Chinese society. Chen was not defensive about the need for violent revolution; rather, he felt more compelled to justify the construction of a new authority structure, after having spent so much of his life battling against one. This was true particularly because this authority was opposed initially by many of the youth Chen hoped to recruit into his new party. Even so, they joined him.

PARTY ORGANIZATION AND SOCIETAL DEVELOPMENT:
CHEN, LENIN, AND MARX

The differences between the ideologies of Chen and Li point up many of the divergences in the thinking of Chen and Lenin, as well. Because of his ambivalent attitudes toward authority,

[42] Meisner, *Li Ta-chao*, pp. 106–7.

Chen could never have the same "jealous pride of the artist"[43] that Lenin has been described as possessing in his attitude toward building the party organization. One of the reasons for Chen's later downfall was his inability to utilize the party organization to ensure his own power. Although Chen might have agreed with Lenin that "a systematic plan of action" was necessary to preserve "the energy, the stability, and continuity of the political struggle,"[44] Chen, unlike Lenin, was continually pondering the question of how the methods of the revolution would affect its ultimate goals. The first to understand the kind of political organization necessary to carry off the revolution in China, Chen was thus nevertheless unable to take advantage of the organization. He continued to view party members not as bureaucrats but as moral examples.

Chen interpreted the Marxist idea that only the proletariat had the vision and organization necessary to carry out the proletarian revolution in terms of his earlier Confucian-influenced belief that revolution had to be made by those pure in intentions and beliefs. Lenin gladly might have seconded Chen Duxiu's insistence that a social revolution would not be able to "abolish the old and institute the new" unless it is carried out among "the organized productive workers," and under certain circumstances Lenin might also have agreed: "Using money to stir up the scum of society (the unemployed, unproductive rascals and thieves) cannot count as a revolution, no matter what its goal, but can only create chaos. . . ." But Lenin never could have gone along with Chen's contention: "Revolution is the work of saints."[45]

Another criticial difference in emphasis between Chen and Lenin was that Lenin emphasized the necessity of organization as a tool for creating the revolution, while Chen emphasized that organization would be necessary after the revolution as a way of building the new society. Lenin always assumed that the revolution he would be leading would be an international

[43] Sheldon Wolin, *Politics and Vision*, p. 425.
[44] As quoted in ibid., p. 424.
[45] Chen Duxiu, "Geming yu zuoluan" [Revolution and chaos], *XQN*, vol. 8, no. 4 (Dec. 1, 1920).

revolution; the rising of the Russian workers would incite their comrades in the more advanced Western European countries and lead to the creation of socialism on a worldwide basis. Lenin therefore rarely thought very concretely about the postrevolutionary government, assuming that after the revolution the government would in effect run itself. On the eve of the Russian revolution, he wrote: "Capitalist culture has created large-scale production, factories, railways, the postal service, telephones, etc., and on this basis the great majority of the functions of the old 'state power' have become so simplified and can be reduced to such exceedingly simple operations by registration, filing, and checking that they can easily be performed by every interested person. . . ."[46] Chen, however, in spite of occasionally mentioning the fact that the Chinese revolution would be part of an international revolution, was very aware of China's industrial underdevelopment. He was concerned primarily with the kind of conditions the revolution would create in China. He did not share Lenin's faith that the revolution would have a cataclysmic effect on society and solve its problems; he felt that the type of postrevolutionary government chosen would be of critical importance in altering the society.

Chen saw in the Bolshevik organization the kind of moral leadership that he had long felt would be necessary to transform Chinese society. The Marxist message, one must remember, came to China during the period following World War I, when Western material culture was being attacked by Liang Qichao and at a time when Chen himself was deeply concerned about the severe recession that had just overtaken China's recently expanded industrial base in the wake of World War I, particularly the effect it had on China's infant proletarian class. Chen's disenchantment with the West as a result of the Versailles Peace Conference in 1919 was one of the last in a series of blows that had begun to shake the faith he and his followers had previously displayed for Western ideas. Given

[46] V. I. Lenin, "The State and Revolution," in *Selected Works*, vol. 2, p. 299.

this situation, it is only natural that Chen and others began to sympathize with the Bolsheviks as the one group resisting the imperialist powers, the people who had betrayed Chen at Versailles. In March 1920 the Soviets published Leo Karakhan's manifesto outlining the new Soviet regime's position concerning the concessions of territory and privileges the previous czarist regime had extracted from the Chinese government. The Karakhan manifesto renounced czarist extraterritorial rights in China and repudiated all unequal treaties. The news of this manifesto heightened the moral standing of the Bolsheviks in the eyes of Chen Duxiu and many other Chinese and increased their attraction to the Bolshevik Revolution. It provided Chen with a model that repudiated what he considered to be the bad aspects of Western society that were then under attack by people such as Liang Qichao.

Moreover, the early socialist doctrines in which Chen had expressed an interest—Dewey's guild socialism, the Korean Christian Socialist movement, the new village movement of Mushakoji Soneatsu, and the Work-and-Learning Mutual Assistance Corps—all had suggested ways of industrializing by redeveloping the "social" cohesion and strengths of the society without the misery created by the capitalist system. Chen therefore assumed that the Marxist revolution of the Bolsheviks, who had created a new government in underdeveloped Russia, had the same aim of developing without capitalism. As Chen Duxiu wrote:

In my opinion, although capitalism . . . has developed industry and education, it has also produced many societal evils. Everyone knows that the war [in Europe] was a product of capitalist development and the imminent revolution is also produced by it. Fortunately, in China, where capitalism has not yet developed . . . we can best use socialism to develop education and industry and avoid the mistakes [of capitalism].[47]

[47] Chen Duxiu, "Zhi Luosi xiansheng dexin" [Letter to Bertrand Russell], in *Shehui zhuyi taolun ji* [*Collection of a discussion on socialism*], pp. 44–45.

This interpretation of Marxism was not uncommon. Intellectuals in so-called developing countries have often taken Marx's descriptions of the horrors of capitalism not as a stage through which all countries must pass, as Marx believed,[48] but as a stage that can be skipped over or otherwise avoided.[49] Marxism in the wake of the Bolshevik revolution even seemed to offer a program for instituting a government of people who could accomplish this. Such a socialist government, Chen believed, which would be controlled by those with the interests of society at heart, could decide where a nation's capital should be concentrated and ensure that it could be used in a productive manner.[50] What Chen was hoping to avoid was the decadent and money-grubbing attitude he had begun to complain about in Shanghai.[51]

Chen Duxiu was not alone with this idea. As Benjamin Schwartz has already noted, the Guomindang rightists Dai Jitao and Hu Hanmin were similarly attracted to Marxism because of their belief in the need to create a strong, new state.[52] And as Herman Mast has shown in his insightful analysis of Dai Jitao, Dai, like Chen, had feelings of revulsion for the developing capitalist forces in Shanghai.[53] The experimentation with socialism by a broad spectrum of the Chinese

[48] This was one of the basic themes of Marx's writings, although in an intriguing letter written by Marx to the editors of *Otechestvenniye zapiski*, a Russian populist journal, he suggested that it might be possible for Russia to bypass capitalism and pass directly into socialism. See Lewis Feuer, ed., *Marx and Engels*, p. 439.

[49] A. Walicki, *The Controversy Over Capitalism*, esp. pp. 107–31, 179–94.

[50] Chen Duxiu, "Maersi renkou lun yu zhongguo renkou wenti" [Malthus's theory of population and the Chinese population problem], *XQN*, vol. 7, no. 5 (April 1, 1920).

[51] Chen Duxiu, "Shanghai shehui" [Shanghai society], *XQN*, vol. 8, no. 1 (Sept. 1, 1920). Also, Chen Duxiu, "Zailun Shanghai shehui" [Again on Shanghai society], *XQN*, vol. 8, no. 2 (Oct. 1, 1920); and Chen Duxiu, "Sanlun Shanghai shehui" [A third time on Shanghai society], *XQN*, vol. 8, no. 3 (Nov. 1, 1920).

[52] Schwartz, *Chinese Communism and the Rise of Mao*, p. 32.

[53] Herman Mast, "Tai Chi-t'ao, Sunism and Marxism During the May Fourth Movement in Shanghai" in *Modern Asian Studies*, pp. 229–31.

intelligentsia in the period prior to the acceptance of Marxism was by itself evidence of their general disillusionment with capitalism and their fear of its effects.

Marx's description of the blatantly economic motivations of mankind's political and social behavior struck a very responsive note in a country where the struggle for existence was a harsh reality for the vast majority of the populace. Moreover, Marx's antipathy with the profit orientation of the bourgeoisie harmonized very well with the Confucian ideas to which Chen and his colleagues were exposed as youths— ideas that ranked merchants as the lowest order of society. Finally, at a time when Liang Qichao and others were persuasively proclaiming the degradation of Western material civilization, Chen, who had been put on the defensive by this attack, could now respond without seeming to be defending the obvious corruption of Western society. Capitalism had failed but material progress was still possible.

Marx had exposed the hypocrisy and pretensions behind the activities of the bourgeoisie—both Western and by analogy also the Chinese—revealing the blatant economic motives behind their "moral" declarations and political behavior. Much of Chen Duxiu's *New Youth* writings had been an attempt to expose the sham in the moral pretensions of his Chinese colleagues. Since it must have been psychologically uncomfortable for Chen to laud the virtues of the West repeatedly while deriding those of the Chinese, he must have welcomed Marxism as a powerful weapon in this battle, one which proclaimed that Westerners were no better morally than the Chinese— and perhaps worse.

Chen was understandably cautious at first in welcoming the notion of a class struggle that might exacerbate the fissures within Chinese society. But once he began to view the bourgeoisie as responsible for China's problems, he was quick to see how their removal would set the stage for a government that could truly lead and inspire the people, since, he felt, their materialist attitudes contributed to a further division of China.

Chen, who so adamantly desired the transformation of Chinese society, saw in Marxism the positive view of progress he had consistently advocated in all his earlier writings. Marxist scientific socialism of course meshed nicely with Chen's own earlier advocacy of science as the solution to China's problems. But he was not simply attracted to the terminology of science used in Marxist writings. Science had always been important for Chen not simply as a method of transforming the world but also as a way of combatting the pessimism of those who believed there was no way of changing Chinese society. Thus, Chen was attracted to Marx's scientific socialism not only because it proclaimed itself to be scientific, but because it interpreted "science" in the same optimistic manner as Chen himself.

One of the first articles Chen wrote after his adoption of Marxism attacked the claims of Malthus, who, like Liang Qichao and other Chinese conservatives, believed that there was a limit to human progress.[54] Chen countered that Malthus wrote before the industrial revolution had really begun, and therefore did not see that in a scientifically improved society production of food can keep pace with a growing population. Although in this essay Chen asserted the transience of all ideologies, including Marxism, it is clear that he felt Marxism was most appropriate for the present precisely because it could help direct the technical powers unleashed by the industrial revolution to remedy the poverty and overpopulation that Malthus saw as insoluble and that threatened China's national essence. Moreover, Marxism seemed to be able to solve these problems without the equally distressing miseries that seemed to have been generated elsewhere by capitalism.

THE COMMUNIST INTERNATIONAL

By now it should be clear that most of the major ideas that drew Chen Duxiu toward Marxism could perhaps just as easily have been found in other socialist doctrines. Indeed, most of the study groups and political societies formed in the wake of the May Fourth movement that later became the basis

[54] Chen Duxiu, "Maersi renkoulun yu zhongguo renkou wenti."

of the different Chinese Communist cells throughout the country were committed originally only to some vaguely socialist or anarchist doctrines. It was Chen Duxiu who convinced most of these people to join the Communist party, writing letters to Li Dazhao and Mao Zedong, urging them to begin its Beijing and Hunan branches; dispatching Liu Bochui to Hubei to begin the party there; and going to Guangzhou himself to organize the local cell.[55] Chen, of course, had already been interested for some time in forming a new party; but it is doubtful that he could have achieved an efficient organization without the aid of the representatives of the Communist International. Given the inadvertent influence of Bertrand Russell in helping to spread the Marxist message in China and the attraction of Chen and many others of the May Fourth period toward foreign ideas, the effect on Chen by visits of a number of representatives from the Communist International—many of whom spent a considerable amount of time with him when he was just beginning to come to grips both with socialism and the idea of forming a political party—was bound to be great.

These visits began in the summer of 1919, when a member of the Russian Communist party, N. Burtman, who had been forced to take refuge in Tianjin, established contact with Li Dazhao. In September, Burtman was joined by another Russian Communist refugee, A. A. Muller, and the two attempted to promote Marxist ideas and to advocate ties between workers and student groups.[56] Over the next year, a number of other Russian émigrés called on Li Dazhao and others interested in Marxism. By late 1919, official Comintern representatives had begun to arrive in China. At least one of these people was informed by Li Dazhao late that same year that the official formation of a Communist party would have to be undertaken by Chen Duxiu, and Li is said to have written Chen a letter to this effect.[57] According to Zhang Guotao, Li

[55] Lin Maosheng, "Dui Chen Duxiu pingjia jige wenti," p. 56.
[56] See Lydia Holubnychy, Michael Borodin, p. 142.
[57] Peng Shuzhi, "Zhongguo diyige gongchan zhuyi xiaozu shi zenyang

did not feel conditions were ripe for the establishment of a party;[58] hence Li's willingness to defer to Chen. In the spring of 1920, the secretary of the Department for Eastern Affairs of the Communist International, Gregori Voitinski, arrived in China at the head of a Comintern delegation; after receiving Li Dazhao's letter of introduction, they journeyed to Shanghai. Voitinski met with Chen, explaining to him the basic structures and purpose of a Chinese Communist party and helping him draft a program for it.[59] With Comintern assistance, Chen was able to construct the first official Communist cell, and in May 1920 he established a provisional Central Committee for the new Communist party.[60] By August a Communist Youth League had been established and the infant party, under Chen's direction, had begun to engage in propaganda work among local labor unions, establishing evening schools and periodicals to further disseminate their message.[61]

Even before the arrival of the Comintern representatives, Chen had taken steps to form a loose, new political party based on what he had assumed to be Marxist principles. But these Comintern representatives were important in helping Chen to reorganize the party and gradually build a Leninist-style organization, convincing him in 1921 to expel the anarchist elements from the party.[62] Although it would be a long time before its organization was to resemble that of its Soviet counterpart, the Chinese Communist party, under the tutelage of the International, gradually began to take on a more orthodox Leninist form.

In spite of his commitment to the idea of a Bolshevik-style

---

xingchengde?" [How did the first Communist group take form?], *Shiyue pinglun [October Magazine]*, vol. 7, no. 5 (June 20, 1980), p. 14.

[58] Chang Kuo-t'ao, *Rise of Chinese Communist Party*, vol. 1, p. 101.

[59] Peng Shuzhi, "Zhongguo diyige gongchan zhuyi xiaozu shi zenyang xingchengde?" Also, Old Man Chi Wu, "Vignettes on the CCP before and after Its Founding," as reprinted in Warren Kuo, *Analytical History of the Chinese Communist Party*, vol. 1, pp. 22–23.

[60] Holubnychy, *Michael Borodin*, p. 144.

[61] Ibid.

[62] See the translations of Russian sources in *Wenshi ziliao [Literary and historical materials]*, vol. 12, issue 4 (Beijing, 1963).

organization, it is clear that Chen was at first too naive about
Leninist organization to be able to organize the party without
Voitinski's help. But having received this aid, Chen was not
prepared for the kind of bureaucratic manipulation that was
necessary to maintain the Leninist-style party he created.

Marxism, as Benjamin Schwartz pointed out over thirty
years ago, came to China with a program for implementation—a Leninist-style party.[63] Without this party, Marxism
would never have been adopted in China. Chen Duxiu initially
saw this party in terms of his past experience—as an instrument for fostering the development of China in a way that
would avoid the evils of Western society. He still wished to
ensure what he considered to be China's most important national essence—the material improvement of the Chinese people.

Chen Duxiu felt that his new party would be composed of
the Chinese radical youth who had been interested in reforming their society. Eventually he came to believe in the need
for class struggle, but even this belief was colored by his older
idea that the sincere example and ideas of members of an elite
dedicated to change could induce their followers to transform
society once the political and social groups that had blocked
progress were removed. Thus Chen had begun the first new-
style party in China; but he was never to understand it fully.

[63] Schwartz, *Chinese Communism and the Rise of Mao.*

CHAPTER SIX

THE UNITED FRONT

The two major themes that Chen had brought together in his Marxist thought—national unification and social transformation—began to unwind almost as soon as they were joined. Under pressure from the Comintern, Chen yielded to political efficacy and conceded the role of national unification to the Guomindang, agreeing that the Chinese Revolution would have to occur in two stages, with the CCP waiting until some unspecified later date before attempting to implement socialism.

Why would Chen, an ardent defender of Chinese national honor and strength, by 1923 in effect allow his infant organization to be dominated by the Russian-controlled Comintern? And—even more difficult to grasp—why would Chen, who initially turned to communism in hopes of placing himself and his followers in a position from which to lead the Chinese Revolution and construct the new Chinese society, agree (albeit at Comintern insistence) to the formation of a United Front between his Communist party and the Guomindang of Sun Yatsen? He had earlier criticized the KMT for its "attaching importance to the upper levels of society rather than to the common people, its utilization of bandits, its opportunistic, crafty nature, which was readily given to making compromises, and the heterogeneity of its membership, which was permeated by open and concealed internal struggles."[1] But by 1923 Chen had to accept the idea advocated by the Comintern that Chinese society, like that of the West, had to undergo a capitalist transformation before it could begin to adopt socialist modes under the leadership of the proletariat.

[1] Chang Kuo-t'ao, *The Rise of the Chinese Communist Party*, vol. 1, p. 221.

Thus he put aside his idea of Marxism as an alternative to capitalist development.

THE DIFFICULTIES OF AN INDEPENDENT PARTY

As would be expected, Chen initially was very insistent about maintaining the independence of his new party. After Chen's meeting with Comintern representative Gregory Voitinski in the spring of 1920, he agreed to form a Communist party that would be associated with the Comintern and he continued to listen to Comintern advice on the organization of his new party.[2] Still, Chen and his associates resisted the initial attempts of the Comintern to dominate the CCP, even at first refusing Comintern offers of financial aid.

But Chen's influence, like that of the traditional intellectual Mandarin, had always stemmed at least in part from his association with outside political forces, whether his family's relations with the upper-level Anhui gentry or the affiliation of Beijing University with the central government. And once again Chen did not remain independent of all political forces for long. In order to retain his own financial and political independence, Chen Duxiu accepted a position offered him by Chen Chiungming, an old associate,[3] as head of the Education Committee that Chen Chiungming established for Guangdong province after his troops took Guangzhou in October 1920.[4] While carrying out activities to improve the educational facilities of the province, particularly to raise the level of scientific skills, Chen also formed the first Guangdong Communist cells and began Communist organizing activities throughout the province.[5] But after the CCP held its First

[2] See chapter 5.

[3] The two Chens had worked together in the Water Conservancy Society (Shuili hui), a front organization set up after the failure of the 1913 revolution to recruit the aid of overseas Chinese in a new revolutionary venture. George Yu, *Party Politics in Republican China: The Kuomintang 1912–1914*, p. 135.

[4] C. M. Wilbur and Julie Lien-ying How, *Documents on Communism, Nationalism, and Soviet Advisors in China*, p. 50. Chang Kuo-t'ao, *The Rise of the Chinese Communist Party*, vol. 1, p. 133.

[5] Ibid.

National Congress in Shanghai in the late spring of 1921 and elected him as the first secretary-general of the party, Chen returned to Shanghai to work for the party full time in August 1921.

At that time he refused to have any dealings with Maring (H. Sneevliet), the new Comintern representative. Chen was resentful of what he considered Maring's clumsy attempts to gain control of the CCP by dangling offers of cash assistance from the Comintern in front of party members.[6] But as Sun Yatsen also was to learn, an independent party was difficult to maintain in the fractured Chinese political environment. Deprived of the security of his position at Beida or of the support of Chen Chiungming, Chen discovered that he was very vulnerable. His attitude about independence changed after the police of the French-run Concession in Shanghai raided his house and seized him, his wife, and several other party members who happened to be there. Although he and his companions were released the next day, the incident apparently convinced Chen that the party was too prone to official harrassment to be able to operate independently and of necessity would have to rely more on Comintern aid.[7] Chen was now also agreeable to a Comintern subsidy of the party.[8] In order to maintain his position, Chen thus accepted foreign support—something he had criticized in earlier Chinese governments but which he found necessary in the Chinese political environment.

Even after accepting Comintern financial assistance, Chen was still critical of Comintern representative Maring's desire for the CCP to enter into a close alliance with the KMT.[9] Chen not only opposed this idea because of his distrust of Maring and his wish to preserve the independence of his new party, but also, one can assume, because of his long-standing distrust of Sun Yatsen. As already noted, in 1905 Chen had

[6] Chang Kuo-t'ao, *Rise of Chinese Communist Party*, vol. 1, pp. 161–63.
[7] Ibid., p. 166.
[8] Ibid., pp. 167–68.
[9] Ibid., p. 221.

been one of the few Chinese revolutionaries to refuse to join Sun's party, Tongmenghui, or Revolutionary Alliance, and in 1913 he had again refused to participate in Sun's new Guomindang, or Revolutionary party.

The issue of CCP cooperation with the KMT came to a head on August 22, 1922, when the party, under pressure by Maring, convened a special plenary session at West Lake in Hangzhou to discuss the question of the CCP-KMT United Front. In his "A Letter to All Comrades of the Party," Chen recalled the situation thus:

> In 1922 . . . the representative of the Youth Communist International, Dailin, came to China, suggesting to the Guomindang the policy of a united front of the revolutionary groups. The head of the Guomindang, Sun Yat-sen, sternly rejected it, allowing only the members of the Chinese Communist party and the Youth League to join and obey the Guomindang. He did not recognize any extraparty alliances. Soon after . . . , the Communist International sent its delegate, Maring, to China, demanding that all the members of the Central Committee of the Chinese Communist party hold a meeting at West Lake in Hangzhou, at which he suggested to the Chinese party that it join the Guomindang organization. He strongly contended that the Guomindang was not a party of the bourgeoisie, but the party of an alliance of all classes and that the proletarian party should join it in order to improve this party and advance the revolution. At that time, all five members of the Central Committee of the Chinese Communist party—Li Dazhao, Zhang Guotao, Cai Hesen, Gao Junyu, and I—unanimously opposed the proposal. The chief reason was: an alliance between the parties would confuse the class organizations and restrain our independent policy. Finally, the delegate of the Third International asked if the Chinese party would obey the decision of the International. Thereupon, for the sake of respecting the decision of the International, the Central

Committee of the CCP could not but accept the proposal of the International and agree to join the Guomindang.[10]

Less inclined to agree with the Comintern position than most of the other members of the Central Committee. Chen finally accepted Comintern instructions after the Central Committee passed a resolution he had sponsored specifying that the CCP would join the KMT only "if Dr. Sun revoked the rule forcing people joining the KMT to take an oath of allegiance to him personally and to sign the oath with their fingerprints, and if he reorganized the KMT so that it was based on democratic principles."[11] The oath of allegiance to the party leader, which Sun had established originally for his Guomindang organization in 1913, had been the major issue cited by Chen and many of his fellow revolutionaries in their original refusal to join this group. Having now achieved this concession, Chen avoided offending Maring, his new benefactor and foreign model, and agreed to the First United Front.

THE FAILURE OF AN ALTERNATIVE TO THE KMT

Following the meeting, Chen allowed himself to be one of the few CCP members to be officially inducted into the Guomindang by Sun Yatsen.[12] A rumor that he had never really joined the Guomindang was only convenient propaganda for the later followers of both Jiang Kaishek and Chen Duxiu, who for independent reasons, insisted that Chen had never really gone along with the United Front policy. In fact, Maring accompanied Chen, Li, and a few other members of the Central Committee (but not Zhang Guotao) to be sworn into the

[10] Chen Duxiu, "Gao chuandang tongzhi shu" [A letter to all party comrades], Dec. 10, 1929; translation adopted from "A Letter to All Comrades of the Party," in *Chinese Studies in History*, Spring 1970, p. 226.

[11] Chang Kuo-t'ao, *Rise of Chinese Communist Party*, vol. 1, pp. 254–55.

[12] Wang Yongchun and Chen Zhixia, "Chen Duxiu zai guogong hezuo wenti shang de sixiang bianhua" [The transformations in Chen Duxiu's thought on the question of cooperation between the Communists and Nationalists], *Dangshi yanjiu* 5 (1980). Chang Kuo-t'ao, *Rise of Chinese Communist Party*, vol. 1, p. 255.

Guomindang in the special ceremony presided over by Sun Yatsen.[13]

Still, though the CCP finally accepted the Comintern's desire for an alliance between the Communists and the Guomindang in late 1922, Chen and his cohorts made no immediate effort to implement that decision. On the contrary, at the time of the Hangzhou conference in August 1922 at which the CCP decision to join the KMT was made, Li Dazhao, also with Maring's backing, suggested that the CCP make an effort to cooperate with Wu Peifu, the newly victorious northern warlord. Under Chen's leadership the party had earlier condemned those on "the liberal professorial staff of Beijing University" who seemed prepared to trust Wu Peifu's government,[14] but now they acted quickly to back Li's suggestion. Although Sun Yatsen's cooperation in this project was elicited and received, the decision to cooperate with Wu Peifu led to the movement of CCP headquarters from Shanghai to Beijing in the fall of 1922, making cooperation with the southern-based Guomindang extremely difficult.[15]

Indeed, in spite of the importance that has been attributed to the decision of the CCP at the Hangzhou conference in August 1922, it would seem that the conference results may have been more of an attempt to humor the International than to affect policy. Although Chen Duxiu and other CCP leaders had long shown themselves willing to cooperate with the KMT, the policy to which they objected—that of asking CCP members to join the KMT as individuals—was something of a dead issue at this point, for the KMT organization was then in

[13] Ibid.

[14] "First Manifesto of the CCP on the Current Situation," June 10, 1922, as reprinted in Conrad Brandt, Benjamin Schwartz, and John K. Fairbank, eds., *A Documentary History of Chinese Communism*. The original Chinese version of this can be seen in a variety of places, most easily in *Gongfei huoguo shiliao huibian*, vol. 1 (Taipei, 1964), pp. 16–17. The document itself was written by Chen Duxiu.

[15] Chang Kuo-t'ao, *Rise of Chinese Communist Party*, vol. 1, p. 273. See also Deng Zhongxia, *Zhongguo zhigong yundong jianshi (A brief history of the Chinese labor movement)*. Also, Conrad Brandt, *Stalin's Failure in China*, pp. 24–26.

considerable disarray. On August 9, 1922, shortly before the CCP decision to cooperate with him, Sun had been driven out of the Guangzhou by Chen Chiungming and forced to take refuge in Shanghai, where, as mentioned earlier, he inducted Chen and other party members into the Guomindang. The decision to honor the Comintern's desire to have the CCP join the Guomindang therefore had little immediate effect on CCP policies. Chen Duxiu himself discussed the conference only as a way of showing the Comintern's responsibility for the United Front policy and of demonstrating that even these efforts by the Comintern did not lead to a meaningful relationship between the CCP and the KMT until almost a year later, when the KMT was reorganized by Borodin.[16] The alliance of Wu Peifu afforded the Communists a chance to cooperate with a so-called "bourgeois" force that was approved by the International without having to subordinate themselves to any group, as they would have had to do with the Guomindang. Chen still needed an outside force to support him, but he correctly feared that dependence on this force could lead to the subordination of his infant party.

A short time before the party headquarters were moved from Shanghai to Beijing in early September, Chen left the country to attend a meeting of the Communist International; while he was out of the country, Zhang Guotao, the head of the labor secretariat, became the acting head of the party. Around the time that Chen returned from Moscow, the party policy of cooperation with Wu Peifu ended with the bloody suppression by Wu's forces of the Hankow Beijing Railway Workers Union on February 7, 1923, resulting in the virtual destruction of the entire northern branch of the party and the relocation of party headquarters back to Shanghai.

It was soon after this incident that Chen began to throw his weight behind Maring's proposal to join the Guomindang. At the Third Congress of the Chinese Communist party held in Guangzhou in June 1923, the United Front between the

---

[16] Chen Duxiu, "Gao chuandang tongzhi shu."

CCP and the KMT was officially approved by the CCP. Chen himself proposed that CCP members should join the Guomindang as individuals and help the Guomindang expand its membership among the urban workers and rural peasants.[17] And it was Chen who cast the decisive vote in the closely split meeting against Zhang Guotao's proposal for an independent Communist labor organization, supposedly remarking that the Chinese working class was too immature and that the Chinese Communist party had been formed too early.[18] Still, Chen insisted on keeping the headquarters of the CCP in Shanghai rather than near the KMT in Guangzhou, as Maring desired, thereby in a small way at least affirming his belief in the future independence of the CCP.

ADVANTAGES OF THE KMT

Chen Duxiu's enthusiastic embrace of the strategy of now joining with the Guomindang cannot be explained simply by saying that, after the northern labor movement failed as a result of Wu Peifu's crackdown on the party, Chen lost faith in the proletariat, as most previous interpretations have maintained.[19] Rather, it is also necessary to look at the comparative advantages enjoyed by each of the two parties by mid-1923. Sun and his party were now in a position to give valuable aid to Chen Duxiu's party, whose strength had been diminished greatly as a result of the attacks by Wu Peifu and his army. On January 15, 1923, Sun Yatsen succeeded in driving Chen Chiungming from Guangzhou, and on February 21 he returned to the city in triumph to reestablish his government

[17] Chang Kuo-t'ao, *Rise of Chinese Communist Party*, pp. 307–8. See also Hu Hua, *Zhongguo geming shi jiangyi [A textbook of the history of the Chinese revolution]*, pp. 76–78.

[18] Ibid.

[19] Cai Hesen, "Lun Chen Duxiu zhuyi" [Concerning Chen Duxiuism], in Chen Dongxiao, *Chen Duxiu pinglun*, p. 14. This has been the standard interpretation of Chen during this period that was followed in one way or another by virtually every other source.

there. Thus the positions of the Chinese Communist party and the Guomindang were now completely reversed from what they had been just six months earlier at the time of the special plenary session in West Lake. The CCP, which had seemed to be expanding rapidly and had before it a potentialy beneficial alliance with Wu Peifu, had received a major setback; it was the Guomindang which could now offer the political benefits that accrue from having an established government with its own territorial base.

Chen's pragmatism therefore quickly overcame whatever doubts he may have had about working with Sun Yatsen, with whom he had cooperated once before from 1921 to 1922 while he served as the head of the Guangdong Education Committee under Chen Chiungming. By supporting the alliance with the KMT, Chen also reaffirmed his own leadership position in the party. Although no one contemplated removing Chen at this time, his Guangzhou supporters, who had once been his most devoted followers, were ousted for supporting Chen Chiunming over Sun Yatsen,[20] and the left, under Zhang Guotao, who had been allied with Chen in opposing the United Front with the KMT, had been discredited. Chen's resumption of his party position was now more dependent on the support of the Comintern and perhaps of Li Dazhao and his cohorts, who also were in favor of an alliance with the KMT, than had previously been the case. Chen's new agreement with the position of Li Dazhao and Maring swept aside any doubts about his leadership ability.

This is not to say that Chen Duxiu agreed to the United Front solely out of negative motives. Rather, he had throughout his life been tempted by alliances or coalitions with groups he felt had the power to back his revolutionary forces, in spite of his apparent disdain for these very groups. Moreover, a Chinese Communist party based solely on the small Chinese proletariat indeed seemed to be a party that needed allies, and at that time the Guomindang offered the best prospect for an alliance.

[20] Chang Kuo-t'ao, *Rise of Chinese Communist Party*, vol. 1, pp. 249–50.

THE "BLOCK WITHIN" STRATEGY

Certainly, the question of whether the Chinese Communists had to actively join the Guomindang as individuals or whether they could have simply allied their party with the Guomindang still remains. Neither Chen nor any of the other Communists had any objections to an external alliance with the Guomindang—a strategy which in retrospect might have served the party much better. But the Comintern at this time touted the idea of Communists joining the Guomindang as individuals and conducting their activities under the Guomindang banner. Since the Comintern was urging this policy upon them and since Sun Yatsen would not agree to an alliance in any other form, it would appear that the Chinese Communists had no choice but to join forces with the Guomindang.

Moreover, the accomplishment of this United Front allowed Chen to return to the same method of operation he had used in his past to good result. As dean of Beijing University, Chen, as noted earlier, had occupied a position of influence similar to that of a Mandarin in the old society. He had been working within and receiving authority from the same political structure he was attacking. This authority had been important in helping him draw young intellectuals to his cause, and he was reluctant to relinquish this traditional authority. Even after leaving his post at Beida, Chen was still interested in retaining his official association, as is evident in his acceptance of a position with Chen Chiungming's government in 1920. But after resigning this post a year later and returning to Shanghai, he lacked an official position within the bureaucracy. He was vividly aware that some of his own intellectual mentors, such as Zhang Binglin, had lost their followings quickly once they slipped out of the political limelight (as indeed he himself had quickly lost the loyalty of his Guangzhou followers after he left Chen Chiungming's government). As has been noted, one of the major attractions of Chen to Leninism was his renewed awareness of the influence of government on social and intellectual change. Chen may therefore have felt that the message of his party would be better received if it had the support of a governmental apparatus, which was something the Guomindang could offer after 1923.

As the executor of the KMT-CCP alliance, Chen, who in speech after speech to the Central Committee stressed the necessity of attracting revolutionary youth, was able to use the CCP-KMT United Front to place himself in a role similar to that from which he had launched the New Culture movement at Beida—the insider desiring reform and change who bemoaned the oppression of the same political and social forces that the students themselves also resented. Thus, even after joining the KMT, Chen did not shrink from attacking that organization or clearly stating his differences with it. Writing in his own defense in 1929, Chen specifically mentioned the fact that during the first period of the United Front with the KMT "we could still severely criticize the compromising policies of the Guomindang."[21] Chen did more than that. On at least five occasions after 1923, he advocated a change in policy of the United Front from within the KMT.[22]

THEORETICAL CONFUSION

What Chen obviously had not counted on was the ideological and organizational confusion that his acceptance of the United Front with the Guomindang would create for his young party. Interestingly, the Chinese themselves have begun to acknowledge this problem over the last few years. In a series of revisionist articles that appeared in Chinese publications in 1979 and 1980, relying largely on earlier Western accounts of the period, several Chinese Communist historians have implied that the ideological immaturity of the party allowed it to be easily misled by the Comintern.[23] Without

[21] Chen Duxiu, "Gao chuandang tongzhi shu."

[22] Ibid.

[23] All these articles are of course remarkably guarded in their conclusions. The two most interesting are by Lin Maosheng: "Guanyu Chen Duxiu yanjiu de yixi wenti," in *Zhongguo renmin daxue dangshixi dangshi jinxiuban jianggao*, no. 6. Also, "Dui Chen Duxiu pingjia de jige wenti" [Several problems in evaluating Chen Duxiu] in Hu Hua, ed., *Zhongguo xiandai shijiao xue*

refuting the earlier charges of opportunism that have been leveled against Chen Duxiu, the new interpretations of his actions have tended to center on the meddling of the International in Chinese affairs during this period.

Implicit in the above-mentioned articles is the idea that one of the difficulties for Chen was that the strategies and ideas that had brought the Bolsheviks to power in Russia did not operate very well in China. The keys to Leninist success in the Soviet revolution—theoretical orthodoxy and tactical innovation—seem to have become twisted when Lenin and his followers began to assess the potential for revolution outside of Russia, particularly in the case of the colonial and semicolonial countries of the world. Lenin had been responsible for three important innovations in Marxism: the necessity of a party of professionals who could lead and organize a proletariat whose spontaneous instincts were not to be trusted; the insistence on the participation of the peasantry in the revolution in alliance with the workers; and a belief that the revolution could first begin in less advanced semicolonial and colonial countries, such as Russia, which were under the exploitation of the imperialist powers. Lenin, however, firmly believed that once begun the Russian Revolution would stir up the proletariat of the advanced countries of Western Europe and thereby lead to the inevitable world revolution. Consequently, Lenin always assumed that his modifications of Marxist theory were merely tactical innovations. Lenin never fully addressed the implications that may have been contained within his writings about the socialist potential of the peasantry or of the colonial and semicolonial countries.

After 1920 when it became clear that the Bolshevik Revolution had not set off a string of echoing revolutions in Western Europe, the Bolsheviks began to urge the development of

cankao ziliao. See also Wang Yongchun and Chen Zhixia, "Chen Duxiu zai guogong hezuo wenti shang de sixiang bianhua." Also Tao Kangle, "Dui Chen Duxiu youqing jihui zhuyi luxian xingcheng de yidian renzhi," Dangshi yanjiu 5 (1980):31–37; and Xiang Qing, "Guanyu gongchan guoji he zhongguo geming wenti" [On the question of the Communist International and the Chinese Revolution], Beijing daxue xuebao 6 (1979).

nationalistic upheavals in the colonial and semicolonial countries of the world in order to divert the attention of imperialist countries from the Soviet Union (this was particularly true in the case of China, which was right on the Soviet border) and also of course to create the necessary preconditions for a worldwide rising of the proletariat. The new Soviet government itself was confused over what kind of foreign policy to undertake, now that it had assumed power yet had failed to stir up the European proletariat.

Lenin himself never confronted the problem. Although Lenin continually insisted that the proletariat needed its own party—namely, the Communists—he also maintained that it was the duty of the proletariat in the colonial and semicolonial countries of Asia to ally with the bourgeoisie in carrying out the national revolution and expelling imperialism.[24] But on the question of how this alliance was to be carried out, Lenin, who had been very specific about tactics in the case of his own party, failed to be clear. To be sure, a possible reason for this lack of clarity was his belief that the rising of the European proletariat would by necessity set off the sparks that would start the world-wide Communist revolution. But the result of this ethnocentrism of Lenin's was that the Comintern officers who came to China were told to carry out a policy of bourgeois revolution to achieve national independence. But the nature of this task left little in the way of a role for the infant Communist party led by Chen Duxiu.

This theoretical confusion is seen first in the proposition developed by Comintern agent Maring (or H. Sneevliet) and later accepted by the International that the Guomindang was a party that represented all four of the classes within Chinese society, i.e., the intelligentsia, the liberal democratic bourgeoisie, the petty bourgeoisie, and the workers.[25] In some ways

[24] V. I. Lenin, "Preliminary Draft of Theses on the National and Colonial Questions," June 5, 1920, and "Report of the Commission on the National and Colonial Questions to the Second Congress of the Communist International," July 26, 1920, in Lenin, *The National-Liberation Movement in the East.*

[25] Dov Bing, "Sneevliet and the Early Years of the CCP," *China Quarterly* 48 (Oct.-Dec. 1971):67–97.

this was simply a logical extension of Lenin's notion of imperialism, which held that as a result of imperialist oppression the colonial and semicolonial countries of the world as a whole were exploited by the advanced European countries, just as the bourgeoisie of these nations exploited their own native proletariat. But the idea that all four classes, if these groups are indeed really classes in the Marxist sense, can be members of the same party is not to be found anywhere in Marxist theory and would seem to obviate the raison d'être of the Communist party as the independent party of the proletariat.

Indeed, in spite of his own lack of familiarity with Marxism, Chen still objected initially to this attempt to depict the Guomindang as a four-class party, insisting that the Guomindang was the party of the bourgeoisie.[26] But Maring stubbornly clung to this formulation, which helped justify his demand that the CCP carry out an alliance with the Guomindang on the basis of the so-called block within, in which CCP members entered the Guomindang as individuals. On at least three separate formal occasions, Maring told Chen Duxiu that this policy had to be carried out, arguing that the proletariat in China was too small to maintain an independent struggle, that the peasantry had no political understanding or needs, and that it was a matter of international discipline that Chen agree to this line.[27] Indeed, the International as a whole put a great deal of pressure on Chen to accept this formulation, even subjecting him and the rest of the Chinese delegation to criticism at the Fourth Congress of the International held in Moscow in early 1923—Chen's first trip outside Asia.[28]

The pressure of the International increased with time. One of the reasons for the obstinacy of the International with respect to China was that the China issue became a basic issue of contention between Stalin and Trotsky in their power struggle. Although Trotsky did not begin to publish his views on the Chinese Revolution until 1927, it is now known that as

[26] Chen Duxiu, "Gao chuandang tongzhi shu."
[27] For an interesting discussion of this by a contemporary Communist historian, see Lin Maosheng, "Guanyu Chen Duxiu yanjiu de yixie wenti."
[28] Liu Renjing, "Huiyi wo canjia gongchan guoji disizi dahui de qingkuang."

early as 1923 Trotsky had written that he was "resolutely opposed to the Communist party joining the Guomindang."[29] This opposition only strengthened Stalin's defense of the policies his representative had advocated in China and made the Comintern representative even more likely to push aside any objections to this idea from the Chinese Communists.

THE INDEPENDENT PROLETARIAN ECONOMIC REVOLUTION

Chen was at a disadvantage in his dealings with Comintern representatives because of his own lack of exposure to a social-democratic tradition. He became committed to Marxism with very little real understanding of what Marxism entailed. As pointed out earlier, Chen initially saw in Marxist doctrines a way of rapidly developing the country by bypassing capitalism, something very different from the original Marxist idea. Chen Gongbo indeed attests to Chen Duxiu's own lack of knowledge of Marxist ideas, describing how he and other members of the Guangzhou cell began to read Marxist works only after Chen became educational commissioner in Guangdong in 1920.[30] There was no social-democratic tradition in China for Chen to fall back upon, and there were few Marxist works that had been translated into Chinese. Chen was therefore by necessity more attracted to the idea of the Marxist revolution emanating out of Russia than by the content of what that revolution stood for; under such conditions it was natural that Chen, who himself was unsure of his own Marxist knowledge, would be deferential to his Soviet advisers.

The lack of knowledge of Marxist ideas was widespread throughout the Communist party in the early years. Wang Fanxi mentions how student circles in Beijing in the 1920s concentrated on the personalities and cultural ideas of Chen Duxiu and Hu Shi in deciding between communism and its liberal alternatives.[31] After becoming Communists, Wang Fanxi

[29] Peng Shu-ts'e, "Introduction," in Leon Trotsky, *Leon Trotsky on China*, p. 32.
[30] Chen Gongbo, *Hanfeng ji [Cold Winter Collection]*, p. 217.
[31] Wang Fan-hsi, *Chinese Revolutionary*, trans. Gregor Benton, p. 15.

relates, party members, even middle-level cadres, knew little if anything about Communist ideology.[32] Party leaders were scarcely more knowledgeable than their followers, and given this situation it was difficult for someone like Chen Duxiu to be anything but confused about the correct line on the situation in China, particularly when faced with the authority of the Comintern.

Still, Chen was not a patsy. The Comintern strategy also happened to accord very nicely with Chen's most basic commitment, namely, his faith that the Chinese Revolution would sooner or later have to be carried out by an independent party of the Chinese proletariat. From the time of his earliest revolutionary involvement, Chen had felt that only a "pure" revolutionary party could save China, once China's political disunity was overcome. Having come to believe in the class struggle, Chen became fully committed to the notion that eventually the party of the Chinese working class would have to undertake the transformation of China. But while Chen believed that China eventually had to undergo a proletarian revolution, he did not believe that this revolution of the proletariat had to be the first step in the revolutionary process. Even at the time of his initial espousal of Marxist thought in 1920, Chen had conceded that China first had to undergo a democratic revolution led by the bourgeoisie to overthrow the feudal system still plaguing China. Immediately after this political revolution, China could begin the task of socialist construction without having had to experience extensive capitalist development. This task of socialist construction, which Chen called China's economic revolution, would be carried out by the proletariat.[33]

Because of this belief that China could move quickly from one historical stage to another, Chen may have been a "proto-Trotskyite," as one writer has described him,[34] but his justification for this rapid transition was totally different from that of Trotsky. Before 1917 Trotsky felt that the initial stage of

[32] Ibid., p. 20, 30–31.

[33] Chen Duxiu, *Shehui zhuyi taolun ji [Collection of a discussion on socialism]*, pp. 132–74.

[34] Benjamin Schwartz, *Chinese Communism and the Rise of Mao*, p. 29.

the revolution would occur in Russia, which had yet to undergo a bourgeois revolution. The Russian Revolution, under the leadership of the proletariat, would spur into action the proletariat of the advanced Western European nations, who would provide the impetus for the transition from capitalism to socialism on a world-wide basis. Chen Duxiu, however, initially viewed the revolution in national terms, seeing the proletariat revolution as complementary to the democratic revolution he had been trying to accomplish in China for the past two decades, the latter being political and the former being economic. Chen therefore believed that the bourgeois and proletarian revolutions could occur in rapid succession in China. Moreover, Chen Duxiu saw the socialist state that would develop with the help of the proletarian revolution as desirable not simply because it would create a more just order but also because it would allow the state to concentrate its capital and organize its labor more efficiently, and thus industrialize more rapidly.[35] Chen never abandoned this idea; as late as his trial in 1933, he still argued that communism would make production more efficient.[36]

What was distinctive about this notion and may have influenced Chen's later relations with the International was his idea that only the proletariat under the leadership of the Communist party had the "purity" of intentions to develop China in a way that would not put their own petty interests first and would thus benefit the society as a whole. Other classes might carry out their revolution first, but then it would be the proletariat who would have to develop China. In 1922, when

[35] See, for instance, Chen Duxiu, "Maersi renkoulun yu zhongguo renkou wenti" [Malthus's theory of population and the Chinese population problem], *XQN*, vol. 7, no. 5 (April 1, 1920). Adam Ulam has suggested that because Marxism embodies what he calls a "passion for material improvement and fanaticism in the service of industrialization," economic development frequently takes center stage after the revolution has passed. See Adam Ulam, *The Unfinished Revolution*, p. 285. In this case, the concern preceded the revolution.

[36] Chen Duxiu, *Chen Duxiu xiansheng biansu zhuang [Mr. Chen Duxiu's written defense statement]* (n.p., 1933).

Chen first began to see the tactical advantage of forming some
kind of alliance between the CCP and a so-called bourgeois
force in China like the KMT,[37] he still insisted that the proletariat was the key to carrying out China's economic development. The alliance with the bourgeoisie was to aid in reu-
nifying the country and carrying out the national democratic
revolution. "But then the Chinese nation will still only be
partly established; the other part is the Chinese republic's
economic establishment."[38] According to Chen: "We must
use national socialism to develop our enterprises after the
completion of the national revolution."[39] This national socialist revolution would of course have to be accomplished by
the proletariat under the leadership of the Chinese Communist
party.

   After 1923, when Chen Duxiu finally had accepted the KMT-
CCP United Front, he went along with Comintern policy as
well and accepted the Stalinist idea of distinct revolutionary
stages to the revolution. Once the United Front was established, Chen began insisting in orthodox fashion that every
society must transform itself from a nomadic into a feudal
and then into a bourgeois state, as Stalin had stated, before
the proletariat could gain hegemony over the society. China,
he felt, first had to undergo a bourgeois democratic revolution,
which the KMT with the aid of the proletariat would accomplish. But even here Chen still did not seem to feel that the
bourgeoisie would also be able to carry out the economic
development of the country. Rather, Chen still reserved the
right to attempt to use "socialism" to carry out the economic
revolution following China's political transformation.

   It is true that Chen also had accepted the formulation of
the KMT as a four-class party and not simply the party of
the bourgeoisie, but he saw no point in quibbling over se-
mantics; he, in fact, still did think of the KMT as the party
of the bourgeoisie. For instance, in his article, "The Chinese

[37] Chen Duxiu, "Zaoguo lun" [On building the nation], *Xiangdao* 2 (Sept.
20, 1922).
[38] Ibid., p. 10.
[39] Ibid.

National Revolution and the Various Social Classes"[40] (on which previous studies of Chen have relied when demonstrating the change in Chen's thought after 1923 and which was an official party paper written by Chen as party leader), Chen did insist on the need for a capitalist revolution in China, to be carried out by the bourgeoisie with the help of the proletariat. But he ended the article by asserting:

> After the completion of the national revolution, under ordinary conditions the capitalist class would monopolize political power. But sometimes if there are special circumstances perhaps there can be a new development in which the proletariat can seize some political power. This depends on the strength of the proletariat during the revolution as well as on the international situation.[41]

Even in this official expression of his new position, Chen was not willing to allow that the bourgeoisie would be able to develop China after the revolution. On the contrary, all of Chen's occasional attacks on the KMT, even after the establishment of the first United Front, made the point that the important revolution to come must be led by the proletariat—a point underscored by Chen's refusal in 1923 to move the headquarters of the Chinese Communist party from Shanghai to Guangzhou near the KMT, thereby retaining at least a measure of independence for the party from the "bourgeois"-dominated Guomindang.[42]

Chen quickly abandoned his faith in what Chinese Communists have criticized as "the two-stage revolution" theory as soon as he felt that the revolution of the KMT was succeeding too well and might endanger the second stage of the revolution. Although he agreed to the United Front in 1923, in December 1924 Chen, under the influence of Peng Shuzhi, asserted that "in the national revolution of those countries

---

[40] Chen Duxiu, "Zhongguo guomin geming yu shehui ge jieji" [China's national revolution and the various social classes], Qianfeng [Vanguard] 2 (Dec. 1, 1923).

[41] Ibid., p. 50.

[42] Chang Kuo-t'ao, Rise of Chinese Communist Party, vol. 1, pp. 314–15.

oppressed by imperialism, the proletariat must assume leadership [of the revolution]."[43] By 1925 Chen had recanted,
insisting that more power be taken by the proletariat even in
the first stage of the revolution. For the first time since the
establishment of the United Front, Chen made a public statement calling for workers to join the CCP, and in October
1925 he proposed to the Central Committee of the CCP that
the Chinese Communist party quit the Guomindang.

THE MEDDLING OF THE INTERNATIONAL

By this time, however, Chen's hands were tied. Party headquarters had remained under his control in Shanghai, but
Soviet advisers were quick to take advantage of the organizational immaturity of the party, usurping much of Chen's
control over party matters in other parts of the country. After
Chen's acceptance and implementation of the First United
Front in June 1923, the International dispatched Borodin and
Galen to Guangzhou to help the Guomindang construct an
efficient party organization and a new army, strengthening
that organization at the expense of the CCP. As Soviet arms
and money poured into Guangzhou and other parts of China,
many members of the infant Communist organization also
became dependent on Comintern advice and money. By early
1924, Borodin, obviously proud of the Communist organization in Guangzhou, was comparing it to the less disciplined
Shanghai apparatus run by Chen, complaining "that things
are not going in Shanghai as well as in Guangzhou."[44] And
later, in defending himself to his Soviet comrades in 1930,
Borodin was to complain that "beginning with the reorganization of the Kuomintang in 1923 . . . there were two lines
in the Chinese Revolution: the Shanghai line, the line of Chen
Duxiu . . . and the Canton line."[45] A contemporary Russian

[43] Chen Duxiu, "Ershiqinian yilai guomin yundong zhong suode jiaoxun"
[Lessons of the National Movement over the past 27 years], *XQN* 4 (Dec.
20, 1924):476.
[44] As quoted in Lydia Holubnychy, *Michael Borodin*, p. 319.
[45] Ibid., p. 377.

source identified the Guangzhou party head, Tan Pingshan, as "Borodin's student," saying that "from 1923 on Comrade Borodin almost step by step instructed and helped T'an P'ingshan."[46] Even allowing for exaggeration on the part of the Russians, it is clear that they often were able to supersede Chen's authority at least in the Guangzhou cell of the party, one of the major party branches.

By late 1924 the International had enough control over the party apparatus to begin to make some policy decisions for the party. An example was the new rule forbidding party members from criticizing the Three Principles of the People, although it was by no means clear what class the principles represented or how Sun's stated opposition to class struggle could be reconciled with CCP ideology after the CCP joined Sun's party.[47]

Still, there is no evidence that Chen objected to this new policy. As long as the United Front seemed to be succeeding, Chen did not oppose Soviet power or policy within the CCP. It was not until early 1925 that Chen again began to raise doubts about the efficacy of the United Front, spurred by the efforts of Sun Yatsen at that time to create an alliance with some of the northern warlords in Beijing.[48] After Sun's death on March 12, 1925, Chen became even more vocal in advocating the independence of the CCP from the Guomindang.[49]

But Sun's death was followed by a flurry of labor organization and activity in China that culminated in the famous May Thirtieth incident, which greatly multiplied the membership of the Chinese Communist party. As these new Communist recruits joined the "block within" delegation in the KMT, Communist influence over the Guomindang began to grow. Increasingly confident of the strength of the Communist

[46] Ibid.

[47] See Lin Maosheng, "Guanyu Chen Duxiu yanjiude yixie wenti."

[48] Chen Duxiu, "Sun-Duan hezuo yu guomindang zhi mingyun" [The Sun-Duan cooperation and the destiny of the Guomindang], *Xiangdao zhoubao* 94 (Dec. 10, 1924).

[49] Chang Kuo-t'ao, *Rise of Chinese Communist Party*, vol. 1, pp. 462–63.

movement, Borodin attempted to push the KMT to the left. Borodin had a considerable amount of influence with the Guomindang because of his work with General Galen (Vasilii Konstantinovich Blücher) in aiding Sun Yatsen in the construction of an efficient party organization and in creating a new Guomindang army. He was convinced that with the aid of the Communists he could build on the support he already had within the KMT to gain a dominant influence within the party. Chen Duxiu objected to this policy, warning that it would alienate the right wing of the Guomindang and lead to a split between the two parties.[50] But Borodin's position within the Guangzhou CCP was so strong that he was able to ignore Chen's warnings and continue his policy.

Chen insisted that before the Communists could even begin to talk about taking over power within the Guomindang, it was first necessary to see to the development of the mass political movement in order to enable the completion of the national democratic revolution.[51] As the power of the right wing of the Guomindang grew in proportion to the amount of pressure that Borodin had begun to put upon the KMT, Chen began to argue that the Chinese Communist party should split with the KMT so they could continue the organization of the national revolution unhampered by their somewhat dubious allies.[52] But support within the party for the Comintern position had become too strong. Chen's proposal in a plenum of the CCP Central Committee in October 1925 that the CCP quit the Guomindang was shunted aside.[53] Not only did Borodin and the Comintern continue to underwrite the alliance, but Chen Duxiu, as the leader of the party, was charged with publicly supporting it. On March 20, 1926, Jiang Kaishek, then the Guomindang military commander, proceeded to take action against the Communist-inspired left-

[50] Ibid.

[51] Chen Duxiu, "Ji Dai Jitao de yifengxin" [A letter to Dai Jitao], *Xiangdao zhoubao* 129 (Sept. 11, 1925).

[52] Chen Duxiu, "Gao chuandang tongzhi shu." See also Zhang Guotao and Peng Shuzhi as quoted in notes 53 and 54 of this chapter.

[53] Peng Shu-ts'e, "Introduction," in *Leon Trotsky on China*, p. 52.

wing tilt of the KMT. Jiang carried out a coup d'état within the Guomindang, taking over the leadership of that organization and at the same time claiming that the Communist commander of the gunboat, *Zhong Shan*, had been involved in a plot against the life of the generalissimo. Jiang used this accusation as an excuse to arrest most of the Communist cadres in the Whampoa Academy (a KMT military training camp), detain the Russian advisers to the Guomindang, and lock up many other prominent Communist leaders in Guangzhou. Though the Communists were released later and Jiang apologized for the incident, Chen took it as clear evidence of the perfidy of Guomindang intentions. Taking advantage of Borodin's absence, Chen and the Central Committee at this time requested that arms be given to the Guangdong peasants and workers to organize a movement independent of Jiang Kaishek.[54] But the Comintern, which controlled the shipment of arms, turned him down, showing where the real power within the party lay. Chen again allowed himself to be bound by Comintern directives. The peasant movement was discouraged, and in accordance with Comintern wishes Chen even wrote a letter stating that "Jiang Kaishek is one of the pillars of the national revolution."[55]

CHEN ON SOCIAL REVOLUTION

Chen's proposal to arm the Guangdong peasantry is interesting in light of later Chinese Communist charges against him of ignoring the peasant movement. In fact, Chen had been one of the first to support the peasant movement, assigning Peng Pai to his position in the countryside when Chen was educational commissioner for Guangdong province,[56] and ar-

[54] Ibid., pp. 52–53. Chang Kuo-t'ao, *Rise of Chinese Communist Party*, vol. 1, p. 306.

[55] Chen Duxiu, "Ji Jiang Jieshi de yifengxin" [A letter to Jiang Kai-shek], *Xiangdao zhoubao* 157 (June 9, 1926).

[56] Interview with Lin Maosheng, Beijing, 1981. I did not personally see the sources for this but was assured that they existed. Chang Kuo-t'ao, however, does confirm Chen's early support for Peng Pai; see his *Rise of Chinese Communist Party*, vol. 1, p. 309.

guing in 1923 and 1925 and then again in 1927 for peasant participation in the revolution, for which he was rebuked each time by the International.[57] It could of course be argued that Chen supported Peng Pai without really understanding what Peng was up to; Chen's attitude toward the Chinese peasantry at this time was certainly far less positive than that of the later Mao Zedong. Still, Chen Duxiu's position on the peasant question was well to the left of the Comintern; by November of 1926 Chen had taken a position as radical as that of anyone else during that period, producing a document calling for the confiscation of the land of large landholders and the arming of the peasants, a document that was suppressed by Bukharin and Stalin.[58] It is true, as has been charged, that Chen always felt that the role of the peasantry in the Chinese revolution had to be subordinate of necessity to that of the Chinese proletariat, but these ideas were still at least as radical as those later approved by Stalin after the Fifth Party Congress.[59]

Indeed, as long as the CCP was tied to a KMT that was being supported by southern warlords from landlord families, it is hard to imagine how Chen could have carried out a more radical policy without alienating his KMT supporters, as indeed he pointed out at the time. Mao himself supported a moderate land reform policy in another period of the United Front after 1937, when, in the face of the anti-Japanese war, the CCP supported so-called enlightened or patriotic landlords and was satisfied in many areas with simply seeking rent reductions rather than outright confiscation of land.

In spite of being thus hampered by the alliance with the KMT, Chen still continued to insist on the importance of the Communists' support for a social revolution. Chen opposed Chinese Communist aid for Jiang Kaishek's Northern Expedition, saying that it was being "carried out by a motley crowd

[57] The best discussion of this is available in Roy Hofheinz, *The Birth of the Rural Strategy*, chaps. 1, 2, and 3.
[58] Ibid., pp. 25–26.
[59] J. V. Stalin, "Questions of the Chinese Revolution: Thesis for Propagandists," in *Works*, vol. 9. See also Robert North, *Moscow and Chinese Communists*, p. 104.

of military adventurers and politicians interested in achieving their own private ambitions; even if victory is achieved, it will only be a victory for the military adventurers and not for the revolution."[60] Chen felt that a successful unification of the country had to be accomplished by the masses of people themselves through a revolutionary uprising. A military expedition could be successful only as an adjunct to this mass uprising, which Chen felt would be led by the workers and the peasants; it could not be a substitute for it.

Regardless of the opposition of Chen, who was then on his sickbed in Shanghai, the Northern Expedition began in July 1926 with the support of Borodin and substantial portions of the CCP. As it turned out, Chen himself was to be surprised pleasantly by the successes of the Northern Expedition and the opportunities it presented for agitation among the masses.[61] But the developing power of Jiang Kaishek as a result of the expedition led to Jiang's increasing aversion to his Communist allies, whose organization of the peasants was sure to alienate Jiang's landlord supporters. This was exacerbated by Borodin's attempts to split the left wing of the KMT from Jiang Kaishek.

Again Chen tried to insist on a social revolution by the Communists. As the Northern Expedition approached Shanghai, Chen Duxiu, alarmed by the spread of anti-Communist pamphlets by Dai Jitao and the KMT rightists, and sure that Jiang Kaishek was about to mount a purge of his Communist allies once he took the city, suggested that the Communist forces in the city arm themselves to resist Jiang.[62] The suggestion, however, was made too late and too tenuously to override the contradictory instructions of the Comintern;[63] the result was the infamous purge of April 12, 1927, in which Jiang's forces liquidated virtually all Communist cadres and

---

[60] Chen Duxiu, "Lun guomin zhengfu zhi beifa" [On the Northern Expedition of the National government], *Xiangdao zhoubao* 161 (July 7, 1926).

[61] Chen Duxiu, "Women xianzai weishenma zhengdou?" [Why are we now fighting?] *Xiangdao zhoubao* 172 (Sept. 25, 1926).

[62] Peng Shu-ts'e, "Introduction," in *Leon Trotsky on China*, pp. 61–63.

[63] Ibid., p. 73.

trade unionists in the city, including Chen Yannian, former party secretary for Guangdong and Chen Duxiu's oldest son.

SCAPEGOAT

Chen Duxiu, who had by this time gone to Wuhan, where the left wing of the Guomindang had established a capital in cooperation with the Communists, again advocated a policy of independence from the Guomindang, but he acquiesced to the Comintern policy of cooperating with the left-wing Guomindang government of Wang Jingwei, which at this time was still at odds with Jiang Kaishek.[64] Broken and dispirited, Chen tried again in mid-June to end the collaboration between the two parties; when this failed, he resigned.[65] On July 19, 1927, however, Wang also turned on his Communist allies and rejoined the Jiang Kaishek government. It was Chen Duxiu who became the scapegoat for the defeat of the United Front with the Guomindang. On August 7, in a special party conference, Chen's "opportunistic" policies were condemned and he was officially removed as a chairman of the Chinese Communist party.[66]

Chen Duxiu was blamed for refusing Stalin's instructions to arm the Chinese workers and peasants. Stalin had stated that the "special characteristic of the Chinese Revolution" was its need for arms, and after the Fifth Party Congress on May 1, 1927, he called for the Chinese Communist party to implement a land reform policy. Still, though Stalin spoke of the need for arms, he and his representatives gave no arms of consequence to the Chinese Communists or to the workers they had organized. Even in 1926, when Chen asked Borodin

[64] Ibid.

[65] Chang Kuo-t'ao, *Rise of Chinese Communist Party*, vol. 1, pp. 667–71, vol. 2, pp. 42–43. "Zhonggong baqi huiyi chuandang dangyuan shu" [A letter to all members from the August 7th Conference of the Chinese Communist party] in Hu Hua, ed., *Zhongguo xinminzhu zhuyi gemingshi cankao ziliao*, pp. 191–223.

[66] J. V. Stalin, "Questions of the Chinese Revolution." For a discussion of this, see Conradt Brandt, *Stalin's Failure in China*, chap. 5.

for arms, Borodin supplied the Guomindang in Guangzhou with arms but gave none to the Chinese Communists.[67] It was not until after 1927 that the Comintern finally began to talk seriously of arming the proletariat; but this was after the April 12, 1927 incident, at which point few troops loyal to the Chinese Communists still existed, and there were no arms to be had since they had all been seized by the KMT.

Still, in spite of the responsibility of the International for the failure of many of the policies of the CCP during this period, it was Chen Duxiu who founded and led the party and who was accountable for accepting the advice of the International for his infant party. This brings up the difficult question of why Chen Duxiu was at this time so solicitous of the ideas and proposals of the International. For one thing he had little choice. It is true that the CCP was better organized by 1925 than it had been in 1920, when it consisted largely of anarchists and other non-Communists, but the party even at this time barely had a Central Committee and almost completely lacked organizational discipline. The Central Committee in Shanghai consisted principally of Chen and Voitinski, sometimes joined by Qu Qiubai and Peng Shuzhi and one or two others.[68] During the period before the April Central Committee meeting in Wuhan when the party had to decide the important question of its attitude toward Jiang Kaishek's Northern Expedition, Chen was handling matters in Shanghai largely on his own. There was no standing committee or Politburo. Although this would seem to have given Chen a great deal of power, in fact it made things very difficult for him, for he had no Politburo to fall back upon for support in any decision that would oppose the Soviets. Moreover, much of the actual party apparatus outside of the Shanghai area was controlled by the Comintern advisers. This was particularly

[67] Chang Kuo-t'ao, *Rise of Chinese Communist Party*, vol. 1, p. 344.

[68] See Li Da, "Huiyi Lao Yuyang li erhao he dangde 'yida', 'erda' " [Remembrances of Number 2 Yuyang Lane and the First and Second Party Congresses], in *Dangshiziliao*, vol. 1 (Shanghai, 1980), pp. 18–20. Also P'eng Shu-ts'e, "Introduction," in *Leon Trotsky on China*, p. 51. Also Chang Kuo-t'ao, *Rise of Chinese Communist Party*, vol. 1, p. 306.

true of the influential southern branch of the party,[69] which was largely under the control of Borodin, who through the force of arms, money, and revolutionary reputation had created an organization of loyal followers.

To be sure, Chen several times angrily attacked Borodin and his supporters. But Chen, who all his life had distrusted organization, had in effect become a victim of the organization he had finally created. Perhaps a Mao Zedong or a Lenin might have fought back organizationally, replacing Soviet supporters in the party with his own, but Chen neither by temperament nor training was equipped for such in-fighting. His tool had been his pen and his personal prestige as a scholar. These were weapons that were hard to use after 1925, when the revolutionary forces were in ascendancy and the Soviet strategy, for all its apparent flaws, seemed to be working; furthermore, Chen Duxiu himself was already being looked at with some resentment by many of the youthful revolutionaries who had joined the party in their revolt against authority and were now inclined to view him as a figure from another generation, somewhat out of touch with those doing the actual party work.

Chen was in many ways a victim of the youthful following he had helped develop. Ironically, he found that his attempts to influence the youth by writing learned articles that challenged party positions—in other words, using the tactics appealing to an intellectual elite that had gained him followers in the first place—did not work now that these youth were within a party organization. As became clear later in Chen's efforts to form a Trotskyist party, most party members, even those who sympathized with Chen, were reluctant to disobey their organizational superiors either because of inertia, monetary considerations, or simply fear. Thus in 1929, when Chen finally began to oppose the party organization that was built for him with the help of Soviet arms and money, he was removed from it.

[69] For a discussion of this, see Lin Maosheng, "Guanyu Chen Duxiu yanjiu wenti." Also Chang Kuo-t'ao, *Rise of Chinese Communist Party*, vol. 1, p. 407.

Some might say that Chen had not been sufficiently ruthless. Unlike Lenin, who saw the party as the instrument of his will that would help him direct the revolution, Chen felt the party to be composed of a group of like-minded people of roughly equal status whose support he needed to carry out the Chinese Revolution. Thus Chen felt much more dependent on maintaining the good will of his party followers than did Lenin. In effect, Chen's ultimate belief in the true revolutionary potential of the masses may be said to be weaker than Lenin's, for at the bottom of his ideas was still the fear that perhaps the Chinese people would not move in the direction he felt was right; thus it was necessary to rely on a group of the elite—even a foreign party—for support.

This comparison between Chen and Lenin reflects the temptation to examine Chen's role in forming and leading the Chinese Communist party in relation to other Communist leaders. Current Chinese scholarship has attempted to compare the role of Chen Duxiu in the Chinese Revolution, particularly during this period, with that of Plekhanov—an analogy begun by Mao Zedong himself.[70] But although both Chen and Plekhanov founded their respective parties and were ultimately replaced by leaders more capable than they of wielding organizational discipline, Chen's sense of party organization was closer to that of the pre-Marxist revolutionary leaders who preceded Plekhanov than of Plekhanov himself. Chen Duxiu's relationship with his followers and their view of him remained locked in the relative position of the Mandarin teacher to his disciples.

Ironically, Chen Duxiu, who went along with the Comintern idea for a United Front with the Guomindang in order to help bolster the fortunes of his newly formed party and his position among his student admirers, ended as victim of this policy, despised by the students he had once led. In the same way at an earlier time, Chen and his own generation had come to despise the student leaders Liang Qichao and Kang Youwei, whom they had once looked up to, as conservative oppor-

---

[70] Quoted in Lin Maosheng, "Guanyu Chen Duxiu."

tunists. Moreover, this was instigated by the same Russian enemy against which Chen Duxiu had struggled so urgently in the two preceding revolutions.

The way in which Chen Duxiu joined a long list of earlier and later Chinese revolutionaries who ultimately were vilified for their "wrong" policies in the Chinese Revolution illustrates the complexities of the problems China confronted in the twentieth century. In the face of domestic strife and imperialist incursions into China, patriotism and social change had been the two major elements in Chen's thought since the early 1900s. Although he was able to unite these two elements into his Marxist ideas, this mixture was not totally successful. In effect, the idea of a "two-stage" revolution was a reseparation of these two sometimes contradictory desires of modern China. Chen was willing to allow the bourgeoisie to reunite China, but then he felt that it was up to his pure party of proletarians to carry out the social revolution and restore the material well-being of the Chinese people—China's true national essence. Although Chen was perhaps right that the social revolution would not be as pure if it simultaneously had to be part of a national revolution, the Chinese, as he was again to discover, were in no mood to wait for them to occur separately. Chen was to fall victim to the conflicts between these two diverging forces, but he was not to be the first nor the last Chinese revolutionary to suffer such a fate.

CHAPTER SEVEN

CHEN DUXIU
IN OPPOSITION

Cast out into the political wilderness following his removal from the party chairmanship, Chen Duxiu after 1927 increasingly found himself in the position of a political has-been who could only watch from the shoreline as the movement he had once headed sailed into waters that he could neither navigate nor tolerate. His two eldest sons, his close friend Li Dazhao, and many other former comrades and students had all been killed in the breakup of the United Front. Moreover, Chen had seen the destruction of the policy for which he had worked hard for the last seven years and for the sake of which he had sacrificed his family and his reputation. Worse yet, Chen himself had been held responsible for the failure of this policy. Even the Soviet Union, which he had once looked to as the leader of world revolution and whose counsel he had once heeded so obediently, had now turned on him as an opportunist.

Of course the biggest blow to Chen's pride was the fact that the students and youth, in whose name he had carried on his revolutionary activities since the early 1900s and who had seemed his most devoted and loyal band of supporters, now showed themselves to be deeply resentful of his "patriarchal" leadership and joined in vehemently denouncing the "opportunism" of his policy. Like his early mentor Kang Youwei, Chen seemingly had lost touch with the generation he had aroused out of political apathy and introduced to revolutionary politics. It is no wonder that Chen had been described during this period as resembling "a lion returned to his lair to lick his wounds."[1]

[1] Wang Fanxi, *Chinese Revolutionary*, p. 121.

Faced with these problems, Chen, as he had done in other periods of despair and disappointment, retreated from politics and turned to the philological researches with which he had intermittently occupied himself since his early student days, conducting research on the origins of dialect differences in China.[2] But Chen also continued to contribute short miscellaneous articles attacking the Guomindang to the new party publication, the *Bolshevik*. Engaging in this writing was no doubt soothing to Chen's wounded psyche; it also helped reestablish his reputation as a cultural Mandarin within those youthful literary circles from which he had previously attracted followers.

TROTSKYIST NEW YOUTH

These were the same youth circles that, by late 1928 or early 1929, introduced Chen Duxiu to a new political influence—that of Leon Trotsky. Trotsky's writings explained to Chen why he had been made the scapegoat of Soviet policy and reconfirmed many of Chen's earlier ideas about the potential for socialist revolution in China, the necessity of an independent political party, and even the need to use democratic slogans to recapture the interest of the masses. Trotsky's ideas thus opened another opportunity for Chen to make his influence felt in those Chinese intellectual circles where he had traditionally operated.

Prior to this time, neither Chen nor any of the other top Chinese Communist leaders had paid much attention to the internal disputes of the Soviet leadership. The only exception was a rather mechanical condemnation of Trotskyism in a party proclamation of 1927, obviously made at the behest of the International.[3] By 1928, however, some of the Chinese Communist students who had been studying in Moscow and who now returned to China brought back with them some

[2] Mao Dun, "Chuangzuo shengya de kaishi" [The beginning of a career in writing], *Renmin ribao [People's Daily]*, April 3, 1981, p. 5.
[3] Ch'en Pi-lan, "Introduction," in Peng Shu-ts'e, *The Chinese Communist Party in Power*, p. 39.

Trotskyist ideas and documents and began to form a secret leftist opposition group within the party. By January of 1929 this group had even managed to hold a small secret conference and to issue the following five slogans:

> First we demand the Central Committee publicly discuss the problem of opposition; second, a national congress should be reconvened to re-elect a Central Committee; third, we demand the Central Committee ask the Comintern for open discussion of the problem of opposition; fourth, Trotsky should be recalled and his leadership restored; and fifth, the erroneous leadership should be corrected on the basis of Trotsky's stand.[4]

This group became the basis of the Chinese Trotskyist faction known as "Women de hua," or "Our Word." They were at first extremely hostile to what they regarded as the opportunistic leadership of Chen Duxiu, whose policies Trotsky had also attacked. Both Trotsky and his Chinese followers initially thought of Chen Duxiu as a Stalinist. In 1927 Trotsky criticized Chen for "the postponement of the agrarian revolution until the territory is secured militarily" and "the postponement of the reorganization of the government until the military victory."[5] Although here Trotsky was criticizing Chen for policies actually ordered by Stalin, this did not prevent Stalin from making similar charges against Chen later that year after the failure of the United Front, as has already been shown. But even after Stalin condemned Chen, the Chinese Trotskyists continued to hold him in contempt.

A generation younger than Chen Duxiu, the members of the Our Word faction had written him off. But throughout his life Chen had been very attuned to the newest trends within Chinese student circles, and it is certain that as Trotskyist

[4] Translation adapted from Warren Kuo, *Analytical History of the Chinese Communist Party*, vol. 2, p. 74. For original, see *Zhongguo gongchandang zhi toushi* [An anatomy of the Chinese Communist party], pp. 135–37.

[5] Leon Trotsky, "First Speech on the Chinese Question," in *Leon Trotsky on China*, p. 232; also his "The Chinese Question after the Sixth Congress," in ibid., p. 349.

ideas began to spread among many former party activists, he began to take an interest in Trotskyism. According to Wang Fanxi, by late 1927 Chen had already come into contact with some of Trotsky's ideas from students returning from Moscow.[6]

Chen soon managed to obtain some Trotskyist documents to read on his own. By the spring of 1929, his chief lieutenant during this period, Peng Shuzhi, had come into possession of two important Trotskyist documents—"The Chinese Revolution: In Retrospect and Prospect" and "The China Problem: After the Sixth National Congress." Peng found the documents to be very persuasive in their explanation of the mistakes of the party, and he "submitted them to Chen Duxiu for his perusal." Chen found his ideas "were in complete accordance with Trotsky's." Peng and Chen began to organize their own "leftist opposition faction within the party."[7] This group soon alarmed party leaders. By June of 1929, the interest of Chen and many others in Trotskyism had become well-known enough for the party to show its concern by adopting a resolution condemning the actions of the opposition and calling for their liquidation, expressing the fear that so-called "residual opportunism"—namely Chen Duxiu—was joining hands with the opposition.[8]

TROTSKYIST CRITIQUE

Chen had become converted to Trotskyist ideas quickly. Although it has been assumed that he joined up with the opposition only as a desperate measure after he was removed

[6] Yi Ding (Wang Fan-hsi), "Pu zhu 'Wo suo zhidao de Chen Duxiu' jiumiu" [Correcting the mistakes in the work by Pu, 'The Chen Duxiu that I knew' "], *Zhongbao yuekan*, p. 102. For the work that Yi Ding criticizes, see Pu Qingguan, "Wo suo zhidao de Chen Duxiu" in *Wenshi ziliao xuanji [Materials on literature and history]*, no. 71, pp. 36–37.

[7] Ch'en Pi-lan, "Introduction," in Peng Shu-ts'e, *The Chinese Communist Party in Power*, pp. 38–39.

[8] "A Circular Letter to All Party Members Issued by the August 7 Conference," as quoted in Wu K'un-jung, "The Leftist Opposition Faction in the Chinese Communist Party," part I, *Issues and Studies* (March 1974), p. 82.

from the party in late 1929,[9] in fact it would appear that one of the factors precipitating Chen's removal from the party was his growing sympathy to Trotskyist ideas by the spring of 1929 at the latest. By the summer of 1929, Chen was even in indirect contact with Trotsky. Liu Renjing, who had stopped in Turkey to visit Trotsky on his way back from his studies in the Soviet Union, had sought out Chen Duxiu and Peng Shuzhi to explain to them more about the Trotskyist movement. Probably Chen's contradictions with the party leadership were irreconcilable even before this time. In May of 1928, when the Central Committee invited Chen Duxiu, Cai Hesen, Luo Zhanglong, Deng Zhongxia, and Zhang Guotao to attend the Sixth World Congress to be held in Moscow, Chen had refused, implying that his ideas already differed too much from those of the other party members.[10]

By July 1929 Chen Duxiu was ready to vocalize these differences. Just as the Russian occupation of Manchuria had first roused Chen into political action in the period after 1900, and as in 1915 Japanese actions in that area had led Chen to his founding of *New Youth*, so once again Russian maneuvers in Manchuria elicited comment from Chen Duxiu. In this case, Chen's comments showed not only his dispute with party policy but also the extent of and some of the reasons for his attraction to Trotsky's ideas. The events in question began when Chinese authorities in Manchuria in May of 1929, probably acting on their own initiative rather than that of the central government, seized the Chinese Eastern Railway, which the Soviets in 1924 had promised would be restored to joint Chinese-Soviet management. The incident provoked several armed clashes between Chinese and Soviet troops in the area. As a result of Soviet prodding, the CCP Central Committee passed a series of resolutions opposing Chinese "attacks" on the Soviet Union and eventually called on party members to rally behind the slogan "Defend the Soviet Union with Arms."

[9] See, for instance, Thomas Kuo, *Ch'en Tu-hsiu and the Chinese Communist Movement*, pp. 203–5.

[10] Chang Kuo-t'ao, *The Rise of the Chinese Communist Party*, vol. 2, p. 65–67.

On July 18, the day after this slogan was first promulgated, Chen sent the first of a series of three letters criticizing party policy.[11]

Chen's first letter, published in the party paper, was very mild. He suggested that the use of such a slogan would alienate the nationalistic feelings of the masses, which he felt had already been aroused by the KMT. Rather than use simple slogans, Chen felt that the party had to explain clearly to the masses the antiprogressive policies of the Guomindang and the differences between the attitude of the Soviet Union toward China and that of the imperialist countries.[12]

The important point about this letter, which has been ignored by most writers on the subject, is that rather than simply rebuking the party about tactical policies, Chen was echoing the Trotskyist position that the revolutionary tide had now ebbed and that the proper policy for the party was to attempt gradually to reinvolve the masses in the political struggle through slogans that exposed the sham democracy of the KMT and the dangers of imperialism.[13] By arguing that the Guomindang had won the support of the majority of the people, Chen was implicitly rejecting the Stalinist line then being followed by the Central Committee, which held that the high tide of the revolution was imminent. In his earlier opposition to the 1927 Canton Insurrection, Chen had expressed his belief that the Central Committee was following an "adventurist" policy. Chen was now not simply condemning the Chinese Communist leadership as an individual but was giving credence to the views of the Trotskyist opposition. It is for this reason that the party responded rather bitterly, proclaiming Chen to be a "liquidationist," insisting that the masses would understand why it was necessary to support the Soviet Union and that Chen's policy was not that of a Communist but was

[11] Chen Duxiu, "Duxiu tongzhi fu zhongyang de xin" [A reply from comrade Chen Duxiu to the Central Committee], in *Zhongguo geming yu jihui zhuyi [The Chinese revolution and opportunism]*, pp. 67–70.

[12] Ibid.

[13] See Trotsky, "The Chinese Question after the Sixth Congress," pp. 345–97. This was one of the two essays given Chen by Peng Shuzhi.

similar to that of the leftist faction of the bourgeoisie of the KMT.[14]

Chen, however, did not wait for a reply; on August 5, 1929, he followed this first letter with a second letter in which he restated his view that party policy on the Chinese Eastern Railway question was divorcing the party from the masses.[15] Barely a week later Chen fired off yet another letter to the Central Committee. This third letter, far from being concerned with the Manchurian Incident, was a far-ranging Trotskyist critique of the "mistaken line of the party."[16] Closely following the basic tenets and in some cases even the subheadings of the two articles by Trotsky that he had read earlier, Chen criticized the "blind adventurism" of Chinese Communist policy since 1927, claiming it had been based falsely on the assumption that the Chinese revolution was in a "high tide." Chen felt that the putschist policy the party was pursuing in the vain hope that the masses just needed a little encouragement to rise in revolution was only serving to alienate the people from the party.[17]

Chen also followed Trotsky's analysis of the Chinese revolution by holding that feudal relations essentially had been abolished in China.[18] Chinese Communists differed among themselves in their assessment of the exact time of the establishment of the feudal period, with Guo Morou insisting that China made the transition from a primitive Communist society to a feudal society at the beginning of the Zhou dynasty

[14] "Zhonggong zhongyang da Duxiu tongzhi guanyu zhongdonglu wenti de diyixin" [A reply from the Central Committee of the Chinese Communist Party to comrade Chen Duxiu's first letter concerning the problem of the Chinese Eastern Railway Incident], in *Zhongguo geming yu jihui zhuyi*, pp. 37–42.

[15] Chen Duxiu, "Duxiu tongzhi fu zhongyang de xin," in ibid., pp. 71–84.

[16] Chen Duxiu, "Duxiu tongzhi guanyu zhongguo geming wenti zhi zhonggong zhongyang xin" [A letter from Comrade Chen Duxiu to the Central Committee of the Chinese Communist Party concerning problems of the Chinese Revolution] in *Zhongguo geming yu jihui zhuyi*, pp. 94–117.

[17] Ibid.

[18] Ibid.

(1122–221 B.C.) and others claiming that it did not occur until the Qin dynasty (221–206 B.C.).[19] But Chen and the Trotskyists focused their attention on the demise of the feudal period, asserting that in fact Chinese society had its own unique development and that the feudal era had ended in China with the Qin. The Qin had ushered in a period denoted by the paradoxical term "bureaucratic feudalism"—though feudal remnants continued in the countryside, market relations were established, and a central bureaucratic government reigned. Chen, après Trotsky, insisted that even this bureaucratic feudalism essentially had ended with the establishment of the Jiang Kaishek regime. To be sure, neither Chen nor Trotsky engaged in considerable debate on this issue, but basically their position was that under the impact of bourgeois market relations, the landlord class in the countryside had rapidly transformed itself into an incipient bourgeoisie, which had come under the thumb of international imperialism.

The Trotskyist position now articulated by Chen Duxiu emphasized that in China only a "democratic revolution of the proletariat as well as the peasantry could fight the imperialists, destroy the feudal remnants in the Chinese countryside, and complete the process of land reform."[20] Chen had long maintained the necessity of an independent Communist party that was the party of the proletariat. In accord with Trotsky's theory of permanent revolution, Chen now asserted that after the victory of the working class, Chinese society could directly experience a socialist revolution (a policy that stood in contrast to the Stalinist idea of the necessity of clear and distinct revolutionary stages). This debate, which still continues, at that time dominated literary circles.[21] It also figured into the important question of deciding what would be the next stage of the Chinese revolution.

---

[19] Most of the articles in this debate, though not Chen's, were published either in the journal *Dushu zazhi [Study Magazine]* or *Xin shengming [New Life]*.

[20] Chen Duxiu, "Duxiu tongzhi guanyu zhongguo geming wenti zhi zhonggong zhongyang xin."

[21] See footnote 19.

Because of his belief that China did not have to undergo a new bourgeois revolution, Chen, like Trotsky, criticized the Central Committee policy of allying with the rich peasants in the countryside, insisting the "rich peasants are the capitalist class of the countryside and are the first manifestation of the capitalist class in the village."[22] Indeed, turning the tables on those who had earlier charged him with opportunism, Chen now insisted that to ally with the rich peasants against the landlords "is the same kind of opportunism as an alliance with the bourgeoisie against imperialism."[23] Allying with the rich peasants, he warned, would result in the defeat of the revolution, as had occurred in 1927 as a result of the party's policy during that period of allying with the bourgeoisie. Rather the party should be working for what Lenin called the "proletariat and peasant democratic revolution." Chen's own call for a "proletariat and peasant democratic revolution" echoed Trotsky's idea that the only way to reinvolve the peasants and workers in the political arena would be to have the Communist party lead the struggle for democracy so that the workers could see the sham of the bourgeois democracy of the Guomindang and would want to take action against it. Finally, Chen also insisted on the necessity of internal democracy, protesting the party's opposition to any dissident opinions and claiming that it could only lead to bureaucratic centralism.

This defense of democracy, this belief in the necessity of educating the workers to the long-term political struggle, and particularly this attempt to see the Communist party as totally independent of the bourgeoisie had long been the crux of Chen's ideology. In Trotsky, Chen now found a foreign source that could lend additional support and legitimacy to his beliefs.

EXPULSION

The fact that most Western writers have failed to comprehend the Trotskyist intentions behind the three letters that

---

[22] Chen Duxiu, "Duxiu tongzhi guanyu zhongguo geming wenti zhi zhonggong zhongyang xin."
[23] Ibid.

Chen wrote prior to his expulsion from the party is a consequence of the writers' misunderstanding of Chen's political
style.[24] As was mentioned earlier in the discussion of his *New
Youth* and New Culture movement activities, Chen had grown
to maturity in a Confucian political culture in which political
ideas and disputes were frequently addressed indirectly. This
indirect style, which worked well for Chen during the New
Culture movement and is still used today by Chinese intellectuals, was not appropriate to the development of a mass movement. But it does explain why, when he wrote his three letters
of protest to the party, Chen did not openly state his Trotskyist
proclivities and that, in fact, he had already organized a leftist
opposition group within the party among those party activists
still loyal to him.[25] Still, by waiting until after his expulsion
from the party to announce openly his Trotskyist beliefs, Chen
alienated many potential supporters, who were easily convinced that Chen's Trotskyist ideas were insincere and opportunistic. Rather than gain followers for his new position,
Chen further broadened the generation gap between himself
and the group of students he had once led.

Under these circumstances it was also easier for the party
to take action against Chen. The party quickly answered the
charges leveled against it in Chen's second letter,[26] as it had
after Chen's first letter, but bided its time before reacting to
the accusations in Chen's third letter. On September 12, Peng
Shuzhi was allowed to attend a joint conference of the delegates of the Central Committee and the various regional

---

[24] For instance, neither Benjamin Schwartz nor Thomas Kuo in their earlier
studies of Chen Duxiu mention the Trotskyist influences on him before he
wrote the three letters or the fact that by the time of the writing he had
already organized a sizable Trotskyist faction within the party. Both writers
seem to assume that Chen stumbled on Trotskyism after his disagreements
with the party had been made public. See Thomas Kuo, *Ch'en Tu-hsiu*, pp.
195–200. Also, Benjamin Schwartz, *Chinese Communism and the Rise of
Mao*, pp. 145–47.

[25] Ch'en Pi-lan, "Introduction," p. 39.

[26] "Peiping Duxiu tongzhi dui zhongdonglu wenti yijian de jihui zhuyi de
cuowu" [Criticism of Comrade Chen Duxiu's opportunistic error in regard
to the Chinese Eastern Railway Incident], in *Zhongguo geming yu jihui zhuyi*,
pp. 45–66.

branches, where he made a vigorous defense of the main points of Chen Duxiu's letter that had attacked the Central Committee for its policies.[27] By this time it had become clear that Chen and Peng were intent on continuing to oppose the party leadership and, more important, that they did not have the support of the majority of the party members in doing so. The party made one more attempt at reconciliation with Chen, offering him his first assignment since he resigned the party chairmanship—the opportunity to author an attack on the leftist opposition faction (i.e., the Trotskyists).[28] Chen's refusal determined his fate. On November 15, 1929, Chen Duxiu, Peng Shuzhi, and a number of their followers were expelled from the party.

Certainly, the party did not undertake this action lightly. As the former party leader, Chen Duxiu still had a considerable following among the party regulars. Moreover, there was much sympathy for some of Chen's positions among many of the party members. Many highly influential Chinese Communist leaders argued against his expulsion.[29] Chen Bilan, Peng Shuzhi's wife, has claimed that even Liu Shaoqi, the future president of the People's Republic of China, called for leniency toward Chen Duxiu, but this claim has been vigorously and convincingly disputed by Wang Fanxi and other Trotskyists.[30] In any case, Chen's support within the party did not save him. Once again Chen had shown his failure to control the Chinese Communist organizational infrastructure in spite of his ability to articulate positions with which many party members could agree. Hence, Chen once again became the victim of a party he had created but could not control.

Chen's fall from grace ended the possibility of restoring the democratic tradition within the party. Despite criticisms of

[27] Warren Kuo, *Analytical History of the Chinese Communist Party*, vol. 2, pp. 66–69.
[28] Chen Duxiu, "Gao chuandang tongzhi shu" [A letter to all party comrades], Shanghai, Dec. 10, 1929.
[29] Ch'en Pi-lan, "Introduction," p. 39.
[30] Ibid. Wang made his refutation of Ch'en Pi-lan's claim in a letter he wrote to me in December of 1981.

his leadership as autocratic and paternalistic, Chen had in fact continually advocated the right of party members to criticize party policy freely. This democratic style of leadership completely changed after 1927 when Chen was removed from the party chairmanship, a change that he criticized severely in his second letter and that was central to Peng's defense of Chen. The approach Chen Duxiu advocated at this time would have led the party on a much more open, democratic path than was subsequently to be its fate. Had such a policy been adopted, it would also have allowed Chen Duxiu to continue to maintain his position as criticial insider to the Chinese Communist party, a role that he had consistently advocated in his earlier relations with other established movements.

In the pre-1911 period, as a former examination candidate and scion of a noted official family, Chen had been able to make his opposition to the policies of the Qing government palatable, since he was in effect a privileged insider rebelling against the system. Similarly, as already noted, one of the reasons for Chen's success during the May Fourth period was that as dean of the Faculty of Arts and Letters at Beijing University, Chen was again a high official criticizing his peers. The CCP-KMT United Front, in spite of all its problems and Chen's opposition to many of its tenets, had provided Chen with the opportunity of continuing to be a critical insider to the growing power of the Guomindang revolution. Once the United Front was eliminated and Chen was removed from his chairmanship, he was deprived of this authority.

Chen's attempts to establish a similar position in his relations with the Chinese Communist party were doomed to failure. For one thing, the party itself was weak at that time. Furthermore, the attitude of party members was now different from that of earlier Chinese revolutionaries. The favorable reception to Chen's criticisms of the Qing dynasty, his attacks on the regime of Yuan Shikai and his successors, and finally his snipes at Jiang Kaishek had relied on the traditional respect for the honest Mandarin who dared to risk his position to remonstrate with his ruler—an obeisance not likely to be effective with young party members in revolt against the older generation and apt to see Chen as the representative of the old values. Indeed, Chen's criticisms of the CCP leadership seemed to many to be simply sour grapes from an old man who had not kept up with the revolutionary struggle. In any case, Chen's attitude during this period may have been somewhat naive; at a time when the KMT had recently reunited China and was cracking down on its enemies, the party could ill afford the luxury of conflicting discussions and differing policies.

Certainly Chen had never been a good follower. Beginning with his refusal to join Sun Yatsen's Tongmenghui in 1905, Chen had always preferred to lead his own independent party or at least to be able to criticize freely the organization to which he belonged. By joining with the so-called leftist opposition, Chen could once again portray himself as leading a group of young revolutionary comrades interested in the most progressive brand of socialism. He felt comfortable being able to maintain a critical stand against both the CCP and the KMT.

Chen probably was also comforted by Trotsky's vilification of the policies of the Communist International, even if Trotsky did not spare Chen for his role in the debacle that eventually befell the party.[31] Chen himself, as he made clear in "A Letter to All Comrades of the Party" written after his expulsion from the party, felt he had been treated unfairly by the International,[32] whose policies he had faithfully executed. Like Trotsky, Chen now felt the policies of the Russian-controlled organization to be hypocrytical, self-serving, and wrong.

Moreover, the tactics Trotsky proposed as an alternative to those of the International were ones Chen endorsed. Chen agreed that the best way to attempt to unify the opposition would be through calls for a national assembly, which would expose the sham of Guomindang democracy. Chen's greatest successes in rallying readers to his cause during the New Culture movement period had been through his attempts to ex-

[31] See footnote 5.
[32] Chen Duxiu, "Gao chuandang tongzhi shu."

pose the false democracies being established by Yuan Shikai and his successors, and Chen knew the appeal of this strategy. He also welcomed the idea of a party not confused by other alliances but based on the urban proletariat.[33] Chen Duxiu had long felt more comfortable with the urban classes, and he, like Trotsky, believed it was now necessary for the Chinese Communist party to organize its followers in the cities. Both Chen and Trotsky had faith that as soon as the revolutionary forces again crested, it would be possible to quickly complete the bourgeois revolution and carry the revolution on to its socialist phase.[34] Finally, Trotsky tended to view the Chinese Revolution in terms of its international setting, examining its prospects and potential in relation to the development of capitalism and imperialism throughout the rest of the world, a perspective Chen had also held since his earliest schools days.

Given the variety of reasons for Chen's attraction to Trotskyist ideas, the question remains as to why more former party members did not follow Chen's lead. In fact, many did. A large percentage, maybe even a majority, of the Chinese Communist students in Moscow, who were somewhat outside the control of the regular Chinese Communist apparatus, did become Trotskyists.[35] Within China itself the position of Chen and his colleagues often generated a great deal of sympathy. Many of the party branches, to the consternation of the Central Committee, refused to prosecute their Trotskyist members, perhaps waiting to see what the outcome of the struggle would be before playing their hand.[36] Others who might have

[33] Ibid. Also Chen Duxiu et al., "Women de zhengzhi yijian shu" [Our political views], Dec. 25, 1929. Also, idem, "Women de zhenglun zhi zhongdian" [The central point of our dispute], *Huohua*, vol. 1, no. 4 (Nov. 7, 1931); and idem, "Zuijin Shanghai de gongren yundong yu dang de lingdao" [The recent Shanghai Workers' Movement and the leadership of the party], *Huohua*, vol. 1, no. 6 (Nov. 30, 1931).

[34] Trotsky, "The Chinese Question After the Sixth Congress."

[35] Wang Fan-hsi, *Chinese Revolutionary*, p. 86. See also translator Gregor Benton's introduction to this work, p. xiii.

[36] CCP Central Committee, "Letter to All Party Branches and All Comrades," April 11, 1930, as quoted in Warren Kuo, *Analytical History*, vol. 2, p. 77.

sympathized with the Trotskyist position had no way of making contact with the movement. Wang Fanxi has related how upon his return to China even he, who had been an active Trotskyist while in the Soviet Union, found it difficult to make contact with the "right" Trotskyist group after he was expelled from the party.[37]

Given these problems, many party members remained in their old positions through sheer bureaucratic inertia or perhaps financial considerations. As Wang Fanxi has also pointed out, many party members could not afford to join with the Trotskyists, since their livelihood depended upon party salaries paid to them by the Soviets.[38] In this respect, the establishment of the Jiangxi Soviet by Mao Zedong, a move opposed by Chen Duxiu and the Trotskyists because they felt it would alienate the party from the proletarian leadership in the cities, was a necessary step in establishing an independent party that could exist free of Soviet subsidies while still assuring the livelihood of its cadres through the taxes it collected from its own government.

THE LEFTIST OPPOSITION

A further reason that the party did not gain more recruits can be found in the disunity of the Trotskyist movement. The Trotskyist groups in China in late 1929 and early 1930 were divided into four major factions, based as much on generational and personal differences as on ideological divisions. The biggest and most important group, centered around Chen Duxiu and Peng Shuzhi, was known as the Proletarian Society, named after the journal that the group began to issue in March 1930. The members of this group, numbering approximately one hundred, consisted of many of those veteran cadres and intellectuals whom Chen had begun to form into an opposition group before his expulsion from the party and who had joined with Chen on December 25, 1929 to issue a political statement

[37] Wang Fan-hsi, *Chinese Revolutionary*, p. 133.
[38] Ibid., p. 125.

attacking the Stalinist leadership. This statement, together with "A Letter to All Comrades of the Party," which Chen had issued a few days earlier in response to his expulsion from the party, marked Chen's first open endorsement of Trotskyism and managed to excite a great deal of interest from many party members. Because of Chen's reputation, this faction came to have the greatest number of members.[39]

The next most important Trotskyist opposition group after Chen Duxiu's Proletarian Society was the previously mentioned Our Word group (Women dehua). This was the earliest Trotskyist group and consisted mostly of students who had come into contact with Trotskyist ideas while at Sun Yatsen University in Moscow. These students returned to China in late 1928, and by early 1929 had begun publishing their own party journal, *Our Word (Women dehua)*. A third group was set up by Liu Renjing, a former student of Chen Duxiu's at Beida who had also studied in the Soviet Union with the Our Word group. Liu, who had personally had a number of discussions with Trotsky before returning to China, was later to be known in the West as the informant for Harold Isaacs' book, *The Tragedy of the Chinese Revolution*. Liu joined together with Wang Fanxi and others to publish the magazine *October (Shiyue)*, and subsequently their group became known as the October Society. A fourth group headed by Liu Ying and Zhao Ji was known as the Militant Society, named for their paper *The Militant (Zhandou bao)*, which ran for only one issue.[40]

The animosities among and lack of unity between the different factions illustrate the difficulties of maintaining a revolutionary organization run by democratic principles under the highly factionalized regional and class differences within Chinese society during a period of repression. As Trotsky himself later insisted, the differences between groups were not

---

[39] Ming-yuan, "Quxiaopai de xingcheng ji moluo" [The rise and fall of the leftist opposition], *Xiandai shiliao [Source materials of modern history]*, vol. 2, Shanghai, 1934, pp. 369–79. Also *Zhongguo gongchandang zhi toshi*, pp. 125–27. Also see Wang Fan-hsi, *Chinese Revolutionary*, pp. 132–50.

[40] Ibid.

really that great, but even so they often resulted in hatred and antagonisms.[41]

The first issue of disagreement between the groups centered around the slogan for a constituent assembly. In his article, "The Chinese Question After the Sixth Congress," Trotsky had maintained that in this period between two revolutionary "high tides," when the forces of revolution had temporarily ebbed, the Communist party had to seize the initiative and help reinvolve the working class in the political process. In order to do so, Trotsky felt the party "should formulate the slogan of the constituent assembly with full powers, elected by universal, equal, direct, and secret suffrage."[42] As we have seen, Chen and the other Trotskyists were quick to accept Trotsky's suggestion and adopt this slogan. The problem was that Liu Renjing felt that the Chinese Revolution would eventually have to go through a short stage in which a government similar to that of Alexsandr Kerensky's would have to be established. Kerensky had been the leader of the democratic provisional government set up in Russia after the revolution of February 1917 and before the October, or Bolshevik, revolution. Liu Renjing cited the example of the Kerensky government because he felt that the assembly, which the Trotskyists were calling for, was something that definitely had to be established before the revolution could proceed to a higher stage.[43]

On the other hand, the Our Word group felt that the assembly was a dream. They believed that the purpose of a slogan calling for a democratically elected constituent assembly as Trotsky had proposed would be to stir up the masses by exposing the illusionary nature of the National Assembly

[41] Ibid., especially Wang Fan-hsi. Leon Trotsky, "Two Letters to China," in *Leon Trotsky on China*, pp. 438–42.

[42] Trotsky, "The Chinese Question after the Sixth Congress," p. 367.

[43] For Chen Duxiu's replies to Liu Renjing see Chen Duxiu, "Da Liuer shi (Ji Liu Renjing) tongzhi" [Answer to Liu Renjing], *Wu zhanje* 9 (Jan. 20, 1931); idem, "Liangge luxian" [The two roads], *Xiaonei shenghuo* 1 (Dec. 1931); idem, "Women de zhenglun zhi zhongdian" [The central point of our dispute], *Huohua*, vol. 1, no. 4 (Nov. 7, 1931). Finally, see Wang Fan-hsi, *Chinese Revolutionary*, pp. 132–50.

then being promised by Jiang Kaishek.[44] Chen's position probably was closest to that of the Our Word group. But in an
effort to settle these grievances, he followed Trotsky's lead
and pointed out that it could not be said for sure whether or
not the assembly would ever actually be established. Even if
the assembly were convened, he maintained, "this is not our
future."[45] Although it might provide the basis through which
the proletariat could gain power, an assembly could not be
the ultimate goal of the revolution, but of the bourgeoisie.
Instead, Chen felt, the dictatorship of the proletariat could
only be realized after soviets were set up.[46]

A second and related issue was that of the nature of the
coming revolution. Trotsky had talked of the "dictatorship
of the proletariat" or the "dictatorship of the proletariat at
the head of the poor peasantry" as a way of distinguishing
his revolutionary goals from those of Stalin, who still saw the
necessity of the "democratic dictatorship of the workers and
peasants" and whose use of this formulation implied the necessity of a democratic bourgeois phase to the revolution.
Chen, in "Our Political Views," the letter he and other senior
party leaders had issued after their expulsion from the party,
had argued that the third revolution would establish a "dictatorship of the proletariat and the poor peasantry,"[47] which
most of the others in the Trotskyist camp felt was too close
to the formulation of the Stalinists and implied the need for
a bourgeois stage to the revolution. Since Chen had already
denied the need for a transitional bourgeois stage to the revolution in his analysis of the nature of Chinese society, the
dispute, as Trotsky pointed out, was nonsensical. Chen's language did not contradict Trotsky's. Chen echoed Trotsky's
sentiments in his attempt to reconcile the dispute.[48]

Yet a third cause for dispute centered around an essay Chen

[44] Ibid.
[45] Ibid.
[46] Ibid.
[47] Chen Duxiu et al., "Women de zhengzhi yijian shu."
[48] Trotsky, "To the Chinese Left Opposition," in *Leon Trotsky on China*,
p. 493. Also, Chen Duxiu, "Da Liuer shi (Ji Liu Renjing) tongzhi."

had written on "The So-called Red Army Question" in July 1930 in the *Proletarian*. In this essay, Chen attacked the Red Army being organized by the CCP. Chen maintained that a revolution based on such an army would be a revolution of the *lumpenproletariat* and not a revolution under the leadership of the working class. The new Red Army, he said, relied on bandits and outlaw elements who would eventually betray the revolution. A peasant revolution, Chen insisted, could only succeed under the leadership of the working class.[49] This formulation, which was to be at the heart of later and present Trotskyist critiques of Maoist leadership, aroused a temporary storm among the Trotskyist groups in China. These groups saw this essay as another example of Chen Duxiu's abandonment of the military and the army, a position that they felt had been responsible for the opportunism that had resulted in the defeat of the Chinese Revolution between 1925 and 1927.[50]

This dissatisfaction with Chen's previous leadership of the party was something that Chen's Trotskyist opponents had in common with their enemies who had taken over the Chinese Communist party. Chen had become the leader of the party as a result of the respect he commanded among the largely disenfranchised and alienated youth. Many of the original party members had once been Chen Duxiu's students, and students or at least former students also formed the bulk of the original Trotskyist membership. This group previously had seen Chen as a figure of authority from the older generation who was nonetheless willing to do battle with the other authorities. Chen's leadership of the Chinese Communist party had created great ambivalence among the youth— an ambivalence Chen himself had symbolized by his seeming unwilling submission to Comintern authority. Although the youth were willing to go along with this authority while he was successful, when Chen failed they were quick to attack him; many of the Trotskyists were as vehement in their de-

[49] Chen Duxiu, "Guanyu suowei 'hongjun' wenti," *Wu zhanje*, July 1, 1930.
[50] Wang Fan-hsi, *Chinese Revolutionary*, pp. 137–38.

nunciations of Chen's "opportunism" as was the Central Committee of the party itself.

Indeed, one of the chief issues dividing the four groups was the demand by those who were not members of the Proletarian Society that Chen Duxiu be more forthright and contrite about his earlier mistakes in leading the party, although he had in fact already acknowledged his own "opportunism." Many felt that Chen's confession did not go far enough. As Trotsky later pointed out, the Our Word group would be satisfied only if Chen in effect was to "kneel down in front of the gate of Our Word's publishing house."[51]

This failure to accept the authority of even their own leaders tends to be a common problem in Trotskyist groups, which typically bring together individuals who have not been willing to accept the bureaucratic leadership of the regular Communist party. Moreover, because of their interest in theoretical matters, Trotskyist groups have usually been less willing to compromise over matters of principle than those members of the regular Communist organization. The result was that the young Trotskyists were hostile and suspicious of Chen's efforts to become a Trotskyist, viewing him as a leader from an older generation whose revolutionary efforts had already failed.

Still, after Chen's expulsion from the party, his formation of the Proletarian Society, and his refusal to compromise with the party—which on February 8, 1930 sent him a cable from the Political Secretariat of the Comintern urging him to attend a meeting to review his expulsion[52]—it was difficult for the other Trotskyist groups to ignore Chen. This was particularly true after the summer of 1930. At this time Trotsky, who had once been highly critical of Chen Duxiu, came into contact with some of the documents written by Chen and the other Trotskyist factions since 1929, and he adopted a more positive attitude toward Chen. Consequently, Trotsky sent the Trot-

[51] "Tuoluociji tongzhi ji 'women de hua' pai xin" [A letter from Comrade Trotsky to the 'Our Talk' faction], *Wu zhanje* 9 (Jan. 30, 1931).

[52] See Chen Duxiu, "Da guoji de xin" [A letter to the International], *Wu Zhanje* 9 (Jan. 30, 1931).

skyists a letter urging the different factions to unify their forces as soon as possible, saying that he saw no basic differences between them.[53]

Even this letter of Trotsky's was not by itself sufficient for unification. A protracted period of negotiation and meetings followed, which required several other interventions from Trotsky before a negotiation committee of the various groups was organized in the winter of 1930. In May 1931, a Leftist Opposition unification congress was finally held in Shanghai.[54] This secret conference left bitter feelings among many of those delegates whose positions and ideas were not represented. One of the disgruntled delegates, Ma Yufu, tipped off the Guomindang secret police as to the hiding place of the conference.[55] As a result, most of the members of the newly organized Central Committee of the leftist opposition, which was once again headed by Chen Duxiu, were arrested by the Guomindang in a series of two raids over the next two months. Although Chen Duxiu escaped the KMT dragnet on this occasion, he and Peng Shuzhi and most of the other remaining oppositionist leaders were arrested on October 15, 1932, effectively eliminating the Trotskyists as a serious political force and for all intents and purposes ending Chen Duxiu's political career.[56]

URBAN REVOLUTIONARY

Before being arrested, Chen had tried to demonstrate the validity of the Trotskyist strategy of attempting to reinvolve

[53] Trotsky, "Two letters to China," pp. 438–42.

[54] "Zhongguo gongchan zhuyi zuopai fanduipai de ganling" [Program of the Chinese Communist leftist opposition faction], *Wu zhanje* 9 (Jan. 30, 1931). Also *Zhongguo gongchandang zhi toushi*, p. 130; and Wang Fan-hsi, *Chinese Revolutionary*, pp. 132–50.

[55] Shitou, "Quxiaopai de xingchen ji molo," pp. 219–21. Wang Fan-hsi, *Chinese Revolutionary*, pp. 132–50.

[56] *Dagong bao [Dagong News]*, Oct. 18, 1932. Also, "Chen Duxiu deng weihai guomin an qisi shu" [The brief of the prosecution against Chen Duxiu et al. for their crime of endangering the security of the Republic], in Chen Dongxiao, *Chen Duxiu pinglun*, pp. 245–46.

the proletariat in the political process with slogans that appealed to their democratic interests and patriotic consciousness. Chen, we will remember, had argued in the three letters he wrote to the Central Committee of the Communist party in 1929 that patriotic slogans were necessary. He felt these appeals should be addressed particularly to the proletariat. After becoming a recognized leader of the Chinese Trotskyist movement, Chen had pointed out how the Chinese Communist party, by removing itself to the countryside, had abandoned the urban labor movement.[57] Chen did not see the advantage of having an independent rural base and was oblivious to the benefits it could provide to the party by supporting itself and its government.

The result, as Chen Duxiu himself pointed out, was that at the time of the Mukden Incident of September 18, 1931, when Japanese troops proceeded to occupy Manchuria, only the Chinese Trotskyists were seriously attempting to organize the workers in the cities. With Jiang Kaishek intent on appeasing the Japanese, the Trotskyists saw themselves as the only viable force willing to fight both the Japanese and their domestic allies. This entailed modifying their program somewhat to allow for the possibility of an alliance between the proletariat and other anti-Japanese classes. Chen was able to argue successfully for a policy in which the Trotskyists would attempt to carry out the internal revolution while leading the patriotic anti-Japanese resistance, a strategy not unlike the one successfully followed by Mao Zedong in the late 1930s and early 1940s. But Chen, in contradistinction to Mao's later policy, insisted that the party must vigorously unite with the poor peasants against the rich peasants.[58]

Despite this insistence on the need for the proletariat to

[57] Chen Duxiu, "Zuijin shanghai de gongren yundong yu dang de lingdao" [The recent Shanghai Workers' Movement and the leadership of the party), *Huohua*, vol. 1, no. 6 (Nov. 30, 1931).

[58] Chen Duxiu, "Nongmin zai zhongguo geming de zuoyung ji chi qiantu" [The function and future of peasants in the Chinese revolution], *Huohua*, vol. 1, no. 9 (April 6, 1932); idem, "Shui he cenmayang jiu zhongguo?" [Who and how to save China], *Huohua*, July 28, 1930.

unite with the poor peasantry, Chen's party succeeded in making headway only among the urban working class in cities like Shanghai. Even this small success proved to be the party's undoing. Throughout the 1930s, whenever the Trotskyists began to reappear as a prominent force among the urban working classes, their members were arrested. To some extent these arrests were a result of intraparty jealousies and hostilities from the Chinese Communists, who, when they could, "jailed or executed" the Trotskyists and otherwise slandered them.[59] A more serious problem, however, was simply that the forces of repression under the Guomindang were too strong; the only real revolutionary alternative at the time was in the countryside. Indeed, though Chen Duxiu spoke of the necessity of the urban working class to unite with the poor peasantry in the countryside, he and his followers made even fewer attempts to implement that policy than did the Chinese Communist party at that time to organize the urban labor movement.

The fact that Chen Duxiu and his Trotskyist followers made virtually no effort to engage in any organizing work in the countryside was symptomatic of their state of mind and of the general cultural milieu in which they operated. People of leftist persuasion who stayed in the cities in the 1930s, whether Trotskyists or otherwise, were generally littérateurs—people who had either left party work or were in the process of leaving party work, or were in any case temporarily abandoning their party affiliation to provide a living for themselves in cultural and literary activities. As Wang Fanxi made clear in his memoirs, one of the reasons that most of those who became Trotskyist activists could afford to do so (and similarly, the reason that many who sympathized with Trotskyist aims were not able to leave the party) is that they were able to support themselves without the party stipend by writing for the growing and ever-popular leftist literary and cultural magazines that flourished in places like Shanghai at the time.[60]

[59] See, for instance, Wang Fan-hsi, *Chinese Revolutionary*, pp. 184.
[60] Ibid., pp. 159–61, 124–26.

Many of those forced to leave the cities probably would have liked to stay, but their literary talents were too meager to allow them to earn a living from this kind of publishing. Certainly, some of those who wrote well performed a valuable task. The writers for these urban literary magazines, such as Lu Xun, were important in helping to draw new student recruits to the party and in keeping the intellectual climate of the times generally sympathetic to the Communists. (Indeed, these periodicals had since the late teens been the most important source of Chen Duxiu's own following and popularity.) Still, the fact remains that most of those who engaged in these tasks were the urban cultured elite, even if leftist ones.

This is not to doubt the revolutionary connections of those who wrote. To be sure, some of those who remained in the cities to write for literary magazines may have been unwilling to engage in the difficult business of revolutionary organization, particularly rural revolution, because of concern for their own safety and comfort. But most of these people were the heirs of the New Culture movement. Their concern with cultural matters had led them to follow Chen Duxiu in the beginning; they continued to model themselves after Chen, viewing themselves as teachers or littérateurs whose influence came from what they wrote. Like the members of the student culture of the early 1900s from which they had descended, these new urban literati were in effect a radical Mandarin group.

The Trotskyists distinguished themselves from most of the rest of the members of this culture because of their willingness to engage in labor agitation and constantly risk arrest and execution in their attempts to organize the proletariat. But few if any were equipped either by outlook or breeding to engage in peasant organization. Their Trotskyist analysis of the importance of the urban working class to the revolution may have reinforced this tendency among them to sidestep the peasantry.

Chen Duxiu in particular had always depended upon this class of urban littérateurs as his special audience and had consistently seen them as holding a special place in the Communist party. It is therefore natural that he was to settle in

among this class after his removal from the party chairmanship in 1927. When Chen remarked in 1928 to the novelist
Mao Dun, who himself had just left the party to return to
literary activities, that he was now mostly interested in philological research, this could be interpreted as his attempt to
reinstate himself with the literati.[61] The party in effect left
Chen Duxiu behind when it moved to the countryside; but
Chen's influence did not leave the party. As the party of the
proletariat, the Chinese Communists continued to carry a torch
for the urban revolution and for the values and ideas of Chen
Duxiu.

LAST ATTEMPTS AT POLITICAL INFLUENCE

Chen's continuing influence over the urban intellectual stratum, even at a time when the revolution had moved on, became evident after his arrest. Virtually the entire non-Communist liberal and leftist establishment of the cities rallied to
his side, demanding that he be given a fair trial and finally
pressuring Jiang Kaishek to allow Chen to be defended by a
group of five lawyers led by his old friend Zhang Shizhao.[62]
Chen was in his natural element, starring impeccably in the
role of the forthright intellectual acting according to his principles. Appealing to the jury with one of the most eloquent
statements of his life, Chen admitted that he had been trying
to overthrow the Guomindang government, but suggested that
his actions were merely designed to aid the Chinese state by
eliminating an organization that had failed to defend China
against Japanese aggression, had suppressed the basic rights
and freedoms of the people, and was in reality betraying Chinese
society.[63] This appeal aroused much personal admiration for
Chen. Yielding to the pressure of public opinion, the Guomindang government, about a week after Chen's trial ended

---

[61] Mao Dun, "Chuangzuo shengya de kaishi" [The beginning of a career
in writing], Renmin ribao [People's Daily], April 3, 1981.
[62] See articles collected in Chen Dongxiao, Chen Duxiu pinglun.
[63] Chen Duxiu, Chen Duxiu xiansheng biansu zhuang.

on April 29, 1933, sentenced Chen not to death but to thirteen years in prison.[64]

In prison, Chen was accorded very favorable treatment, living in a special ward that had been built for him and his friends. Given his own private cell, Chen was also allowed to share the ward with his old comrade Peng Shuzhi and to receive a constant stream of visitors, including many top Guomindang figures as well as his current female companion.[65] Chen's third son, Chen Songnian, saw his father in prison for the first time since 1912, when Chen Songnian was two years old. So emotional was their reconciliation, that the now grown son broke down, sobbing at his father's feet.[66]

Chen's jailers gave him freedom to pursue the philological research to which he had returned intermittently throughout his life as befits a true Chinese scholar, and he published several new articles. He also began the first chapters of his never-completed but highly iconoclastic and interesting autobiography.[67] Moreover, it seems Chen continued to write articles commenting on Trotskyist affairs, contributing to the debate on the question of national assembly and soviets.[68] In all these activities, Chen showed his continued desire to influence the leftist cultural and intellectual youth world.

Still, by August 8, 1937, when Chen was released from prison nine years early as a result of the implementation of the Second United Front between the Communists and the Guomindang, even he could now recognize that urban littérateurs were not to be of much use in the next stage of the

[64] "Chen Duxiu ankai shenji" [A record of the trial of Chen Duxiu], *Guowen zhoubao* [*National News Weekly*] 17 (May 1933).

[65] Pu Qingquan, "Wo suo zhidao de Chen Duxiu" [The Chen Duxiu that I knew], in *Wenshi xiliao xuanji* [*Materials on literature and history*], p. 68.

[66] "Fangwen Chen Songnian tongzhi jilu" [Record of interviews with Chen Songnian]. Manuscript of interview by Xi Xu and Sun Qiming, Anqing, April 18–20, 1979.

[67] See chapter 2. Chen's work is discussed somewhat in ibid.; also in Pu Qingquan, "Wo suo zhidao de Chen Duxiu."

[68] Pu Qingquan, "Wo suo zhidao de Chen Duxiu," p. 71. The articles in question were written in 1933 and 1934 for the *Guominhui yu suweiai* [*National Assembly and Soviets*] under the penname Xueyi.

Chinese Revolution. With Japanese troops occupying Shanghai and much of North China, it was clear that the urban-oriented strategy of the Chinese Trotskyists was no longer sufficient, as Chen himself explained to Wang Fanxi. Moreover, Chen's own relations with the new leadership of the Trotskyist movement, particularly his former cell mate Peng Shuzhi, had become extremely bad. Upon leaving prison, Chen spoke contemptuously of his former Trotskyist colleagues, complaining to Wang Fanxi that they seemed interested in making revolution primarily by engaging in scholarly conversations in a room in Shanghai. Chen insisted that he was no longer a Trotskyist.[69]

In fact, however, Chen remained passionately interested in Trotskyist affairs, obsessively talking to Wang Fanxi about Lenin in late 1937 and early 1938, and even responding with a personal letter to Trotsky when the Chinese Trotskyists criticized his strategy and statements.[70] Chen realized that only by supporting the military opposition to Japan could any group hope to mobilize the masses at this time. He explained that the best way to unite the opposition against Japanese imperialism was around a program emphasizing "freedom and democracy."[71] Chen therefore returned to Warrior-Yue-Society-style attempts to regain a following among the military. He hoped to utilize the armies of an already existing commander, in this case General He Jifeng, a commander sympathetic to Chen's ideas. Chen suggested that he and his followers serve as educational commissars for He's troops while developing a program of agrarian reform in the areas He controlled. Unfortunately, General He was removed from his command before this program could come to fruition. Chen then attempted to approach the democratic parties for an

[69] Wang Fan-hsi, *Chinese Revolutionary*, pp. 208–9.
[70] Ibid., pp. 208–10.
[71] Ibid., pp. 210–14. At the end of his life, Chen wrote a series of essays and letters to friends expressing his views on the war of resistance and the relative merits of communism and bourgeois democracy. The most complete collection of these letters may be found in Zhang Yongtong and Liu Chuanxue, eds., *Houqi de Chen Duxiu jiqi wenzhang xuanbian [A collected edition of Chen Duxiu's later essays]*, Sichuan, 1980, pp. 35–234.

alliance with which to develop his political movement. These negotiations, however, were broken off when the Communists began a smear campaign against Chen in mid-1938, accusing him of being a Japanese traitor.[72]

This campaign was apparently begun as a result of the backfiring efforts of Chen's friend and former disciple, Luo Han. Luo felt that Chen's proposals for a United Front against the Japanese were essentially similar to the positions of the Chinese Communists and proposed a reconciliation between the two sides.[73] Chen did not oppose the effort. In his attempts to unite with the non-Communist, non-KMT democratic parties, Chen had repeatedly stated that he was no longer a member of any Trotskyist party and had endorsed a broad-based anti-Japanese movement—statements that made a reconciliation with his former comrades possible.[74] Chen, of course, was a proud man. As founder of the party, he had no intention of humbly apologizing to his former students, nor did he think much of their opinions. His denials of Trotskyist affiliation were thus also filled with recriminations against the charges leveled against him by his former colleagues and he made no overt effort to satisfy the Communists' terms.

These terms were set forth after September 1937, when Luo Han contacted the Communist representative in Nanjing, Ye Jianying. Ye Jianying encouraged Luo in the idea that Chen Duxiu could rejoin the party and suggested that Luo go to Yennan to speak with the party leaders about it. Luo's trip

[72] Wang Fan-hsi, *Chinese Revolutionary*, pp. 210–17.

[73] Ibid., pp. 205–6. See also Luo Han, "Zhi Zhou Enlai deng yifeng gongkai xin" [An open letter to Zhou Enlai and others], *Zhengbao [Upright Daily]*, April 24–25, 1938. Also "Ye Jianying, Bo Gu, Dong Biwu gei 'Xinhua ribao' de xin" [A letter to the *Peoples' Daily* from Ye Jianying, Bo Gu, and Dong Biwu], in Zhang and Liu, eds., *Houqi de Chen Duxiu jiqi wenzhang xuanbian*, pp. 235–36. See also Sun Qiming, "Chen Duxiu shifou hanjian wenti de tantao" [An inquiry into the question of whether or not Chen Duxiu was a traitor], *Anhui daxue xuebao* 2 (1980), pp. 29–30.

[74] Chen Duxiu, "Gei Chen Qichang deng de xin" [A letter to Chen Qichang and others], Nov. 21, 1937, as reprinted in *Houqi de Chen Duxiu jiqi wenzhang xuanbian*, p. 70. Also, "Gei 'Xinhua ribao' de xin," in ibid. (written in March 1938), pp. 112–33. Chen Duxiu made a similar statement to Bao Huiceng in 1939, as printed in Wang Yilin, "Chen Duxiu yu tuopai" [Chen Duxiu and the Trotskyists], *Anhui daxue xuebao* 2 (1980):32.

to Yennan was delayed because of a flood, and negotiations had to be conducted by telegraph. In one telegram, Mao issued a statement saying that Chen could rejoin the party if he renounced the Trotskyist movement and admitted his past mistakes.[75] Wang Fanxi has said that this statement only angered Chen Duxiu and dashed any hope of reconciliation,[76] although recent Chinese Communist sources have maintained that Chen tried to satisfy most of these conditions.[77]

Certainly the Chinese Communists considered that there was a good chance for this reconciliation. But Stalin found the possibility of this reconciliation alarming in view of the anti-Trotskyist campaign then being waged in the Soviet Union. The Chinese Stalinist Wang Ming, who returned from the Soviet Union in early 1938, attempted to undermine Mao's position in the party by seizing on these negotiations to attack Mao. Wang Ming launched a smear campaign against Chen Duxiu as a Japanese traitor, attacking Mao by innuendo for negotiating with traitors. Mao was able to counter these charges by accusing Wang Ming of duplicating Chen Duxiu's "right opportunism." By that time, however, the charges had had their effect. Reconciliation between Chen and the party he had founded was out of the question.[78] Moreover, the smears against Chen Duxiu were not easily forgotten. The old charges of traitor were to be repeated against him during the Cultural Revolution of the late 1960s.

THE END

The last years of Chen's life were filled with defeat and disappointment. Frustrated in his efforts to effect an alliance with the Chinese Democratic League and accused of being a

[75] Luo Han, "Zhi Zhou Enlai deng yifeng gongkai xin." See also Gregor Benton, "The 'Second Wang Mang Line'," *China Quarterly*, March 1975, p. 81.

[76] Wang Fan-hsi, *Chinese Revolutionary*, pp. 205–6.

[77] Sun Qimeng, "Chen Duxiu shifou hanjian wenti de tantao." Also Zhang Yongtong and Liu Chuanxue, "Women dui Chen Duxiu zai kangri zhanzheng shiqi de yidian liaojie he renzhi," in *Houqi de Chen Duxiu jiqi wenzhang xuanbian*, p. 6.

[78] Ibid. See also Wang Fan-hsi, *Chinese Revolutionary*, pp. 210–17.

traitor by his old comrades in the Chinese Communist party, in 1939 Chen fled from the Japanese invasion with the retreating Guomindang forces. Chen moved from Wuhan, where he had first gone upon his release from prison, to Sichuan. Accompanying Chen to Sichuan were his stepmother, his older sister, and Chen's third son, Chen Songnian, as well as Chen's third "wife," Pan Lanzhen. Pan Lanzhen had been a worker in the British-American Tobacco Company in Shanghai when she came to live with Chen in the early 1930s, in the period before his arrest. An ordinary worker who needed money, she had been procured for Chen, whose earlier wives had both left him, by comrades in the party. For her own protection and Chen's, she had not even been told Chen Duxiu's true identity until his arrest.[79] During Chen's incarceration, his family was touched by the devotion Pan showed to Chen. As a consequence, Pan was not only allowed to accompany Chen to Sichuan but, in a traditional gesture of gratitude, she was honored by having her name included in the family genealogy that the Chen family began to prepare in the 1930s.[80]

Chen and his family did not stay in Chongqing, the nationalist capital during the war, but settled in the small town of Jiangjin, about fifty miles from Chongqing. Living simply in an unpretentious dwelling, Chen continued to express his increasingly conservative political views in letters to his former Trotskyist comrades, many of whom still considered him to be part of the movement, and to the small group of political disciples who still gathered around him. In his last years, Chen seems to have begun a movement further and further away from his Communist positions, falling back on the old issues of "democracy and freedom" that had first attracted him to the revolutionary cause.[81] As his health weakened in 1941–42, Chen in his last letters and statements became, as his old friend Hu Shi later maintained, a late-in-life reconvert to democracy.

But most of Chen's energy was devoted to completing the

---

[79] "Chen Duxiu jiashi gaolue," in *Chen Duxiu yanjiu cankao ziliao*, vol. 1, p. 194.

[80] Ibid. Also, my interview with Lin Maosheng, Beijing, Feb. 1981.

[81] See footnote 70.

dictionary of etymological reconstructions on which he now labored, as well as to conducting his phonological research.[82] This was a traditional retirement occupation for officials whose careers had ended, one that previously had been followed by such illustrious predecessors as the famous Song dynasty reformer Wang Anshi. Chen's goals of course were different. Chen apparently hoped, as he told his young cousin, that these philological labors would pave the ground for the eventual romanization of the Chinese language. In this way, Chen continued to labor for the reconstruction of an original national essence, which he saw as connected with social reform in China and which he still felt was intimately connected to a "rectification" of the language.[83]

Ironically, even the influence of these last labors has been colored by Chen's political reputation. Although his dictionary has been used as a basic textbook in many middle schools and colleges in both Taiwan and China, the true identity of the work's author has been concealed by the authorities, who may still be worried about the effect of Chen's influence on Chinese youth.

The fate of these works merely reflects the general misery of Chen's life during these last years. This misery may also be seen in the diminution of the optimistic faith in the future that had characterized the previous twenty years of Chen's Communist activities. This pessimism may have been the result of Chen's personal situation. In 1939 Chen's stepmother, who had kept house for Chen and cared for his children for almost forty years, died.[84] Despite Chen's lifelong public criticisms of the influence of the traditional Chinese family on Chinese life, he had remained very attached to and dependent

[82] Chen Duxiu, "Xiaoxue shezi jiaoben [A textbook on recognizing characters]. The book is actually more ambitious than the title would indicate, for it gives the etymology of all the characters it mentions. Although never finished, it has been reprinted in various forms in both the People's Republic of China and in Taiwan. Chen also published a number of phonological and philological articles in *Dongfang zazhi* between 1937 and 1942.

[83] Pu Qingquan, "Wo suo zhidao de Chen Duxiu," p. 52.

[84] "Zai fang Chen Songnian tanhua jilu," in *Anhui geming shi yanjiu ziliao* 1:11–12.

on this old woman, who has been compared in the reminiscences of some of Chen's family members with the old matron
of the family in *Dream of the Red Chamber*. Following her
death, another tragedy struck the family—the death of Chen's
older sister, to whom he was also greatly attached and whose
lingering illness Chen movingly described in an essay he wrote
for his sister's funeral.[85]

Perhaps influenced by these deaths and his own pathetic
situation, Chen's own health began to deteriorate. Suffering
from high blood pressure and heart disease, Chen made repeated trips to the hospitals of Chongqing, but to no avail.
On May 27, 1942, at 9:40 P.M., Chen died at the age of sixty-
two, his death barely warranting mention in the press of the
Chinese Communist party that he had founded and that would
soon achieve final victory.[86]

Chen had been, in the words of Trotsky in a letter to the
Chinese oppositionists, an "acute observer" of the Chinese
scene.[87] Even toward the end of his life, he had shown his
prescience on current political events, urging his Trotskyist
followers to join the United Front against the Japanese. Although the Trotskyist movement was broad and democratic
enough to tolerate even Chen Duxiu's dissident ideas, some
of his former comrades had begun to feel that it would be
better, as they complained to Trotsky, for Chen to "go to
America" to visit Trotsky in his exile than to remain in China,
where his fame and reputation would "mislead" those who
might be interested in the movement.[88]

Chen's Trotskyist activities had demonstrated both the limits and the potential of Chen Duxiu's style of operation. His
authority had been dependent on his status with urban intel-

[85] He Zhiyou, "Duxiu xiansheng sheng yishi simo ji" [A remembrance of
the full circumstances of Chen Duxiu's sickness and death], in *Chen Duxiu
yanjiu cankao ziliao*, vol. 1, pp. 99–104.

[86] Ibid.

[87] As quoted in Wang Fan-hsi, *Chinese Revolutionary*, p. 209.

[88] "Bowei makesi zhuyi" [Protect Marxism]. This is a collection of Chen
Duxiu's letters written from 1939 to 1941 and published by the Chinese
Trotskyists. Trotsky was actually in Mexico at the time.

lectual youth. This authority could be a decisive force when the situation was ripe, as it was in the early 1920s, when Chen pushed his student followers to go out to the factories to organize and mobilize the labor movement. After his expulsion from the party, Chen was able to use this authority among Chinese youth to help unify the various Trotskyist factions and settle their differences.

The Trotskyists were in a sense Chen's natural constituency—young iconoclastic intellectuals, many of whom even wore outlandish clothes. They were the heirs to the student culture in which Chen had participated since the early 1900s. To be sure, both Chen and the culture had changed much in the forty-odd years since Chen had first encountered the ideas of Kang Youwei and Liang Qichao. Chen had begun as an iconoclastic traditionalist influenced by the *kaozheng* school and he had ended up as an iconoclastic Marxist. Still, Chen had retained a commitment to the material betterment of the Chinese people and an interest in searching for the roots of the Chinese language in order to unify and romanize Chinese speech.

But Chen's concern for traditional values had now given way to a commitment to a socialist revolution led by the proletariat. He had come to know this proletariat during his stays in Tokyo, Shanghai, and other newly developing cities. To be sure, the revolution he called for was to be led by the stratum of urban intellectual youth whom he had long dazzled as a result of his ability and traditional mannerisms. But Chen had now come to understand that these youth could only be effective when they had the kind of disciplined political organization provided by a Leninist-style party. Still Chen, who had grown to maturity thinking of political parties as groups of moral individuals pledged to common principles and leaders, was reluctant to operate such a party without an adherence to democratic values—a foreign idea he had come to cherish.

But not all of Chen's legacy is positive. The iconoclastic attacks on culture begun by Chen Duxiu may also have influenced future party policy. Chen's use of devastating cultural critique as a way of making political points was a style imitated in the Great Proletarian Cultural Revolution of the late 1960s, when once again the young used cultural attacks to castigate older revolutionaries.

Chen's authority within the Chinese Communist party had been largely derived from the common perception of him as a morally steadfast individual willing to speak out even against the government or party that he served. This was a role similar to that followed by those brave Confucians of the past who had inspired devotion and loyalty in their followers because of their willingness to remonstrate with leaders who had erred. But Chen's attempts to continue this role within the Chinese Communist party as the head of a Communist opposition faction were doomed to fail. Ironically, Chen's successor within the party, Mao Zedong, would define, in the last years of his life, a similar role for himself, with the hope of influencing a new generation of students. Mao did not have Chen Duxiu's intellectual background; but, like Chen, he did attempt to establish his authority among rebellious youths by creating an image of himself as a steadfast individual willing to criticize his own government and party. In the Mandarin tradition, Mao, in his last years, wrote traditional poetry and allowed himself to be photographed in his study surrounded by books. And Mao's efforts were to become unraveled over a difference similar to that which had been Chen Duxiu's undoing—the difficulty of concurrently carrying out national development and the social revolution under conditions of underdevelopment.

EPILOGUE

Since liberation, the Chinese Communist party has shown little public acknowledgment of its indebtedness to Chen Duxiu, but it has been willing to honor Chen Duxiu's descendents. In 1953, during a visit to Anqing, Chen Duxiu's birthplace, Mao Zedong ordered that a plaque be put up outside the residence of Chen Songnian, Chen Duxiu's sole surviving son by his first marriage. In a bizarre footnote on life in the Chinese outreaches, the plaque, which proclaims Chen Songnian's house to be the residence of the "sole surviving son of a martyr to the Chinese Revolution," has been maintained undisturbed to the present—even during the Cultural Revolution, when the Red Guards in Anqing desecrated Chen Duxiu's tomb. Also untouched by the Cultural Revolution was the special stipend that has been paid monthly to Chen Songnian (in addition to his regular salary) following Mao's visit to Anqing.[1] But no special treatment has been meted out to the children of Chen's second wife, Gao Zhunman.

Unfortunately, Chen's political and intellectual contributions have received less attention in China than has his surviving legitimate heir. In spite of the interest in Chen that again has been revived in China in the last few years, Chen has still not been sufficiently credited for his tremendous influence over the course of modern Chinese history—an influence which is probably second in this century only to that of Mao Zedong. Even if Chen had died as early as 1911, he would still occupy an important place in the history of the Chinese Revolution for his role in helping to pioneer the vernacular revolution and his efforts to introduce Western ideas into China, as well as for his work in organizing the revolutionary opposition to the Qing dynasty in the central Yangzi Valley, particularly in Anhui.

[1] Chen Songnian, "Fangwen Chen Songnian tanhua jilu" [Record of an interview with Chen Songnian], May 25–26, 1979.

There are several reasons for the previous obscurity of Chen Duxiu's activities during this period, one of which is simply the lack of research that has been done in the West on the pre-1911 Anhui revolutionary movement. Chen himself, as well as many of the others with whom he worked during the early period and who rose to prominence after 1911, such as Cai Yuanpei, may also have been somewhat reluctant to admit their earlier involvement in the assassination squads and the paramilitary adventures that characterized their early activities. Furthermore, Chen's activities during this period have been obscured because of his refusal to join Sun Yatsen's Tongmenghui, or Alliance Society—discussions of which dominated most of the official histories of the early Republican revolutionary movement. Most important, because Chen Duxiu became something of a pariah in both Chinese Communist and Guomindang circles, many of his former comrades have been fearful about discussing their early associations with him.

Indeed, many of Chen's old allies have become vindictive in their efforts to wipe out all traces of the influence of Chen Duxiu. The most notorious person in this regard was the former anarchist and later Guomindang supporter, Wu Zhihui, who was responsible for the execution of Chen's elder son, Chen Yannian, in 1927. Chen Yannian, using a pseudonym, had been jailed for a minor offense during the Guomindang roundup of Communists and their sympathizers after the collapse of the First United Front. Chen Duxiu's friends, knowing of Wu Zhihui's former association with him, appealed to Wu for aid in getting Chen Yannian released from prison where he was being held. Instead, Wu revealed Chen Yannian's name to the Guomindang authorities, allegedly maintaining that the son was far more dangerous than his father.[2]

[2] There are several different versions of this same story, all of which fault Wu Zhihui. In the version told to me by Tai Jingnong (Taipei, 1975), Chen Yannian actually went to Wu Zhihui's house to hide out and was betrayed by him to the Guomindang. According to Chen Songnian, the police did not know Chen Yannian's true identity when he was first arrested. Since the charges against him were not that serious, Chen Yannian appealed to his

The problem, of course, has been that Chen's post-1911 activities alienated many of his old friends and associates. Still, because of Chen's role in founding *New Youth* magazine and propagandizing the new culture while serving as dean of the Faculty of Arts and Letters at Beijing University, few would be willing to deny Chen a leading place in the events which ended with the founding of the Chinese Communist party and the transformation of China's traditional culture. Chinese historians have debated the relative roles of Hu Shi and Chen Duxiu in leading the New Culture movement. Chen and Hu themselves even briefly, in the 1920s, argued over whether the objective historical forces were more important in creating the vernacular revolution than the individuals involved in promoting this change.[3] But these disputations do not shed as much light on the importance of Chen's activities at this time as Mao Zedong's description of Chen Duxiu as "commander-in-chief" of the May Fourth movement.[4]

The extraordinary thing about Chen Duxiu was the way he took advantage of traditional relations between teacher and students, official and subjects, and scholar and disciples to influence the political direction and organization of the Chinese student body during the May Fourth and New Culture movements and to pave the way for the founding of the Chinese Communist party. Later, Chen used this authority to motivate leftist intellectual youth to join the party, to popularize Marxist thought in China, and to convince his followers to organize the infrastructure among the masses that was necessary for the eventual success of the party. It is unlikely that any other person had the authority or perspicacity to accomplish this task.

Chen's life shows both the possibilities and limitations that

---

father's friend, Wang Mengzou, for bail money. Wang accordingly informed Hu Shi, who in turn wired Wu Zhihui for help in springing Chen Yannian from jail. Instead, Wu turned Chen Yannian over to the police. Chen Songnian, ibid. Also, my interview with Lin Maosheng, Beijing, Spring 1981.

[3] Chen Duxiu, "Kexue yu rensheng guan xu" [A preface to *Science and the View of Life*], XQN, Dec. 20, 1923.

[4] See chapter 5, footnote 1.

existed within the traditional culture. Chen did not suddenly emerge out of a traditional background to embrace icono-clastic Western ideas. His interest in Western concepts was initially spurred by his involvement with iconoclastic Chinese ideas. He originally viewed many of the Western ideas he imbibed in terms of these early Chinese iconoclastic notions. Throughout his life, Chen's interest in language reform and his belief that this reform was vitally connected with the improvement of the Chinese nation stemmed from his earlier idea that the Chinese language was a Chinese national essence that had to be recovered in its original purity. Chen's lifelong devotion to social change stemmed from his idea that the Chinese people were China's most basic national essence. The material improvement of the Chinese people took precedence over virtually all of Chen's other commitments.

Though Chen remained loyal to his interests and commitments, he was flexible in his thought. Unlike most of his early contemporaries who remained mired in the ideas of their youth, Chen developed his thought at he grew older. He constantly embellished and refined his youthful commitment to the restoration of a Chinese national essence. He gradually moved from *kaozheng* notions to democracy and science and then to Marxism. To be sure, Chen did not have the benefit of coming from a society with a social-democratic or even a democratic tradition and tended to interpret these new ideas in terms of contexts and events that were familiar to him. But ideas, whatever their origin, are always reinterpreted and developed in new contexts. It was Chen's special talent to be able to adapt first democratic and then Marxist ideas to a Chinese framework.

Unfortunately, Chen was not so successful in implementing these ideas in the manner that he desired. He was able to use his tremendous prestige as an intellectual to gain a following; yet he was not able to build a government of his own. Without a government of his own that could collect taxes and clothe and feed his followers, Chen was always dependent on outside forces, whether warlords like Duan Qirui, Chen Chiungming, and Wu Peifu or the Soviets. Chen was limited to followers like himself—urban littérateurs who could earn their living in the heady Chinese urban areas. By establishing a rural soviet, Mao Zedong would later be able to broaden his following and win the revolution. But the urban literati were still to be an important—and potentially the most troublesome—part of Mao's power base, as indeed they must be for any Chinese regime. And it was to these people that Chen passed on his legacy.

Chen's legacy—good and bad—must be seen in the existence of the Chinese Communist party today. The tendency within the party for an obscurantist elite vocabulary and the assumption of a relationship between moral and political behavior may have had their origin in the party with Chen Duxiu, though their continuing existence today must be traced to the political and intellectual climate in China. A more direct result of Chen's influence is the continuing effect on the party of student activism—something that Chen Duxiu more than any other person helped to encourage and develop in China. Indeed, the relationship between these student activists and their leaders as well as the continuing search on the part of these student activists for outside political support suggest a strong continuity with Chen's time. An equally important result of Chen's legacy is the continuing desire within and without the party for democratic reforms. Many of those, particularly in cultural and literary circles, who have been at the forefront of demanding democratic reforms within the party and who have resisted attempts to put a political straitjacket around literary activities include people like Wang Shiwei, Ding Ling, and other former associates and students of Chen Duxiu. It is perhaps no accident, then, that today, when these democratic demands are once again mounting within China, people are again interested in Chen Duxiu and the whole Chinese Trotskyist period.

Indeed, there is much about latter-day Chinese policies that would have pleased Chen Duxiu. The recent insistence in China that ultimately the only way to protect the Chinese nation and identity is through the material development of the Chinese people is an idea once expressed eloquently by Chen Duxiu, though few in China today would be willing to trace the origin of this idea to Chen's dabbles in the national essence movement. Moreover, the repudiation of the Chinese policies of the last twenty years has awakened doubts about the course of the Chinese Revolution that hark back to Chen Duxiu. In particular, these include recent articles questioning the efficacy of a peasant revolution that had abandoned the urban proletariat in attempting to create a socialist society—an idea that had been the basis of Chen's critiques of the Chinese Communist party in the early 1930s.[5] And as people have become aware that their own ideas bear some similarity to those of Chen Duxiu, they have begun to question the whole policy that led to Chen's expulsion from the Chinese Communist party in 1929.[6]

At the beginning of this book, an analogy was made between Chen Duxiu and Trotsky. Both were instrumental in developing the Communist parties of their two countries and introducing Marxist theories into their respective nations. Moreover, their Marxist theories had much in common. Both men believed in the critical role to be played in the revolution by the urban working class, both men were concerned about the effect the backwardness of their two countries would have on the revolutionary process, and both men eventually came to believe that revolutionary stages could be quickly telescoped.

But Trotsky was a brilliant orator and organizer who was at home in the factory as much as in the university. His audience consisted of workers as much as students. Not so Chen.

[5] Two of the most interesting articles are: Ying Yueli and Sun Hui, "Guanyu woguo shehui zhuyi gaizao houqi de jige lilun wenti" [On several theoretical problems in the later period of our nation's socialist transformation], *Nanjing daxue xuebao* [*Nanjing University Journal*] 4 (1980):98. Also Liu Chang, "Shilun zhongguo fengjian shehui changqi yanyu de yuanyin" [A preliminary discussion of the reasons for the continuation of China's feudal society for such a long period], *Lishi yanjiu* [*History and Research*] 2 (1981):24.

[6] See particularly Guo Xuyin, "Ping Chen Duxiu gei dangzhongyang sanfeng xin" [A criticism of the three letters Chen Duxiu sent to the party Central Committee], *Shanghai shifan xueyuan xuebao* [*Journal of Shanghai Teacher's College*] 2 (1979):14–20.

The highly refined contents of his writings, even his Communist writings, appealed primarily to an elite audience of upper-class intellectuals. The fact that a Communist party could be founded on such a basis is indicative of the tremendous influence of the traditional intellectual class on modern Chinese history.

If a historical analogy has to be made between Chen Duxiu and a Western figure, then it perhaps should be with one from outside of Marxist tradition. Chen was more the Moses than the Trotsky or even the Plekhanov of the Chinese Revolution. After helping to introduce his people to the new doctrines, a task he was able to perform in large part because of the training he had received in the houses of the privileged leaders, Chen, like Moses, was destined to be left behind by his people when they entered the "promised land" (a land that was to be filled with more turmoil and heartache than genuine milk and honey). And Chen's importance, like that of Moses, was as a spiritual leader who could transform and focus the aspirations of rebellious youth into a coherent movement. The movement, however, still needed a Joshua who, having not been as profoundly discouraged by the "sins" of his people during their captivity and therefore not as affected by occasional retrogressions in his thought as was the original leader, could guide his people out of the wilderness and embark on the military conquest that would be necessary before the chosen people could again settle in their old land. After leading the struggle for forty years, Chen, like Moses, could only stand on the cliffs and view the new land from afar. A prophet more than a priest, he was not destined to lead the political organization necessary to sustain his followers.

GLOSSARY OF IMPORTANT TERMS

Aiguo xuexiao	愛國學校
Aiguo hui	愛國會
Anhui aiguo hui	安徽愛國會
Anhui baihua bao	安徽白話報
Anhui gongxue	安徽公學
Anhui suhua bao	安徽俗話報
Anhui wubei xuetang	安徽武備學堂
Ba Jin	巴金
Bo Wenwei	柏文蔚
Buren	不忍
Cai Hesen	蔡和森
Cai Yuankang	蔡元康
Cai Yuanpei	蔡元培
Can shijie	慘世界
Chang Hengfang	常恒芳
Chang Naide	常乃悳
Chen Chiungming	陳烱明
Chen Duxiu	陳獨秀
Chen Gongbo	陳公博
Chen Mengji	陳孟吉
Chen Qimei	陳其美
Chen Songnian	陳松年
Chen Wangdao	陳望道
Chen Xifan	陳昔凡
Chen Yannian	陳延年
Chien Xuantong	錢玄同
Chouan hui	籌安會
Chu Pucheng	褚輔成
Chiushi Shuyuan	求是書院

Dai Jitao	戴季陶
Deng Zhongxia	登中夏
Ding Ling	丁玲
Du Fu	杜甫
Duan Fang	端方
Duan Qirui	段祺瑞
Enming	恩銘
Eshi jingwen ribao	俄事警聞日報
Fan Zhongjia	范中甲
Fang Zhiwu	房秩五
Feng Ziyou	馮自由
Fu Sinian	傅斯年
Gao Junman	高君曼
Gao Junyu	高君宇
Gao Yihan	高一涵
Gao Yuhan	高語罕
Geming dang	革命黨
Geming jun	革命軍
Gong Baochuan	龔寶銓
Gongyan bao	公言報
Guangfu hui	光復會
Gui Bohua	桂伯華
Guocui xuebao	國粹學報
Guomin riri bao	國民日日報
Guo Morou	郭沫若
Han Yan	韓衍
Hangzhou baihua bao	杭州白話報
He Jifeng	何基澧
He Meishi	何梅士
Heian shijie	黑暗世界
Hezhun	和羣
Hu Hanmin	胡漢民
Hu Shi	胡適

Hu Ying	胡瑛
Huang Xing	黃興
Huaxing hui	華興會
Huazu hui	華族會
Hubei xuesheng jie	湖北學生界
Huoyou	夥友
Jia	家
Jiayin zazhi	甲寅雜誌
Jiang Kaishek (Jieshi)	蔣介石
Jiang Monlin (Menglin)	蔣夢麟
Jiangxi	江西
Jin Huang	金黃
Jin Xiaofu	金少甫
Jin Weixi	金維繫
Jingjin shuju	鏡今書局
Jingshi bao	經世報
Juren	舉人
Jushi	居士
Kang Youwei	康有爲
Kaozheng	考證
Ke Wenzhong	葛溫仲
Kuai Guangtian	蒯光典
Laodong jie	勞動界
Lao Zi	老子
Li Dazhao	李大釗
Li Genyuan	李根源
Li Guangjiung	李光烔
Li Hongzhang	李鴻章
Li Jingfang	李經方
Li Jingmai	李經邁
Li Liejun	李烈鈞
Li Shucheng	李書城
Li Yuanhong	黎元洪

Liang Qichao	梁啓超
Liang Shuming	梁漱溟
Lin Shu	林懈
Lin Xie	林紓
Liu Bei	劉備
Liu Fu	劉復
Liu Kuiyi	劉揆一
Liu Renjing	劉仁靜
Liu San	劉三
Liu Shaoqi	劉少奇
Liu Shipei	劉師培
Liu Yazi	柳亞子
Liu Ying	劉英
Lizhi hui	勵志會
Lujun xuexiao	陸軍學校
Lu Xun	魯迅
Luo Han	羅漢
Luo Jialun	羅家倫
Luo Zhanglong	羅章龍
Lushi xuetang	陸師學堂
Ma Yubao	馬毓寶
Ma Yufu	馬玉夫
Mao Dun	茅盾
Mao Zedong	毛澤東
Matsumoto Hideki	松本英紀
Meizhou pinglun	每週評論
Meng Ben	孟賁
Mieguo	滅國
Nakajima Nagafumi	中島長文
Ni Je	薛節
Niu Zhuang	牛莊
Oushi yanjiu hui	歐事研究會
Pan Lanzhen	潘蘭珍

Peng Pai	彭湃
Peng Shuzhi	彭述之
Qingnian	青年
Qingnian lizhi xueshe	青年勵志學社
Qingnian hui	青年會
Qingshi guan	清史官
Qiu Jin	秋瑾
Qu Qiubai	瞿秋白
Rulin waishi	儒林外史
Shehui zhuyi jiangxi hui	社會主義講習會
Shen Er	沈二
Shen Yinmo	沈尹默
Shihua bao	實話報
Shiwu bao	時務報
Song Yulin	宋玉琳
Su Manshu	蘇曼殊
Subao	蘇報
Sun Yatsen (Zhongshan)	孫中山
Sun Yuyun	孫毓筠
Tang Erhe	湯爾和
Tang Caichang	唐才常
Tao Chengzhang	陶成章
Tieliang	鐵艮
Tienyi bao	天義報
Tongcheng	桐城
Tongcheng gongxue	桐城公學
Tongmenghui	同盟會
Wang Fanxi	王凡西
Wang Jingwei	汪精衛
Wang Mengzou	汪孟鄒
Wang Ming	王明
Wang Shiwei	王實味
Wang Xiaoxu	王小徐

Wang Xiyan	汪希顏
Wang Zhengting	王正廷
Wang Zijin	王子晉
Wangguo	亡國
Weixin hui	維新會
Weixin hui	慰心會
Women de hua	我們的話
Wu Cigu	吳賜谷
Wu Jiyan	吳繼嚴
Wu Peifu	吳佩孚
Wu Rulun	吳汝綸
Wu Yue	吳樾
Wu Zhenhuang	吳振黃
Wu Zhihui	吳稚暉
Xie Wuliang	謝旡量
Xijiang	西江
Xinchao	新潮
Xin qingnian	新青年
Xingzhong hui	興中會
Xiucai	秀才
Xiung Chengji	熊成基
Xu Shan	許善
Xu Shichang	徐世昌
Xu Xilin	徐錫麟
Xun Zi	荀子
Yan Fu	嚴復
Yan Yuan	顏元
Yang Changji	楊昌濟
Yang Yulin	楊毓麟
Yadong tushuguan	亞東圖書館
Yao	堯
Yao Nai	姚鼐
Yao Wenfu	姚文甫

Ye Dehui	葉德輝
Ye Jianying	葉劍英
Yi	羿
Yi Baisha	易白沙
Yu	禹
Yuan Mei	袁枚
Yuan Shikai	袁世凱
Yue Fei	岳飛
Yuewang hui	岳王會
Yuzhou feng	宇宙風
Zhang Binglin	章炳麟
Zhang Dong	張動
Zhang Ertian	張爾田
Zhang Guotao	張國燾
Zhang Ji	張繼
Zhang Jingfu	張經夫
Zhang Shizhao	章士釗
Zhang Xun	張勳
Zhang Zhidong	張之洞
Zhang Zuolin	張作霖
Zhao Ji	趙濟
Zhaoming wenxuan	昭明文選
Zheng Chaolin	鄭超麟
Zhongguo baihua bao	中國白話報
Zhongguo jiaoyu hui	中國教育會
Zhongguo liuxuesheng huiguan	中國留學生會館
Zhonghua geming dang	中華革命黨
Zhonghua xinbao	中華新報
Zhong Shan	中山
Zhong Xianchang	鍾憲鬯
Zhou Ling	周靈
Zhou Yawei	周亞圍
Zhu Xi	朱熹

Zhuang Zi	莊子
Zhu Lingxi	朱菱溪
Zhuge Liang	諸葛亮
Zijue	自覺
Zou Rong	鄒容

Abrams, Philip. "Rites de Passage: The Conflict of Generations in Industrial Society." *Journal of Contemporary History* 5 (1970).

AHSHB: see *Anhui suhua bao.*

Alitto, Guy S. *The Last Confucian: Liang Shu-ming and the Chinese Dilemma of Modernity.* Berkeley, 1979.

"Anhui aiguohui nizhang" [Proposed constitution of the Anhui Patriotic Society]. *Subao*, June 7, 1903.

"Anhui aiguohui zhi chengjiu" [The establishment of the Anhui Patriotic Society]. *Subao*, May 25, 1903.

"Anhui daxuetang zuzhi xuesheng jue qingxing" [The circumstances of the Anhui Higher School's hindering of students involved in expelling the Russians]. *Subao*, May 29, 1903.

Anhui gemingshi yanjiu ziliao: see Anhui sheng shehui kexuesuo lishi yanshi.

Anhui kexue fen yuan lishi yanjiu shi jindaishi zu diaocha [The investigative branch for modern history in the Anhui Scientific Institute's Department of Historical Research], "Wuhu dichu de xinhai geming" [The 1911 revolution in the Wuhu area]. *Anhui shixue tongsu [The Anhui Historical Studies Bulletin]*, vol. 14, no. 1 (Dec. 1959).

"Anhui shengcheng daxuetang di yici chengtu zhi yuanyin" [The reasons for the first conflict at the Anhui Higher School in the Anhui capitol]. *Subao*, May 26, 1903.

Anhui sheng shehui kexuesuo lishi yanshi [Anhui provincial social science group historical research bureau], ed., *Anhui gemingshi yanjiu ziliao [Materials on the history of the revolution in Anhui]*. Vol. 1. Wuhu, 1980.

Anhui shixue tongsu [The Anhui Historical Studies Bulletin]. Wuhu, 1959.

Anhui suhua bao [Anhui Vernacular Paper]. Wuxi, 1904.

"Anhui suyu bao zhi xiaolu" [The circulation of the Anhui vernacular journal]. *Jingzhong ribao*, June 11, 1904.

"Anhui tongxiang hui caozhang" [A draft constitution of the Anhui Provincial Society]. *Subao*, June 23, 1903.

Anhui wenxian [Anhui literary collections]. Anhui, 1933–48, intermittently; published again in Taiwan, 1971–72.

Anqing shihua [A historical discussion of Anqing]. Anqing, 1979.

Anqing shi lishi xuehui [Anqing municipal historical committee] and Anqingshi tushuguan [Anhui municipal library], joint eds., *Chen Duxiu yanjiu cankao ziliao [Research materials on Chen Duxiu]*. Anqing, 1981.

Ba Jin. *The Family*. Beijing, 1979.

Baihua bao [Vernacular Journal]. Shanghai, 1904.

Benton, Gregor. "The 'Second Wang Mang Line.' " *China Quarterly*, March 1975, pp. 61–95.

Bereznii, L. A. *A Critique of American Bourgeois Historiography on China: Problems of Social Development in the Nineteenth and Early Twentieth Centuries*. Leningrad, 1968; digested by Ellen Widner, Cambridge, 1968.

Bernal, Martin. *Chinese Socialism to 1907*. Ithaca, 1976.

Boorman, Howard, ed. *Biographical Dictionary of Republican China*. Vols. 1 and 2. New York, 1967.

Brandt, Conrad. *Stalin's Failure in China*. New York, 1958.

Brandt, Conrad; Schwartz, Benjamin; and Fairbank, John K., eds. *A Documentary History of Chinese Communism*. Cambridge, 1952.

Britton, Roswell S. *The Chinese Periodical Press*. Hong Kong, 1933.

Buren [I Cannot Bear It]. Shanghai, 1913–17.

Cai Hesen. "Lun Chen Duxiu Zhuyi" (On Chen Duxiuism). In Chen Dongxiao, *Chen Duxiu pinglun*.

"Caiji anqing daxuetang wubei xuetang tongcheng xuetang chengtu shi" [Another account of the conflict at Anqing's Upper Level School, the Military Preparatory Academy, and the Tongcheng Academy]. *Subao*, May 30, 1903.

Cai Yuanpei. "Preface." *Xin qingnian [New Youth]*. Vol. 1, 1935. Reprint.

————. *Cai Yuanpei zishu [Cai Yuanpei's autobiography]*. Taipei, 1971.

Chai Degeng et al., comps. *Xinhai geming [The revolution of 1911]*. Vol. 1. Shanghai, 1936.

Chang Hao. *Liang Ch'i-ch'ao and the Intellectual Transition in China, 1890–1907*. Cambridge, 1971.

Chang Hengfang. "Ji Anhui yuewang hui" [Remembrances of the Anhui Warrior Yue Society]. *Xinhai geming huiyi lu* 4:431–37.

————. "Shi lieshi jingwu zhuan" [The biography of martyr Shi Jingwu]. *Anhui wenxian*, vol. 4, no. 5 (1937).

Chang Kuo-t'ao. *The Rise of the Chinese Communist Party.* Vols. 1 and 2. Wichita, Kansas, 1971.

Chen Chunsheng. "Anhui zhi geming wenhua yundong" [The cultural movement during the revolution in Anhui]. *Guangxi yulin ribao*, Feb. 1, 1943.

Chen Dongxiao. *Chen Duxiu pinglun [Commentaries of Chen Duxiu].* Beijing, 1933.

Chen Duxiu. "Aiguoxin yu zijuexin" [Patriotism and self-consciousness]. *Jiayin zazhi* 4 (April 1915).

———. "Anhui aiguohui yanshuo" [Lecture to the Anhui Patriotic Society]. *Subao*, May 26, 1903.

———. "Anhui de meikuang" [Coal mining in Anhui]. *AHSHB* 2 (March 13, 1904).

———. "Baoshou zhuyi yu jinlue zhuyi" [Conservatism and invasionism]. *Xin qingnian*, vol. 7, no. 2 (Jan. 1, 1920).

———. "Beizhi wushen gaolun" [On being common rather than too lofty]. *XQN*, vol. 9, no. 3 (July 1, 1921):3.

———. "Bo Kang Youwei zhi zongtong zongli shu" [Refuting Kang Youwei's petition to the President and the Premier]. *XQN*, vol. 2, no. 2 (Oct. 1, 1916).

———. "Bowei makesi zhuyi" [Protect Marxism]. This is a collection of Chen Duxiu's letters from 1939 to 1941, published by the Chinese Trotskyites. No publication place or date given.

———. "Cai Zimin xiansheng cheshi houganyan" [Words on Cai Yuanpei's death]. In *Shian zizhuan.*

———. "Chaoxian duli yundong zhi ganxian" [Feelings about the Korean independence movement]. *MZPL* 14 (March 23, 1919).

———. *Chen Duxiu de zuihou jianjie* [Chen Duxiu's last opinions]. Taipei, 1959.

———. *Chen Duxiu xiansheng biansu zhuang* [Mr. Chen's written defense statement]. N.p., 1933.

———. *Chen Duxiu xiansheng jiangyan ji [Chen Duxiu's collected speeches].* Canton, 1923.

———. "Chu sanhai" [Eliminating the three evils]. *MZPL* 5 (Jan. 19, 1919); also in *DXWC*, vol. 1.

———. "Da guoji de xin" [A letter to the International]. *Wu zhanje* 9 (Jan. 30, 1931).

———. "Da Liuer shi (Ji Liu Renjing) tongzhi" [Answer to Liu Renjing]. *Wu zhanje* 9 (Jan. 20, 1931).

———. "Dangdai er da kexuejia zhi sixiang" [Thought of two great scientists of the present era]. *XQN*, vol. 2, no. 1 (Sept. 1, 1910) and vol. 2, no. 3 (Nov. 1, 1916).

———. "Diaohe lun yu jin daode" [The theory of compromise and the old ethics]. *XQN*, vol. 7, no. 1 (Dec. 1, 1919).

———. "Dikang li" [Power of resistance]. *XQN*, vol. 1, no. 3 (Nov. 1, 1915).

———. "Dongxi minzu genben sixiang zhi chayi" [The differences between the basic thought of the Eastern and Western peoples]. *XQN*, vol. 1, no. 4 (Dec. 15, 1915).

———. "Duide waijiao" [Relations with Germany]. *XQN*, vol. 3, no. 1 (March 1, 1917).

———. *Duxiu wencun [Chen Duxiu's collected writings]*. Vols. 1 and 2. Shanghai, 1922.

———. "Eluosi geming yu wo guomin zhi juewu" [The Russian revolution and our national awakening]. *XQN*, vol. 3, no. 2 (April 1, 1917).

———. "Eluosi yu wo guomin juewu" [The Russian revolution and our national awakening]. *XQN*, vol. 3, no. 2 (April 1, 1917).

———. "Ershi shijie eluosi de geming" [The twentieth century Russian revolution]. *MZPL* 18 (April 18, 1919).

———. "E supian" [Essay on evil customs]. Articles 1–4. *AHSHB* 3, 4, 6, and 7 (1904).

———. "Falanxi ren yu jinshi wenming" [The French and modern civilization]. *QN*, vol. 1, no. 1 (Sept. 15, 1915).

———. "Fan wendian tishi" [Preface to the Sanskrit Grammar]. *Tianyi bao* 6 (Sept. 1, 1907).

———. "Fubi yu zunkong" [Restoration and worshipping Confucius]. *XQN*, vol. 13, no. 6 (Aug. 1, 1917).

———. "Gangchang mingjiao" [The famous teachings of the three bonds]. *MZPL* 16 (April 6, 1919).

———. "Gao chuandang tongzhi shu" [A letter to all party comrades]. Shanghai, Dec. 10, 1929.

———. "Geming yu zuoluan" [Revolution and chaos]. *XQN*, vol. 8, no. 4 (Dec. 1, 1920).

———. "Guanggao" [Announcement]. *AHSHB* 12 (Aug. 1, 1904).

———. "Guanyu beijing daxue de yaoyan" [As to the rumors regarding Beijing University]. *MZPL* 13 (April 13, 1919).

———. "Guanyu shehui zhuyi de taolun" [A discussion of Socialism]. *XQN*, vol. 8, no. 4 (Dec. 1, 1920).

———. "Guanyu suowei hongjun wenti" [On the Question of the so-called Red Army]. *Wu zhanje*, July 1, 1930.

————. "Guoji pai yu shijie heping" [The Bolsheviks and world peace]. *XQN*, vol. 7, no. 1 (Dec. 1, 1919).

————. "Guomindang shi shenma?" [What is the Guomindang?]. *Xiangdao* 2 (Sept. 20, 1922).

————. "Guoqing jinian de jiazhi" [The value of celebrating the founding of the Republic]. *XQN*, vol. 8, no. 2 (Oct. 1, 1920).

————. "Guoyu jiaoyu" [The teaching of Mandarin]. *AHSHB* 3 (April 1, 1904).

————. "Hangzhou xing kushu jihuai Liu San Shen Er" [A hot summer day in Hangzhou thinking of Liu San and Shen Er]. *Jiayin zazhi*, vol. 1, no. 3 (Oct. 8, 1914).

————. "Hei tianguo" [Black Paradise]. *AHSHB* 11–15 (Aug. 1–Oct. 1, 1904).

————. "Honglou meng xinxu" [A new preface]. In Cao Xueqin, *Honglou meng [Dream of the Red Chamber]*. Shanghai, 1921.

————. "Huagong" [Chinese workers]. *XQN*, vol. 8, no. 4 (Dec. 1, 1920).

————. "Jiangshiyi xu" [Preface to Remembrances of Red Gauze]. *Jiayin zazhi*, vol. 1, no. 7 (Oct. 7, 1915).

————. "Ji Chen Zhongfu guanyu Su Manshu de tanhua" [Transcripts of a discussion with Chen Zhongfu concerning Su Manshu]. In Liu Wuji, *Su Manshu nianpu qi qita [A yearly record of Su Manshu and other items]*.

————. "Jidu jiao yu zhongguo ren" [Christianity and the Chinese]. *XQN*, vol. 7, no. 3 (Feb. 1, 1920).

————. "Ji Dai Jitao de yifengxin" [A letter to Dai Jitao]. *Xiangdao zhoubao* 129 (Sept. 11, 1925).

————. "Ji Jiang Jieshi de yifengxin" [A letter to Jiang Kai-shek]. *Xiangdao zhoubao* 157 (June 9, 1926).

————. "Jinri zhi jiaoyu fangzhen" [Present-day educational directions]. *QN*, vol. 1, no. 2 (Oct. 15, 1915); also in *DXWC*, vol. 1.

————. "Jinri zhongguo zhi zhengzhi wenti" [Present-day Chinese political problems]. *XQN*, vol. 5, no. 1 (July 15, 1918).

————. "Kaiban anhui suhuabao deyuan" [Reasons for publishing the *Anhui Common Speech Journal*]. *Anhui suhua bao* 1 (Feb. 1, 1904).

————. *Kangri zhanzheng zhi yiyi [The meaning of the war against Japan]*. Shanghai, 1937.

————. "Kexue yu rensheng guan xu" [A preface to science and the view of life]. *XQN*, Dec. 20, 1923.

Chen Duxiu. "Ku He Meishi." [Crying over Ku He Meishi]. *Jing-zhong ribao*, April 15, 1904.

———. "Ku Wang Xiyan" [Crying over Wang Xiyan]. *Guomin riri bao*, August 8, 1903.

———. "Kongzi zhidao yu xiandai shenghuo" [Confucianism and present-day life]. *XQN*, vol. 2, no. 4 (Dec. 1, 1916); also *DXWC*, vol. 1.

———. "Laodongzhe de juewu" [The awakening of the workers]. *XQN*, vol. 7, no. 6 (May 1, 1920).

———. "Liangge luxian" [The two roads]. *Xiaonei shenghuo* 1 (Dec. 1931).

———. "Lingyinshou qian" [In front of Hidden Spirit Temple]. *Jiayin zazhi*, vol. 1, no. 3 (Oct. 8, 1914).

———. "Lun anhui de guangwu" [On mining affairs in Anhui]. *AHSHB* 2 (March 15, 1904).

———. "Lun guomin zhengfu zhi beifa" [On the Northern Expedition of the national government]. *Xiangdao zhoubao* 161 (July 7, 1926).

———. "Lun xiqu" [On plays]. *AHSHB* 11 (Aug. 1, 1904).

———. "Maersi renkou lun yu zhongguo renkou wenti" [Malthus' theory of population and the Chinese population problem]. *XQN*, vol. 7, no. 5 (April 1, 1920).

———. "Meizhou pinglun fakan zu" [A statement on the publication of the *Weekly Critic*]. *Meizhou pinglun [Weekly Critic]* 1 (Dec. 22, 1918).

———. "Minzhudang yu gongchandang" [Democrats and Communists]. *XQN*, vol. 8, no. 4 (Dec. 1, 1920).

———. "Nongmin zai zhongguo geming de zuoyung ji chi qiantu" [The function and future of peasants in the Chinese Revolution]. *Huohua*, vol. 1, no. 9 (April 6, 1932).

———. "Ouzhan hou dongyang minzu juewu qi yaojin" [The aftermath of the European war and the awakening and demands of the Eastern people]. *MZPL* 2 (Dec. 29, 1918).

———. "Pinmin de kusheng" [The cry of the poor]. *MZPL* 19 (April 27, 1919).

———. "Pingmin jiaoyu" [Commoner's education]. Originally pub. March 5, 1922 in *Funu sheng* [Women's Voice] 3; republished in *DXWC*, vol. 1.

———. "Qinggao qingnian" [Call to Youth]. *Qingnian zazhi*, vol. 1, no. 1 (Sept. 15, 1915); also in *DXWC*.

————. "Rulin waishi xinxu" [A new preface to *The Scholars*]. In Wu Jingzi, *Rulin waishi* [The Scholars]. Shanghai, 1920.

————. "Sanlun Shanghai shehui" [A third time on Shanghai society]. *XQN*, vol. 8, no. 3 (Nov. 1, 1920).

————. "Shanghai housheng fangsha chang Hunan nugong wenti" [The Shanghai Benefit the Masses Spinning and Weaving Factory and the problem of the Hunan women workers]. *XQN*, vol. 7, no. 6 (May 1, 1920).

————. "Shanghai shehui" [Shanghai society]. *XQN*, vol. 8, no. 1 (Sept. 1, 1920).

————. *Shehui zhuyi taolun ji* [Collection of a discussion on socialism]. Guangzhou, 1922.

————. *Shian zizhuan* [Chen Duxiu's autobiography]. Taipei, 1967.

————. "Shiju zagan" [Miscellaneous feelings about the governmental situation]. *XQN*, vol. 3, no. 4 (June 1, 1917).

————. "Shixing minzhi de jichu" [The basis for the realization of democracy]. *XQN*, vol. 7, no. 1 (Dec. 1, 1919).

————. "Shu ai" [An expression of my grief]. *Jiayin zazhi*, vol. 1, no. 5 (May 10, 1913).

————. "Shui he cenmayang jiu zhongguo?" [Who and how to save China]. *Huohua*, July 28, 1930.

————. "Shuihu xinxu" [A new preface]. In Shi Naian, *Shuihu zhuan* [The Water Margin]. Shanghai, 1920.

————. "Shuuwen yin shen yixiao" [The speaking and writing inferred from the Yili and the Xiaojing]. *Guocui xuebao* [National Essence Journal] 6 and 7 (1910).

————. "Sun-Duan hezuo yu guomindang zhi mingyun" [The Sun-Duan cooperation and the destiny of the Guomindang]. *Xiangdao zhoubao* 94 (Dec. 10, 1924).

————. "Tan zhengzhi" [Talking politics]. *XQN*, vol. 8, no. 1 (Sept. 1, 1920).

————. "Ti Su Shanran tianwan tianshi" [Verse preface to Su Manshu's Sanskrit dictionary]. *Tianyi bao*, Sept. 1, 1907.

————. "Ti Xixiang nanzhou youlie tu" [An inscription for the hunting picture of General Saigo Nanshu]. *Guomin riri bao*, Aug. 17, 1903.

————. "Wangguo de yuanyin" [The reasons for lost country]. *AHSHB* 14 (Sept. 15, 1904), chap. 3.

————. "Wangguo pian" [Lost country article]. *AHSHB* 8 (June 15, 1904), chap. 1.

————. "Wang Yangming xiansheng xunmeng dayi dejie" [An ex-

planation of Wang Yangming's opinion on enlightening the youth].
AHSHB 14 and 16 (Sept. 15 and Oct. 1, 1904).

―――. "Wenxue geming lun" [On the literary revolution]. *XQN*, vol. 2, no. 6 (Feb. 1, 1917); also in *DXWC*, vol. 1.

―――. *Wo duiyu kangzhan de yijian [My opinion of the war of resistance].* Wuhan, 1938.

―――. "Women de zhenglun zhi zhongdian" [The central point of our dispute]. *Huohua*, vol. 1, no. 4 (Nov. 7, 1931).

―――. "Women xianzai weishenma zhengdou?" [Why are we now fighting?]. *Xiangdao zhoubao* 172 (Sept. 25, 1926).

―――. "Wo ren zuihou zhi juewu" [Our people's most recent awakening]. *XQN*, vol. 1, no. 6 (Feb. 15, 1916); also in *DXWC*, vol. 1.

―――. "Xiandai ouzhou wenhua shitan" [A discussion of the history of contemporary European literature]. *QN* 1:3 (Nov. 15, 1915) and 1:4 (Dec. 15, 1915).

―――, trans. "Xiandai wenming shi" [Histoire de la Civilisation Contemporaine]. *QN*, vol. 1, no. 1 (Sept. 15, 1915).

―――. "Xianfa yu kongjiao" [The constitution and Confucius]. *XQN* 2:3 (Nov. 1, 1916).

―――. *Xiaoxue shizi jiaoben [A textbook on recognizing characters].* Taipei, 1942.

―――. "Xianzai jiaoyu shang de quedian, yi zhuguan zhuyi, er xingshi zhuyi" [Present-day educational defects: One, objectivity; two, formalism]. *Minguo ribao*, March 21, 1920.

―――. "Xiaping de wuzhengfu dang" [Lower class anarchism]. *XQN*, vol. 9, no. 2 (June 1, 1921).

―――. "Xin jiaoyu de jingshen" [The spirit of the new education]. *Juewu*, Feb. 15, 1920.

―――. "Xin jiaoyu shi shenma?" [What is the new education?]. *XQN*, vol. 8, no. 6 (April 1, 1921).

―――. "Xin qingnian" [New Youth]. *XQN*, vol. 2, no. 1 (Sept. 1, 1916).

―――. "Xin wenhua yundong shi shenma?" [What is the New Culture movement?]. *XQN*, vol. 7, no. 5 (April 1, 1920).

―――. "Xuezhong xin youren deng wushan" [In the snow with friends climbing Wu mountain]. *Jiayin*, vol. 1, no. 3 (Oct. 8, 1914).

―――. *Yangzi jiang xingshi lunlue [An Account of the Topography of the Yangzi River].* Anqing, 1897.

―――. "Yemang wangyou He Meishi jue er fuci" [A night dream

about my lost friend He Meishi and then awakening and committing it to verse]. *Jingzhong ribao [The Alarm Bell Daily]*, May 7, 1904.

———. "Yeyu guangge da Shen Er" [Evening rain wild singing reply to Shen Er]. *Jiayin zazhi*, vol. 1, no. 7 (Oct. 7, 1915).

———. "Yi jiu yi liu nian." *QN*, vol. 1, no. 5 (1916); also in *DXWC*, vol. 1.

———. "Yonghe" [In praise of the crane]. *Jiayin zazhi*, vol. 1, no. 3 (Oct. 3, 1914).

———. "You hubao" [Traveling on Running Tiger Mountain]. *Jiayin zazhi*, vol. 1, no. 3 (Oct. 8, 1914).

———. "Yuanyu" [Distant Travel]. *Jiayin zazhi*, vol. 1, no. 7 (Oct. 7, 1915).

———. "Zailun kongjiao wenti" [Again on the problems of Confucianism]. *XQN*, vol. 2, no. 3 (Jan. 1, 1917).

———. "Zailun Shanghai shehui" [Again on Shanghai society]. *XQN*, vol. 8, no. 2 (Oct. 1, 1920).

———. "Zaoguo lun" [On building the nation]. *Xiangdao* 2 (Sept. 20, 1922).

———. "Zhengzhi gaizao yu zhengdang gaizao" [Governmental and political party change]. *XQN*, vol. 9, no. 3 (July 1, 1921).

———. "Zhi jiayin jizhe han" [A letter to the editor]. *Jiayin zazhi*, vol. 1, no. 2 (Oct. 6, 1914).

———. "Zhongguo guomin geming yu shehui ge jieji" [China's national revolution and the various social classes]. *Qianfeng [Vanguard]* 2 (Dec. 1, 1923).

———. "Zhongguo lidai de dashi" [Great events of Chinese history]. *AHSHB* 3–5 (April 1904).

———. "Zisha lun" [On Suicide]. *XQN*, vol. 7, no. 2 (Jan. 1, 1920).

———. *Ziyi leili* [Sample study of synonyms]. Shanghai, 1925.

———. "Zuijin Shanghai de gongren yundong yu dang de lingdao" [The recent Shanghai Worker's Movement and the leadership of the party]. *Huohua*, vol. 1, no. 6 (Nov. 30, 1931).

——— et al. "Women de zhengzhi yijian shu" [Our political views]. Dec. 25, 1929.

"Chen Duxiu ankai shenji" [A record of the trial of Chen Duxiu]. *Guowen zhoubao [National News Weekly]* 17 (May 1933).

Chen Duxiu yanjiu cankao ziliao, vol. 1: see *Anqingshi lishi xuehui*.

Chen Gongbo: see Ch'en K'ung-po.

Ch'en K'ung-po. *The Communist Movement in China*. New York, 1960.

Ch'en K'ung-po. *Hanfeng ji [Cold winter collection]*. Shanghai, 1944.

Chen Pan-tsu. "Reminiscences of the First Congress of the Communist Party of·China." *The Communist International*, Oct. 1936.

Ch'en Pi-lan (Chen Bilan). "Introduction." In Peng Shu-ts'e, *The Chinese Communist Party in Power*. New York, 1981.

Chen Shu. "Nuzi fuchou lun" [On women's revenge]. *Tianyi bao* 4. (July 25, 1907).

————. "Fangwen Chen Songnian tanhua jilu" [Record of an interview with Chen Songnian]. Draft prepared in manuscript form, confirmed and signed by Chen Songnian, May 25–26, 1979.

Chen Songnian. "Fangwen Chen Songnian tongzhi jilu" [Record of interviews with Chen Songnian]. Manuscript of an interview by Xi Xu and Sun Qiming, April 18–20, 1979, Anqing.

————. "Guanyu jiachan xingbai de huiyi" [Recalling the rise and fall of the family fortune]. Draft of an interview with Chen Songnian, July 29, 1980.

————. "Zaifang Chen Songnian tanhua jilu" [Another record of an interview with Chen Songnian], Nov. 1979. In *Anhui gemingshi yanjiu ziliao [Materials on the history of the revolution in Anhui]*, vol. 1; edited by Anhui sheng shehui kexuesuo lishi yanshi [Anhui provincial social science group historical research bureau].

Chen Xiawen. "Chen Xiawen tan Chen Duxiu" [Chen Xiawen discusses Chen Duxiu]. Interview by Chen Songnian, Zhang Dong, and Wan Fengyan in *Chen Duxiu yanjiu cankao ziliao*, vol. 1.

Chen Zhu. *Zhongguo sanwenshi [History of Chinese essays]*. Shanghai, 1936.

Chen Zifeng, "Bo Liewu xiansheng geming tanhua gao" [An outline of a discussion with Bo Wenwei]. 1941. Guomindang Historical Archives, Taiwan.

————. "Bo Wenwei jiu hen anhui dudu jingguo" [The proceedings in Bo Wenwei's assumption of the Anhui governorship]. In *Zhonghua minguo kaiguo wushinian wenxian*. Vol. 2, bk. 4.

Chesneaux, Jean. *The Chinese Labor Movement 1919–1927*. Stanford, 1968.

Chih Yu-ju (Zhi Youru). *Chen Duxiu nianpu [Yearly chronology of Chen Duxiu]*. Hong Kong, 1974.

————. "Ch'en Tu-hsiu: His Career and Political Ideas." In Chuntu Hsueh, *Revolutionary Leaders of Modern China*. Toronto, 1971, pp. 335–67.

Chow Tse-tsung. *The May Fourth Movement*. Stanford, 1967.
———. *Research Guide to the May Fourth Movement*. Cambridge, 1963.
Chu Minyi. "Hao gu" [Loving antiquity]. *Xin shijie* 24 (Nov. 30, 1907).
Chuanguo zhongwen qikan lianhe mulu [A union catalogue for the entire country's Chinese language material]. Beijing, 1961.
"Daotong ban" [The handling of the orthodoxy of precepts]. *Guomin riri bao* 2:33.
Dazhonghua [Great China]. Shanghai, 1915–16.
deBary, Wm. Theodore. *Self and Society in Ming Thought*. New York, 1970.
———. *Sources of Chinese Tradition*. Vol. 2. New York, 1960.
Deng Zhongxia. *Zhongguo zhigong yundong jianshi [A brief history of the Chinese labor movement]*. Beijing, 1953.
Deutscher, Isaac. *Lenin's Childhood*. New York, 1970.
———. *The Prophet Armed: Trotsky, 1879–1921*. New York, 1954.
———. *The Prophet Outcast: Trotsky, 1929–1949*. New York, 1963.
———. *The Prophet Unarmed: Trotsky, 1921–1929*. New York, 1959.
———. *Stalin*. New York, 1967.
Dov Bing. "Sneevliet and the Early Years of the CCP." *China Quarterly* 48 (Oct.-Dec. 1971).
DXWC: see Chen Duxiu, *Duxiu wencun*.
Elman, Benjamin. *From Philosophy to Philology: Intellectual and Social Aspects of Change in Late Imperial China*. Forthcoming, Harvard Univ. Press.
Engels, Friedrich. *The German Revolutions*. Chicago, 1967.
Erikson, Erik, ed. *The Challenge of Youth*. Garden City, N.Y., 1966.
Ershi jingwen bao [Warning on Russian Affairs News]. Shanghai, 1903–1904.
Fang Zhaoying. *Qingmo minchu yang xuesheng timing lu [A list of Chinese overseas students at the end of the Qing and the beginning of the Republic]*. Taipei, 1961.
Fang Zhiwu. "Fang Zhiwu huiyi Suhua bao shi yishou" [A poem on Fang Zhiwu's remembrances of the *Common Speech Journal*]. In *Anhui gemingshi yanjiu ziliao*, vol. 1.
Feng De. "Guanyu shian zizhuan" [Regarding Chen Duxiu's autobiography]. *Gujin [Old and New]* 6 (Feb. 20, 1942).
Feng Xu. "Zai wuhu ban xuetang" [The establishment of revolu-

tionary schools in Wuhu]. Manuscript from the Anhui Historical Society, Hefei, Anhui.

Feng Ziyou. *Geming yishi [Fragments of revolutionary history]*. Vols. 1–3. Taipei, 1965.

———. *Zhongguo geming yundong ershiliunian zuzhi shi [Twenty-six years' organizational history of the Chinese revolutionary movement]*. Shanghai, 1948.

———. *Zhonghua minguo kaiguo qian geming shi [A history of the revolution prior to the founding of the Republic of China]*. Shanghai, 1930.

Friedman, Edward. *Backwards towards Revolution*. Berkeley, 1974.

Fu Sinian. "Chen Duxiu an" [The Chen Duxiu case]. In Chen Dongxiao, *Chen Duxiu pinglun*.

Furth, Charlotte, ed. *The Limits of Change: Essays on Conservative Alternatives in Republican China*. Cambridge, 1976.

Gan Rou. "Jiaoyu" [Education]. *Baihua bao* 4 (Oct. 1904).

Gao Pingshu, ed. *Cai Yuanpei nianpu* [A yearly chronology of Cai Yuanpei]. Beijing, 1980.

Gao Yuhan. *Baihua dingpan [The hundred flowers pavilion path]*. Shanghai, 1933.

———. "Canyu Chen Duxiu xiansheng zangyi ganyan" [A grieved statement on Chen Duxiu's funeral]. *Da Gongbao*, June 4, 1942.

Gasster, Michael. *Chinese Intellectuals and the Revolution of 1911*. Seattle, 1968.

Ge Jingen. "Xinhai geming zai zhejiang" [The 1911 revolution in Chekiang]. In *Xinhai geming huiyi lu*, vol. 4, pp. 91–126.

Geming wenxian: see Luo Jialun, ed., *Geming wenxian*.

Geming xianlie zhuanji [Biographies of revolutionary martyrs]. Ed. by Comm. for Comp. of Materials on the Party History of the Central Committee of the KMT. Taipei, 1950.

Goldman, Merle, ed. *Modern Chinese Literature in the May Fourth Era*. Cambridge, 1971.

Grieder, Jerome, *Hu Shih and the Chinese Renaissance*. Cambridge, 1970.

———. *Intellectuals and the State in Modern China*. New York, 1981.

Guan Peng. "Anhui geming jishi" (Remembrances of the Revolution in Anhui). In *Zhonghua minguo kaiguo wushinian wenxian*. Set 2, vol. 15, pp. 253–57.

"Guanyu Chen Duxiu yinqin de xie qingkuang" [A few circumstances according to Chen Duxiu's relatives]. Draft of a series of interviews conducted in Aug. 1980, in author's possession.

Guo Xuyin. "Ping Chen Duxiu gei dangzhongyang sanfeng xin" [A criticism of the three letters Chen Duxiu sent to the Party Central Committee]. *Shanghai shifan xueyuan xuebao [Journal of Shanghai Teacher's College]* 2, 1979.

Guomin riri bao [China National Gazette]. Shanghai, 1907.

Guowen zhoubao [National News Weekly]. Tientsin, 1924–37.

Hackett, Roger. "Chinese Students in Japan, 1900–1910." In *Papers on China.* Vol. 3. Harvard University, East Asian Research Center. Cambridge, Mass., 1949.

Han Yi. "Huijia lun" [On the destruction of the family]. *Tianyi bao* 4 (July 25, 1907).

Harrison, James Pinckney. *The Long March to Power: A History of the Chinese Communist Party, 1921–1972.* New York, 1972.

Hatano Kenichi. *Chugoku hyosanto shi [A history of the Chinese Communist Party].* Vols. 1–5. Tokyo, 1961.

He Zhiyou, "Duxiu xiansheng sheng yishi shimo ji" [A remembrance of the full circumstances of Chen Duxiu's sickness and death]. In *Chen Duxiu yanjiu cankao ziliao,* vol. 1.

———. "Duxiu zhuzuo nian biao" [A chronology of Chen Duxiu]. In *Duxiu qizhong [Seven works by Duxiu].* Vol. 1, Galley proof copy, available at Library of Congress. Shanghai, 1948.

"Heian shijie xianzhuang" [Dark world supplement]. *Guomin riri bao* 4.

Hofheinz, Roy. *The Birth of the Rural Strategy.* Chaps. 1–3. Cambridge, 1977.

Holubnychy, Lydia. *Michael Borodin and the Chinese Revolution, 1923–1925.* Ann Arbor, 1979.

How, Julie Lien-ying. *The Development of Ch'en Tu-hsiu's Thought, 1915–1938.* Master's thesis, Columbia Univ., 1949.

Hsueh Chun-tu. *Huang Hsing and the Chinese Revolution.* Stanford, 1961.

———. *Revolutionary Leaders of Modern China.* London, 1971.

Hu Hanmin. "Zizhuan" [Autobiography]. In Luo Jialun, *Geming wenxian,* vol. 3.

Hu Hua. *Zhongguo geming shi jiangyi [A textbook of the history of the Chinese revolution].* Shanghai, 1951.

———. *Zhongguo renmin daxue dangshixi dangshi jinxiuban jianggao [An outline of a lecture for a class of advanced studies in party history for the party history department of People's University]*, no. 6, Beijing, Sept. 23, 1980.

———, ed. *Zhongguo xin minzhu zhuyi geming shi cankao ziliao [Reference materials on the history of China's new democratic revolution]*. Shanghai, 1951.

Hu Shi, "Chen Duxiu yu wenxue geming" [Chen Duxiu and the literary revolution]. In Chen Dongxiao, *Chen Duxiu pinglun*.

———. "Duo yanjiu xie wenti, xiao tan xie zhuyi" [More study of problems, less talk of isms]. *MZPL* 31 (July 20, 1919).

———. "Wenxue gailiang zhuyi" [Tentative proposals for the improvement of literature]. *XQN*, vol. 2, no. 5 (Jan. 1, 1917).

Huang Jilu. "Cai Yuanpei yu guofu de guanxi" [Cai Yuanpei's relations with Sun Yatsen]. *Zhuanji wenxue*, vol. 5, no. 3 (Sept. 1964).

Huang Mingji. *Su Manshu pingzhuan [A critical biography of Su Manshu]*. Shanghai, 1949.

Hubei xuesheng jie [Hubei Student world]. Tokyo, 1903.

Hummel, Arthur W. *Eminent Chinese of the Ch'ing*. Taipei, 1972.

Huohua [Spark]. Shanghai, Sept. 1931–Jan. 1937.

Isaacs, Harold, *The Tragedy of the Chinese Revolution*. New York, 1968.

Israel, John. *Student Nationalism in China, 1927–1937*. Stanford, 1966.

———. *Rebels and Bureaucrats: China's December 9ers*. Berkeley, 1976.

Jacobs, Dan. *Borodin: Stalin's Man in China*. Cambridge, 1981.

Jiang Menglin. "Tan zhongguo xin wenyi yundong" [A discussion of the Chinese new literature movement]. *Zhuanji wenxue [Biographical Literature]*, vol. 11, no. 3 (Sept. 1967).

Jiang Weiqiao. "Zhongguo jiaoyu huizhi huiyi" [Reminiscences of the Chinese Educational Society]. In Zhongguo shi xue hui.

Jiayin zazhi [The Tiger Magazine]. Tokyo and Shanghai, 1914–15.

Jiayin zhoukan [The Tiger Weekly]. Beijing, 1926–28.

"Jinggao Bo dudu qi ge sheng xingcheng ting" [Telling about Governor Bo Wenwei's administration]. *Duli zhoubao [Independence Weekly]* 10 (Nov. 24, 1912).

Jingzhong ribao [The Alarm Bell Daily]. Shanghai, 1904.

Kagan, Richard, trans. "Ch'en Tu-hsiu's Unfinished Autobiography." *China Quarterly* 50 (April–June 1972).

———. "The Chinese Trotskyist Movement and Ch'en Tu-hsiu: Culture, Revolution, and Polity." Ph.D. diss., Univ. of Pennsylvania, 1969.

―――. "From Revolutionary Iconoclasm to National Revolution: Ch'en Tu-hsiu and the Chinese Communist Movement." In F. Gilbert Chan and Thomas Etzold, *China in the 1920s: Nationalism and Revolution*, pp. 55–73. London, 1976.

Kang Ming. "Huidao Chen Duxiu furen" [Meeting Chen Duxiu's wife]. *Shehui xinwen [Societal Mercury]* vol. 1, no. 3 (Jan. 5, 1933), p. 59.

Kang Youwei. "Ni zhonghua minguo xianfa zaoan fafan" [Preface to a proposal of a constitution for the Republic of China]. *Buren* 3 (April 1913).

―――. "Zhonghua jiuguolun" [On the salvation of China]. *Buren* 1 (Feb. 1913).

Kimura Yasuko. "Chin Dokushu shippitsu katsudo nempu" [A chronology of the writing of Chen Duxiu]. *Kindai chugoko kenkyu senta iho* 2 (April 1963):17–28.

Kirby, E. Stuart. *Russian Studies of China*. Totawa, N.J., 1976.

Kovalev, E. F., ed. "Congress of the Communist Party in China." *Chinese Studies in History*, Spring 1974.

Krebs, Edward S. "Assassination in the Republican Revolutionary Movement." *Ch'ing-shih wen-t'i*, Dec. 1981, pp. 45–81.

Kuo, Thomas. *Ch'en Tu-hsiu and the Chinese Communist Movement*. South Orange, N.J., 1975.

Kuo, Warren. *Analytical History of the Chinese Communist Party*. Vols. 1 and 2. Taipei, 1968.

Kwok, D.W.Y. *Scientism in Chinese Thought*. New Haven, 1965.

Lang, Olga. *Pa Chin and His Writings: Chinese Youth Between Two Generations*. Cambridge, 1967.

Lee, Leo Ou-fan. *The Romantic Generation of Modern Chinese Writers*. Cambridge, 1973.

Lenin, V. I. *The National Liberation Movement in the East*. Moscow, 1957.

―――. *Selected Works*. Vols. 1–3. New York, 1967.

Levenson, Joseph. *Confucian China and Its Modern Fate*. 3 vols. Berkeley, 1958–1963.

―――. *Liang Ch'i-ch'ao and the Mind of Modern China*. Berkeley, 1967.

Levy, Marion. *The Family Revolution in Modern China*. New York, 1968.

Lewis, Charlton. "The Hunanese Elite and the Reform Movement, 1845–1898." *Journal of Asian Studies*, 39 (Nov. 1969).

———. *Prologue to the Chinese Revolution: The Transformation of Ideas and Institutions in Hunan Province, 1891–1907.* Cambridge, 1976.

Li Chien-nung. *The Political History of China.* Stanford, 1967.

Li Da. "Huiyi lao yuyang li erhao he dangde 'yida,' 'erda' " [Remembrances of Number 2 Yuyang Lane and the First and Second Party Congresses]. In *Dangshi ziliao* [Materials on party history]. Vol. 1. Shanghai, 1980.

Li Dazhao. "Fae geming shi bijiaoguan" [A comparison of the French and Russian revolutions]. In *Zhongguo jindai sixiang shi cankao ziliao jianbian*, edited by Shi Cun.

———. "Yanshi xin yu zijue xin" [Pessimism and self-consciousness]. *Jiayin zazhi*, vol. 1, no. 9 (Aug. 10, 1915).

———. "Zai lun wenti yu zhuyi" [Again on problems and isms]. *MZPL* 35 (Aug. 17, 1919).

Li Eng. *Hongse wutai [The red stage].* Beijing, 1946.

Li Fangun, ed. "Chen Duxiu nianbiao buzheng" [A correction of Chen Duxiu's yearly chronology]. In *Chen Duxiu yanjiu cankao ziliao*, vol. 1.

Li Shucheng. "Xuesheng zhi jingzheng" [Student struggle]. *Hubei xuesheng jie [Hubei Student World]* 2 (1903).

Liang Qichao. "Ouyou xinyinlu" [Impressions of a European journey]. *Shishi xinbao [The China Times]*, Shanghai, March 1919.

Lin Maosheng. "Guanyu Chen Duxiu yanjiu de yixie wenti" [A few problems in researching Chen Duxiu]. In *Zhongguo renmin daxue dangshixi dangshi jinxiuban jianggao [An outline of a lecture for a class of advanced studies in party history for the party history department of People's University]*, no. 6, Sept. 23, 1980.

———. "Dui Chen Duxiu pingjia de jige wenti" [Several problems in evaluating Chen Duxiu]. In *Zhongguo xiandai shijiao xue cankao ziliao*, edited by Hu Hua. Beijing, 1980.

Lin Yu-sheng. "Radical Iconoclasm in the May Fourth Period and the Failure of Chinese Liberalism." In *Reflections on the May Fourth Movement*, edited by Benjamin Schwartz.

———. *The Crisis of Chinese Consciousness: Radical Anti-Traditionalism in the May Fourth Era.* Madison, 1979.

Link, Perry. *Mandarin Ducks and Butterflies: Popular Fiction in Twentieth Century Chinese Cities.* Berkeley, 1981.

Liu Chang. "Shilun zhongguo fengjian shehui changqi yanyu de yu-

anyin" [A preliminary discussion of the reasons for the continuation of China's feudal society for such a long time]. *Lishi
yanjiu [History and Research]* 2, 1981.

Liu Shipei. *Liu Shenshu xiansheng yishu [Complete works of Liu
Shipei]*. Taipei, 1965.

———. "Wuzhengfu zhuyi zhi pingdengguan" [The anarchist's view
of equality]. *Tianyi bao* 5, Aug. 10, 1907.

Liu Wu-chi (Liu Wuji). *Su Man-shu*. New York, 1972.

———. *Su Manshu nianpu ji qida [A yearly record of Su Manshu
and other items]*. Shanghai, 1927.

Liu Yazi. *Su Manshu nianpu ji qida [Yearly chronology of Su Manshu
and others]*. Shanghai, 1927.

Lu Manyan. *Shixian bianji [Another record of contemporary wor-
thies]*. Chongqing, 1943.

"Lun baihuabao yu zhongguo qiantu zhi guanxi" [On the relationship between the vernacular papers and China's future road].
Jingzhong ribao [Alarm Bell Daily], April 5, 1904.

"Lun zike de jiaoyu" [On assassination education]. *Zhongguo baihua
bao [Chinese Vernacular Paper]* 8 (1904).

Luo Han. "Zhi Zhou Enlai deng yifeng gongkai xin" [An open letter
to Zhou Enlai and others]. *Zhengbao [Upright Daily]*, April 24–
25, 1938.

Luo Jialun. "Jinri zhi shijie xinjie" [The new tide of the present
world]. *Xinchao [New Tide]*, vol. 1, no. 1 (Jan. 1919).

———, ed. *Geming wenxian [A literary collection of the 1911 rev-
olution]*. Taipei, 1953–56.

Luo Jung-pang. *K'ang Yu-wei: A Biography and Symposium*. Tucson, 1967.

Lust, J. "The *Subao* Case: An Episode in the Early Chinese National
Movement." *Bulletin of the School of Oriental and African
Studies* 27, pp. 408–29.

Ma Xuhun. "Guanyou xinhai geming zhejiang shengcheng guangfu
jishi di buchong ziliao" [Supplementary material on the 1911
Revolution in the provincial capital of Chekiang]. *Jindai shi
ziliao* 1 (1957):47–57.

McAleavy, Henry. *Su Manshu: A Sino-Japanese Genius*. London,
1960.

Macrae, Donald. "The Culture of a Generation: Students and Others."
The Journal of Contemporary History, vol. 2, no. 3 (July 1967).

Malia, Martin. *Alexander Herzen and the Birth of Russian Socialism*.
New York, 1965.

Mao Dun. "Chuangzuo shengya de kaishi" [The beginning of a career in writing]. *Renmin ribao [People's Daily]*, April 3, 1981.
—— (Ershibahua). "Tiyu zhi yanjiu" [A study of athletics]. *XQN*, vol. 3, no. 2 (April 1, 1917).
Marx, Karl, and Engels, Friedrich. *Marx and Engels: Basic Writings on Politics and Philosophy*. Edited by Lewis S. Feuer. New York, 1959.
——. *Selected Works*. New York, 1968.
——. "Theses on Feuerbach." In K. Marx, *The German Ideology*, edited by C. J. Arthur. New York, 1970.
Mast, Herman. "Tai Chi-t'ao, Sunism and Marxism During the May Fourth Movement in Shanghai." In *Modern Asian Studies*, vol. 5, no. 3 (1971), pp. 227–49.
Matsumoto, Hideki. "Shin bunka undo ni sura Chin Dokushu no rikyu shiron" [Chen Duxiu's critique of Confucianism during the New Culture movement]. *Ritsumeikan Bunganku* 299 (May 1970).
Meisner, Maurice. *Li Ta-chao and the Origins of Chinese Marxism*. Cambridge, 1967.
—— and Murphey, Rhoads, eds. *The Mozartian Historian: Essays on the Works of Joseph R. Levenson*. Berkeley, 1976.
Meizhou pinglun [Weekly Critic]. Beijing, Dec. 1918–Aug. 1919.
Metzger, Thomas. *Escape from Predicament: Neo-Confucianism and China's Evolving Political Culture*. New York, 1977.
Miller, Joseph Thomas. *The Politics of Chinese Trotskyism: The Role of a Permanent Opposition in Communism*. Ph.D. diss., Univ. of Illinois at Urbana, 1979.
Ming-yuan. "Quxiaopai de xingcheng ji moluo" [The rise and fall of the leftist opposition]. In *Xiandai shiliao [Source materials of modern history]*, vol. 2. Shanghai, 1934.
Minguo ribao [Republic Daily]. Shanghai, 1915–31.
Moore, Barrington, *Social Origins of Dictatorship and Democracy: Lord and Peasant in the Making of the Modern World*. Boston, 1966.
Morse, H. B. *The International Relations of the Chinese Empire*. Shanghai, 1910.
MZPL: see *Meizhou pinglun*.
Nakajima Nagafumi. *Chin Dokushu ninpu chohen skoku [A first draft of a yearly chronology of Chen Duxiu]*. Kyoto Sangyo Daigaku Ronshu (Kyoto Industrial University Papers), no. 3.

Gaikokugo to Bunka Keiretsu [Foreign language and cultural series], vol. 2, no. 1 (March 1972).

Nakamuro Tadayuki. "Shin Chingoku miraiki kusetsu chugoku bungei ni oyoberu Nippon bungei no eit yo no ichirei" [A study of *Xin Zhongguo weilai ji*]. *Tenri daigaku gakuho*, vol. 1, no. 1 (May 1949).

Nanjing Linshi Jengfu Gongbao [The proclamations of the Nanjing temporary government], no. 24 (Feb. 28, 1912), as published in *Xinhai geming ziliao [Material on the 1911 revolution]*, Beijing, 1961.

Nihon University Bulletin. Tokyo, 1971–72.

Nivinson, David. "The Problem of 'Knowledge' and 'Action' in Chinese Thought Since Wang Yang-ming." In *Studies in Chinese Thought*, edited by Arthur C. Wright. Chicago, 1967.

North, Robert. *Moscow and Chinese Communists.* Stanford, 1953.

"Novye materialy of pervom s'ezde Kommunisteskoi Partii Kitaia" [New materials on the first Congress of the Communist Party of China]. *Norody Azii i Africa [Peoples of Asia and Africa]* 6 (1972):50–58.

"Nuli yu xu" [A preface to slave jail]. In *Guomin riribao*, vol. 1, no. 4.

Peng Ming. "Wusi shiqi de Li Dazhao he Chen Duxiu" [Li Dazhao and Chen Duxiu in the May Fourth period]. *Lishi yanjiu* 6 (1962):52.

P'eng Shu-ts'e (Peng Shuzhi). "Introduction." In Leon Trotsky, *Leon Trotsky on China.*

————. *The Chinese Communist Party in Power.* New York, 1981.

Peng Shuzhi. "Zhongguo diyige gongchan zhuyi xiaozu shi zenyang xingchengde?" [How did the first communist group take form?]. *Shiyue pinglun [October Magazine]*, vol. 7, no. 5 (June 20, 1980).

Price, Donald C. *Russia and the Roots of the Chinese Revolution, 1896–1911.* Cambridge, 1974.

Pu Qingquan. "Wo suo zhidao de Chen Duxiu" [The Chen Duxiu that I knew]. In *Wenshi ziliao xuanji [Materials on literature and history]*, no. 71. Beijing, 1980.

Qingnian [Youth]: see also *Xin Qingnian*.

"Qingnian jun" [The Youth Army]. *Xue Feng* 4 (July 1, 1934).

Qiwu laoren. "Zhongguo gongchanandang chengli qianhou de jianwen" [That seen and heard after the establishment of the Chinese

Communist party]. *Xin guancha [New Observer]* 13 (July 1, 1937).

QN: see *Xin Qingnian.*

Rankin, Mary Backus. *Early Chinese Revolutionaries: Radical Intellectuals in Shanghai and Chekiang, 1902–1911.* Cambridge, 1971.

Ren Jianshi, Wu Xinzhong, and Zhang Tongmo. "Chen Duxiu he Anhui suhua bao" [Chen Duxiu and the *Anhui Vernacular Journal*]. In *Dangshi ziliao [Materials on party history]*, vol. 1 (1980).

"Ruhe pingjie Chen Duxiu gong yu guo?" [How do we evaluate the contributions of Chen Duxiu?]. *Jiefang junbao [Liberation Army News]*, Oct. 14, 1979.

Russell, Bertrand. *The Problem of China.* New York, 1966.

Sanai. See Chen Duxiu.

Scalapino, Robert, and Yu, George. *The Chinese Anarchist Movement.* Berkeley, 1961.

Schiffrin, Harold. *Sun Yat-sen and the Origins of the Chinese Revolution.* Berkeley, 1970.

Schneider, Lawrence A. *Ku Chieh-kang and China's New History.* Los Angeles, 1971.

Schram, Stuart. *Chairman Mao Talks to the People.* New York, 1974.

Schwartz, Benjamin. "Ch'en Tu-hsiu and the Acceptance of the Modern West." *Journal of the History of Ideas*, Jan. 1951.

———. *Chinese Communism and the Rise of Mao.* Cambridge, 1952.

———. "The Intelligentsia in Communist China: A Tentative Comparison." *Daedalus*, Summer 1960, pp. 604–21.

———. *In Search of Wealth and Power: Yen Fu and the West.* Cambridge, 1964.

———, ed. *Reflections on the May Fourth Movement.* Cambridge, 1972.

———. "Some Polarities in Confucian Thought." In *Confucianism in Action*, edited by D. S. Nivison and A. F. Wright. Stanford, 1959.

Seignobos, Charles. *History of Contemporary Civilization.* Trans. by James Alton James. New York, 1909.

Shen Ji. "Chen Duxiu he Anhui suhua bao" [Chen Duxiu and the *Anhui Common Speech Journal*]. In *Anhui gemingshi yanjiu ziliao*, vol. 1.

Shen Ji. "Xinhai geming shiqi de yuewang hui" [The Warrior Yue

Society at the time of the 1911 Revolution]. *Lishi yanjiu [Historical Research]* 10 (1979).

Shen Yinmo. "Wo he Chen Duxiu" [Chen Duxiu and I]. In *Chen Duxiu yanjiu cankao ziliao.*

Shi Diemin. "Ji Guangfu hui ersan shi" [Recollections of two or three things about the Restoration Society]. *Xinhai geming huiyi lu* 4:131–34.

Shi Jun. *Zhongguo gongchangdang zhi laiyuan [The origin of the Chinese Communist Party].* Beijing, 1957.

———, ed. *Zhongguo jindai sixiang shi cankao ziliao jianbian [Source materials for the study of modern China].* Beijing, 1957.

Shimizu Yasuzo. *Shina Todei Shih jin wu [New personages in China].* Tokyo, 1924.

Shiyue pinglun [October Magazine]. Hong Kong, 1976–82.

Snow, Edgar. *Red Star over China.* New York, 1961.

Spector, Stanley. *Li Hung-chang and the Huai Army.* Seattle, 1964.

Stalin, J. V. "Questions of the Chinese Revolution: Thesis for Propagandists." In *Works,* vol. 9. Moscow, 1955.

Su bao [The Kiangsu Journal]. Shanghai, May 6–July 7, 1903; reprint ed., Taipei, 1965.

Su Manshu, trans. *Beican shijie [Les Misérables].* In *Su Manshu chuanji.*

———. *Manshu dashi chuanji [The collected works of the Reverend Manshu].* Edited by Wen Gongzhi. Shanghai, 1934.

———. *Su Manshu chuanji [The complete works of Su Manshu].* Taipei, 1973.

Sun Dezhong. *Cai Yuanpei xiansheng yiwen leichao [A topical selection of Cai Yuanpei's writings].* Taipei, 1960.

Sun Qiming. "Chen Duxiu shifou hanjian wenti de tantao" [An inquiry into the question of whether or not Chen Duxiu was a traitor]. *Anhui daxue xuebao [Anhui University Journal]* 2 (1980).

Sun Zhuanyuan. "Anhui geming jilue." [Remembrances of the revolution in Anhui]. *Xue Feng [Literary Current],* Jan. 1934.

———. "Xinhai geming qian anhui wen jiao jie de geming huodong" [The revolutionary cultural movement in Anhui before the 1911 revolution]. In *Zhonghua minguo kaiguo wushinian wenxian,* vol. 2, chap. 15.

T'ang Leang-li. *The Inner History of the Chinese Revolution.* London, 1930.

Tang Lushi [Zheng Chaolin]. "Weixin yundong de jieji jichu he jiefang yiyi" [The class basis and liberation intentions in the reform movement]. *Jiuzhen [Seeking the Truth]* 3 (July 1, 1946).

Tao Kangle, "Dui Chen Duxiu youqing jihui zhuyi luxian xingcheng de yidian renzhi" [A little understanding of the circumstances behind Chen Duxiu's right-wing opportunism]. *Dangshi yanjiu* 5 (1980).

Tianyi bao [Journal of Natural Rights]. Tokyo, 1907–8; reprint ed., Tokyo 1966.

Trotsky, Leon. *Leon Trotsky on China*. New York, 1976.

————. *Tuoluociji danganzhong zhi zhongguo tongzhi dexin [From the Trotsky archives, letters sent to the Chinese comrades]*. Trans. by Shaungshan (Wang Fanxi). Hong Kong, 1981.

————. "Tuoluociji tongzhi ji 'women di hua' pai xin" [A letter from comrade Trotsky to the 'Our Talk' faction]. *Wu zhanje* 9 (Jan. 30, 1931).

Wakeman, Frederick, Jr. *History and Will: Philosophical Perspectives of Mao Tse-tung's Thought*. Berkeley, 1973.

———— and Grant, Carolyn, eds. *Conflict and Control in Late Imperial China*. Berkeley, 1975.

Walicki, A. *The Controversy Over Capitalism*. Oxford, 1969.

Wang Fan-hsi. *Chinese Revolutionary*. Trans. by Gregor Benton. Oxford, 1980.

———— (Yi Ding). "Pu zhu 'wo suo zhidao de Chen Duxiu' jiumiu" [Correcting the mistakes in the work by Pu 'The Chen Duxiu that I Knew']. In *Zhongbao yuekan*. Hong Kong, 1980.

————. *Shuangshan huiyi lu [Shuangshan's (Wang Fan-hsi) memoirs]*. Hong Kong, 1977.

Wang Mengzou. "Dongya jianshi" [A brief history of the East Asian Publishing House]. In *Anhui geming yanjiu ziliao*, vol. 1.

Wang Senran. *Jindai ershi jia pingzhuan [Critical biographies of twenty contemporary Chinese]*. Beijing, 1934.

Wang Yilin. "Chen Duxiu yu tuopai" [Chen Duxiu and the Trotskyites]. *Anhui daxue xuebao* 2 (1980).

Wang Yimin. "Anhui guangfu jingguo yu dudu de jingdou" [The struggle for the governorship in the 1911 revolution in Anhui]. In *Xinhai geming huiyi lu*, vol. 4.

Wang Yongchun and Chen Jiaxia. "Chen Duxiu zai guogong hezuo wenti shang de sixiang bianhua" [The transformations in Chen Duxiu's thought on the question of cooperation between the Communists and the Nationalists]. *Dangshi yanjiu* 5 (1980).

Wang Yugao. "Bo Wenwei zhuan" [Biography of Bo Wenwei]. *Anhui wenxian*, vol. 1, no. 4 (Jan. 1948).

Wen Gongzhi: see Su Manshu.

Wilbur, C. M., and How, Julie Lien-ying. *Documents on Communism, Nationalism, and Soviet Advisors in China*. New York, 1956.

Wolin, Sheldon. *Hobbes*. Los Angeles, 1970.

———. *Politics and Vision*. Boston, 1960.

Wright, Mary C. *China in Revolution, the First Phase*. New Haven, 1968.

———. *The Last Stand of Chinese Conservatism*. New York, 1966.

Wu K'un-jung. "The Leftist Opposition Faction in the Chinese Communist Party." *Issues and Studies*, pt. 1, March 1974.

Wu Xiangxiang. *Minguo bairen zhuan [Biographies of 100 people of the Republic]*. Vols. 1–3. Taipei, 1971.

Wu Yue. "Zixu" [Personal introduction]. In Feng Ziyou, *Geming yishi*, vol. 3.

Wu zhanje [The Proletariat]. Shanghai, March 1930–March 1931.

Wu Zhihui. "Zhang Shizhao—Chen Duxiu—Liang Qichao." In *Wu Zhihui xiansheng wencun*. Taipei, 1969.

Xiang Qing. "Guanyu gongchan guoji he zhongguo geming wenti" [On the question of the Communist International and the Chinese revolution]. *Beijing daxue xuebao* 6 (1979).

Xiangdao zhoubao [Guide Weekly]. Shanghai, 1922–27.

Xiaonei shenghuo [School Life]. Shanghai, May 1932–April 1934.

Xiebin. *Mingguo zhengdang shi [A political history of the Republican period]*. Taipei, 1962.

Xinchao [New Tide]. Beijing, 1919–22.

Xin guancha [New Observer]. Beijing, 1954–58.

Xinhai geming huiyi lu: see Zhongguo renmin zhengzhi xieshang huiyi chuanguo yanjiu weiyuan hui.

XQN: see *Xin Qingnian*.

Xin Qingnian [New Youth]. Shanghai, Beijing, and Canton, 1915–26.

Yan Duhou. "Xinhai geming shiqi Shanghai xinwenjie dongtai" [Developments in Shanghai newspaper circles around the time of the 1911 revolution]. In *Xinhai geming huiyi lu*, vol. 4.

"Yang Dusheng zhuan" [Biography of Yang Dusheng]. *Geming xian lie jinzhuan [Biographies of revolutionary martyrs]*. Taipei, 1950.

Yang Yuchiung. *Zhongguo zhengdang shi [The history of China's political party]*. Shanghai, 1937.

Yang Zhihua, ed. *Wentan shiliao [Historical materials in the literary world]*. Shanghai, 1944.

Yi Baisha. "Kongzi pingyi" [An appraisal of Confucius]. *XQN*, vol. 2, no. 1 (Sept. 1, 1916).

Ying Yueli and Sun Hui, "Guanyu woguo shehui zhuyi gaizao houqi de jige lilun wenti" [On several theoretical problems in the later period of our nation's socialist transformation]. *Nanjing daxue xuebao [Nanjing University Journal]* 4 (1980).

Young, Ernest. *The Presidency of Yuan Shih-k'ai*. Ann Arbor, 1977.

Yu, George. *Party Politics in Republican China: The Kuomintang 1912–1914*. Berkeley, 1966.

Yu Yechu. "Yu Yechu cang Liu Yazi Zhu Shaopin shu" [Letter from Yu Yechu to Liu Yazi and Zhu Shaopin]. In *Manshu dashi jinian ji* [Memorial collection of Master Su Manshu], edited by Liu Wuji. Shanghai, 1949.

Yu Yimi, ed. *Wuhu Xianzhi [Wuhu District Gazette]*. Wuhu, 1919.

Zhang Binglin: see Zhang Taiyan.

Zhang Jinglu. *Zhongguo xiandai chuben shiliao [Source materials for the publication history of contemporary China]*. Shanghai, 1954.

Zhang Jun, Xie Xunsheng, and Shi Dunnan. "Chen Duxiu jiashi gaolue" [A brief study of Chen Duxiu's family history]. *Chen Duxiu yanjiu ziliao*.

Zhang Pengyuan. "Liang Qichao dui shehui zhuyi de renshi qi zhongguo xiandaihua de jianjie" [An understanding of Liang Qichao's recognition of socialism and China's modernization]. *Shihuo yuekan*, vol. 3, no. 10 (Jan. 15, 1974).

Zhang Shizhao. "Zijue" [Self-consciousness]. *Jiayin*, vol. 1, no. 3 (July 10, 1918).

——— (Chiutong). "Kongjiao" [Confucianism as a religion]. *Jiayin zazhi*, vol. 1, no. 1 (May 1914).

———. "Shuangping ji" [A record of both sides of the chess board]. *Jiayin zazhi*, vol. 1, no. 4 (Oct. 11, 1914).

———. "Shu huangdi hun" [Comments on the spirit of the yellow emperor]. In *Xinhai geming huiyi lu*, vol. 1, pp. 212–304.

———. "Subao an shimo jixu" [A complete narration of the *Subao* case]. In *Xinhai geming [The revolution of 1911]*. Vol. 1. Compiled by Chai Degeng et al. Shanghai, 1956.

———. "Wu Zhuhui—Liang Qichao—Chen Duxiu." *Jiayin zhoukan*, vol. 1, no. 30 (Feb. 6, 1926).

———. "Yu Huang keqiang xiangjiao shimo" [The complete account of my interchange with Huang Xing]. *Xinhai geming huiyi lu*, vol. 2, pp. 138–50.

Zhang Taiyan. *Qiushu [Book of raillery]*. Shanghai, 1958.

————. "Yanshuo lu" [A record of a speech]. *Minbao [People's Paper]* 6 (July 1906):10–11.

————. *Zhangshi congshu [The complete works of Zhang Taiyan]*. Chengtu, 1943.

————. *Zhang Taiyan nianpu zhangpian [A yearly chronology of Zhang Taiyan]*. Edited by Tang Zhidiao. Beijing, 1979.

Zhang Yongtong and Liu Chuanxue, eds. *Houqi de Chen Duxiu jiqi wenzhang xuanbian [A collection edition of Chen Duxiu's later essays]*. Sichuan, 1980.

Zhao Guo. "Qingmo anhui zhi zhongdeng jiaoyu" [Middle school education in Anhui at the end of the Qing]. *Xue Feng*, July 1, 1955.

Zheng Chaolin: see Tang Lushi.

Zhengxie anhui sheng weiyuanwei wenshi ziliao gongzuo zu [The literary and historical materials work organization of the United Anhui Provincial Consultative Committee]. "Ji Hanyan" [Remembrance of Han Yan]. In *Xinhai geming huiyi lu*, vol. 4.

Zheng Xuejia, *Zhonggong xingwang shi [A history of the rise and fall of the Chinese Communist party]*. Vols. 1 and 2. Taipei, 1970.

"Zhen nuli" [An exhortation to slaves]. *Guomin riri bao*, vol. 1, no. 1.

"Zhen xiaonian" [Admonition to youth]. *Guomin riri bao*, vol. 1, no. 4.

Zhi Yuru: see Chih Yu-ju.

Zhiguang. "Chen Duxiu de shengping ji chi zhengzhi zhuzhang" [The life and political views of Chen Duxiu]. In Chen Dongxiao, *Chen Duxiu pinglun*.

"Zhonggong zhongyang da Duxiu tongzhi guanyu zhongdonglu wenti de diyixin" [A reply from the Central Committee of the Chinese Communist Party to comrade Chen Duxiu's first letter concerning the problem of the Chinese Eastern Railway Incident]. In *Zhongguo geming yu jihui zhuyi*.

Zhongguo baihua bao [Chinese Vernacular Paper]. Shanghai, 1903–1904.

Zhongguo geming wenti lunwen ji [A collection of essays on the problems of the Chinese revolution]. Shanghai, 1927.

Zhongguo geming yu jihui zhuyi [The Chinese revolution and opportunism]. Shanghai, 1929.

"Zhongguo gongchan zhuyi zuopai fanduipai de ganling" [Program of the Chinese leftist opposition faction]. *Wu zhanje* 9 (Jan. 30, 1931).

Zhongguo gongchandang zhi toushi [An anatomy of the Chinese Communist Party]. Nanjing, 1935.

Zhongguo guomindang zhongyang jiancha weiyuan hui [Chinese Guomindang Central Control Commission], *Danhe gongchandang liangda yaoan [Two important documents impeaching the Chinese Communist party]*. N.p., 1927.

Zhongguo renmin zhengzhi xieshang huiyi chuanguo yanjiu weiyuan hui wenshi ziliao yanjiu weiyuan hui [Committee on written materials of the national committee of Chinese People's Political Consultative Conference), ed. *Xinhai geming huiyi lu [Remembrances of the 1911 Revolution]*. Vols. 1–5. Beijing, 1961–63.

Zhongguo shi xue hui [Chinese historical society]. *Xinhai geming* [The 1911 Revolution]. Vols. 1–5. Shanghai, 1957.

Zhonghua minguo kaiguo wushinian wenxian bianzuan weiyuan hui [Committee on compilation of documents on the 50th anniversary of the founding of the Republic of China]. *Zhonghua minguo kaiguo wushinian wenxian [Documents on the fiftieth anniversary of the founding of the Republic of China]*. Series 1, 18 vols. Taipei, 1964.

"Zhonghua minguo zhiqian Anhui yu geming dangren zhi huodong" [The movement of the revolutionary party in Anhui before the founding of the Republic]. In *Zhonghua minguo kaiguo wushinian wenxian*. Series 1, vol. 12. Taipei, 1963.

Zhou Fuhai. *Wangyi ji [Recollections of my past]*. Hong Kong, 1955.

Zhou Yawei. "Guangfu jianwen zayi" [Miscellaneous remembrances seen and heard during the revolution]. In *Xinhai geming huiyilu*, vol. 1.

Zhou Zouran. *Zhitang huixiang lu [Remembrances of Zhitang]*. Hong Kong, 1970.

Zhuanji wenxue [Biographical literature]. Taipei, 1962–77.

INDEX

agrarian revolution, 198
Alarm Bell, 68, 70, 100n.8
Alliance Society. *See* Tongmenghui
anarchism, 56, 85, 148, 153–56,
   163, 192, 231
anarchists, 85, 148, 192, 231
anarcho-socialist doctrines, 142
Anhui, 25, 29, 33–34,37n.47, 39,
   48, 56, 61, 65, 70–73, 76–77,
   79–80, 82, 86, 88–90; gentry of,
   76, 90, 167; Qing forces of, 91;
   revolutionary movements of, 93,
   231; scholar-gentry class of, 88,
   89n.95
Anhui Academy, 47
Anhui Army, 93
Anhui Common Speech Journal,
   56, 60–68, 71–78, 80, 84, 88,
   91, 100–101, 107, 111–12, 123,
   127, 135, 150; circulation of,
   88–90; in vernacular, 61–62
Anhui Military Academy, 81
Anhui Mining Company, 65
Anhui Patriotic Society, 37n.47,
   39–42, 44, 48–49, 57, 59–61,
   90, 94; and *Subao*, 49
Anhui Public School, 75–76,
   81n.70, 93
Anhui Upper Level School, 40–41,
   92
Anhui Vernacular Journal, 81n.70
Anqing, 25, 29, 32, 34, 61, 79, 81,
   91n.100, 230
Asian Cousins Society, 85–86
Asian Study Society, 83n.76
assassination, 55, 80; squads, 111,
   231

Ba Jin, 26
Beida. *See* Beijing University

Beijing, 25, 79, 92, 101, 111, 121,
   129–30, 142, 154–56, 163, 171–
   72, 180, 186
Beijing University, 68, 77, 98, 109,
   111–12, 130–32, 167–68, 175,
   207, 211, 232; and Cai Yuanpei,
   68
Beiyang military, 110
Bolsheviks, 138, 140, 147, 159,
   164–65, 177, 197; organization
   of, 148, 158; and nationalistic
   upheavals, 177
Bolshevik Revolution, 4, 7, 16,
   137, 139, 141–42, 159–60, 177
Borodin, 18, 172, 185–88, 190,
   191–93
Boxer Rebellion, 42
Bo Wenwei, 76, 79–81, 91n.100,
   92–93
British, 76–77, 88, 89n.95, 90
Bronstein, Leon. *See* Trotsky
Buddhism, 10, 67–68, 74, 84–85
Bukharin, 189
bureaucracy, xiii, 93, 157, 165,
   203, 215
Burtman, N., 163

Cai Hesen, 17, 169, 200
Cai Yuankang, 55
Cai Yuanpei, 41, 55–56, 62, 76,
   111–12, 130, 142, 231, 237; and
   Beijing University, 68
Canton Insurrection, 201
Canton line, 185
censorship, 132
Central Committee, 164, 169–70,
   176, 185, 188, 192, 198, 201–4,
   206, 209, 214–215, 217; of the
   leftist opposition, 216
Chan Buddhism. *See* Zen Buddhism

nonreligious utilitarian doctrine, 121; and political culture, 205; and tradition, 105; and Western ideas, 105
Cultural Revolution, 224, 229–30

Dai Jitao, 19, 107, 142, 160, 190
Daoism, 96
Deng Zhongxia, 200
Dewey, John, 145–47, 159
Ding Ling, 234
dictatorship of the proletariat, 153–54
Dream of the Red Chamber, 71, 86, 226–27
Duan Fang, 81
Duan Qirui, 109–11, 115, 234; government of, 112

East Asia Book Company, 61
Elman, Benjamin, 14
Enming, 81–82
etymology, 225–26
examination system, 28–29, 31–33, 88; abolition of, 58

family, 77, 120–21, 134–35, 225–26; and Chinese tradition, 66, 104; and nation, 67, 86
February Revolution, 129–30, 138, 140
Feng Yuxiang, 144
Feng Ziyou, 38
Fifth Party Congress, 189, 191
First National Congress, 167–68
First United Front, 185
Fourth Congress of the International, 179
France, 82n.74, 83, 106–8, 115, 135, 142; Chen Duxiu's devotion to, 82–83
French Revolution, 138, 140
Furth, Charlotte, 63–64

Galen, General, 185, 187

Gao Junman, 53, 85
Gao Junyu, 169
Gao Xiaomen, 34
Gao Yihan, 113
gentry, 30, 86–88, 91, 94, 103, 125; and youth, 49
German Social Democrats, 155
Germany, 106, 108–10, 115, 135, 138; and anti-imperialism, 108
Gong Baochuan, 55
Gongyang school, 9
Good Friends Society, 109–10
Great China, The, 100n.8
Great Proletarian Cultural Revolution. *See* Cultural Revolution
Guangzhou naval academy, 33
Gui Bohua, 84
Guo Morou, 202
Guomindang, 109, 111–12, 139, 153, 160, 166, 169–70, 173–76, 178–80, 184–88, 191–92, 194, 197, 201, 204, 207, 217, 220–22, 231, 232n.2; and Chen Duxiu, 160, 166, 169–70; criticism of democracy by, 208–9; forces of, 225; leaders of, 221; secret police of, 216; and United Front, 17. *See also* KMT

Han dynasty, 58
Han learning, 28, 33, 73–74, 121
Han Yan, 238; and Youth Army, 91n.100
Hangzhou conference, 171
Hankow Beijing Railway Workers Union, 172
He Haiqiao, 55
He Jifeng, 222
He Meishi, 52
Hu Hanmin, 11, 160
Hu Shi, 98, 112–13, 128, 130, 154–55, 180, 225, 231n.2, 232; and literary reform, 124–25
Huai Army. *See* Li Hongzhang
Huaining district, 88

Huang Di. *See* yellow ancestor
Huang Xing, 75, 92
Hubei Student World, 39–40, 46
Hundred Days of Reform, 31, 33

iconoclasm, 21, 29, 32, 35, 54, 57,
70, 221, 228, 234; teachings of,
35–36; tradition of, 59; and
Chinese tradition, 97
imperialism, 10, 12, 18, 28, 42,
58–59, 62, 64, 85, 94, 110, 138,
144, 159, 177–79, 184–85, 195,
201, 203–4, 209; and German
opposition to, 108; and new government, 94
industry, 182n.35; in cities, 146;
and revolution, 162; underdevelopment of, 158
intelligentsia, 29–30, 104, 106–7,
114, 178
Isaacs, Harold, 211

Japan, 34, 37–40, 67, 74, 81n.70,
82n.74, 83–84, 93, 138, 140–41,
200, 217, 223, 227; aggression
of, 220; invasion of, 225; threat
of, 148; troops of, 221–22; and
Western ideas, 95; and Youth
Society, 51
Jiang Kaishek, 17, 170, 187–92,
203, 207, 212–13, 217, 220
Jiang Menglin. *See* Jiang Monlin
Jiang Monlin, 132
Jiangnan area, 58
Jiangxi soviet, 210
junzi, 105, 115, 129
Jurcheds, 78
juren, 33, 87

Kagan, Richard, 103n.11
Kerensky, Alexsandr, 212
Kang Youwei, 9–11, 32, 34, 66,
69, 73, 102, 117, 119, 120–22,
136, 141, 143, 194, 196, 228;
and Confucian society, 118; and

reform groups, 30, 32–33
kaozhen, 10, 28, 36, 58, 69, 117,
121, 228, 234; scholarships of,
127; school of evidential research, 14
Karakhan manifesto, 159
Ke Wenzhong, 239
KMT, 18, 23n, 110, 131, 142,
168–74, 176, 183–84, 189, 192,
201–2, 208; dragnet of, 216; organization of, 171; and sham democracy, 201. *See also* Guomindang
Korean Christian Socialist movement, 146, 159
Korean independence movement,
143
Kuo, Thomas, 82n.74, 205n.24

labor secretariat, 172
land reform policy, 189, 191, 203
Lenin, xii, 102, 138, 147, 153,
164, 175, 177–78, 193–94,
204, 222, 228; on imperialism,
178–79; Leninist organization,
157
Les Misérables, 54–55
Levenson, Joseph, 12
Li Dazhao, 43, 98, 108, 112–13,
129, 138–40, 148–49, 154–56,
163–64, 169–70, 174, 196
Li Guangjiung, 75, 80, 93
Li Hongzhang, 75–76, 86, 88,
89n.95, 93; and Huai Army, 88,
93
Li Jingmai, 75
Li Shucen, 40
Li Yuanhong, 109
Li Zhi, 34, 58
Liang Qichao, xi, 9, 19, 32–33,
103, 110, 131, 141–42, 145,
152, 158–59, 161–62, 194, 228;
and *Chinese Progress*, 32; and
Progressive party, 110; and re-
form groups, 32–33

Liang Shuming, 11, 44
Lin Maosheng, 231–32n.2
Lin Shu, 119
Lin Yu-sheng, 6, 100, 133
Liu Bochui, 163
Liu Fu, 112
Liu Renjing, 200, 211–12
Liu Shaoqi, 206
Liu Shipei, 9, 11, 15, 76, 80, 85, 102; in Japan, 83n.76; and Qing dynasty, 83n.78
Liu Ying, 211
Lu Xun, 219
Luo Han, 223–24
Luo Jialun, 140
Luo Zhanglong, 200
Luzhou, 88–89, 91

Ma Yufu, 216
Malthus, 162, 182n.35
Manchuria, 27, 33, 35, 38, 40, 80, 200, 202, 217; and Russia, 38
Manchus, 64–65, 80. See also Qing dynasty
Mandarin, 167, 175, 194, 197, 207, 219, 229
Mao Dun, 220
Mao Zedong, xii–xiii, 3, 26, 42, 44, 98, 115, 119, 137, 163, 189, 193–94, 210, 217, 229–30, 232, 234; ideology of, 214; Maoism, 19
Marx, Karl. See Marxism
Marxism, xi–xii, 3, 19, 22, 59, 134, 140, 142–45, 147, 151, 155–57, 159–65, 167, 177, 179–81, 182n.35, 232, 234–38; seen as alternative to capitalism, 167; and literature, 160n.48
Matsumoto Hideki, 8, 10
May Fourth movement, 7, 20–21, 24, 98, 101, 113, 115, 131, 133, 137, 146, 162–63, 207. See also New Culture movement
May Thirtieth incident, 186

Meisner, Maurice, 5, 13, 155
Meng Ben, 126
Metzger, Thomas, 45, 90
Militant Society, 211
Military Preparatory Academy, 40–41
Ming dynasty, 73
monarchism, 103, 138–39
Mongolia, 27
Mukden Incident, 217
Mushakoji Soneatsu, 142, 144, 146, 159

nation, 62, 67, 93–94, 99, 125, 234; and family, 67ff
National Assembly, 212–13
national essence, 9ff, 60, 63, 78, 84–85, 95, 122ff. 135, 137–38, 162, 165, 195, 226, 234; and China, 60ff
National Essence Journal, 83n.78, 84
National Purpose party, 131
national revolution, 177–78, 184–85, 188
nationalism, 41, 44–45, 47, 65, 84ff, 149, 201; and youth, 45
neo-Confucianism. See Confucianism
New Citizen Magazine, 100n.8
New Culture movement, xi, 3, 5, 7–8, 15, 19, 49, 70, 97–99, 102, 114, 131, 134–35, 139, 142, 176, 205, 208, 219, 232; and Chinese tradition, 5
New Text movement, 9–10
new village movement, 159
New Youth, 15, 42, 44, 49–50, 61, 66, 68, 72–73, 77, 82, 99, 100n.8, 101–2, 105–6, 109–10, 112–13, 115–16, 119, 122–24, 127–29, 131–34, 142, 150, 155, 161, 200, 205, 232; and *China National Gazette*, 49; and Confucianism, 68; manifesto of, 113

Sneevliet, Maring H., 168–72, 178–79

social-democratic tradition, 180

socialism, 19, 59, 85, 139–48, 152–53, 158–60, 160n.48, 162–63, 166, 177, 181–83, 208–9, 228; doctrines of, 141–42; revolution of, 59

Soviet Union, 19, 141, 159, 177–78, 180, 185–86, 192–93, 196–97, 200–201, 210–11, 213, 221, 224, 234; advisers from, 180; arms and money from, 193; clashes with China over Manchuria, 200; government of, 178; policy of, 197; power of, 186; and revolutions, 177. See also Russia

Stalin, Joseph, 179–80, 191, 213, 224. See also Stalinism

Stalinism, 183, 198, 201, 203, 210–11, 213, 224; Chinese Stalinism, 224

Su Manshu, 38, 51–52, 54–55, 76, 81n.70, 84–85, 96; in Japan, 81n.70

Subao, 39, 41, 49, 51, 100n.8; and Anhui Patriotic Society, 49; and Zhang Shizhao, 51

Sun Bocun, 83n.76

Sun Yatsen, 17, 76, 87, 92–93, 102–3, 107, 110–11, 131, 139, 142, 147, 153, 166, 168–75, 186–87, 208, 231; and independent revolutionary group, 92; and Revolutionary Alliance, 76; and Revolutionary party, 103; and violent revolutionism, 102

Sun Yatsen University, 211

Sun Yuyun, 15, 79–81, 91n.100, 92, 102; and Warrior Yue Society, 81n.70

Tai Jingnong, 23n.1, 24n.6, 231–32n.2

Taihu, 88

Tan Pingshan, 186

Third Congress of the Chinese Communist Party, 172

Third International, 169

Three Principles of the People, 186

Tiger Magazine, 100n.8, 117, 132, 148

Tongchen, 40–41, 70n.36, 70–71, 88, 125–26, 130; district of, 70, 88; faction of, 70–71, 126, 130; Tongcheng Public School, 40–41

Tongmenghui, 103n.11, 208, 231

Tongshan, 76, 89

tradition, xii–xiii, 20, 24, 36, 49, 51, 53, 66, 68, 74, 77, 84, 95–97, 100, 104–7, 115, 127, 134, 141, 146, 167, 226–28, 232, 236; and Chinese society, 100; and family, 66, 104; and relationships in accord with, 107; and scholarship, 107; and women, 53

Treaty of Shimonoseki, 30

Trotsky, Leon, xii, 3–4, 20–21, 27, 58–59, 179–82, 193, 197–206, 205n.24, 208–19, 221–27, 234–36; critique of Chinese Communist party by, 202, 214; documents of, 199; exile from Russia, 4, 59; ideas of, 197–99, 204–5, 209–10; Trotskyist factions, 198, 215, 228; Trotskyist movement, 200, 210, 222, 227; Trotskyist opposition groups, 193, 197, 201–3, 205–7, 209–11, 218–19, 222–25

Twenty-one Demands, 148

United Front, 16, 18, 166, 169–70, 172, 174–76, 183–86, 191, 194, 196, 198, 207, 221, 223, 227, 231; collapse of, 16, 196; policy of, 170ff

United States, 141

urban labor movement, 217–18

utilitarianism, 116–17, 121

vernacular revolution, 61–62, 98, 116, 122–24, 126–27, 142, 230, 232; and *Anhui Common Speech Journal*, 61–62
Versailles Peace Conference, 16, 140, 159
Voitinski, Gregori, 164–65, 167, 192

Wan Jiang Middle School, 77
Wang Anshi, 226
Wang Fanxi, 180–81, 199, 206, 210–11, 218, 222, 224
Wang Jingwei, 191
Wang Mengzhou, 37, 61, 231–32n.2
Wang Ming, 224
Wang Shiwei, 234
Wang Xiaoxu, 55
Wang Yangming, 73–74, 84
Wang Zhengting, 111
Wang Zijin, 96
warlords, 112–13, 120, 130
Warrior Yue Society, 76–77, 79–81, 81n.70, 82n.71, 87, 92–93, 101, 222; and assassinations, 80; history of, 77; and Wu Yue, 101
Water Conservatory Society, 167n.3
Weekly Critic, 129, 131
West Lake, 169, 174
Whampoa Academy, 188
Wilson, President Woodrow, 129, 140–43; democracy of, 142; idealism of, 140–41
women, 29, 34, 53–54; and Chinese tradition, 53–54
Work-and-Learning Mutual Assistance Corps, 144–46, 159
World War I, xi, 106, 108–10, 139–40, 158; and China, 108–10
Wu Jingzi, 34, 58
Wu Peifu, 171–74, 233
Wu Rulun, 75
Wu Yue, 56, 79–80, 101; and

Warrior Yu Society, 101
Wu Zhihui, 231, 231–32n.2
Wuhan, 90, 191–92, 225
Wuhu, 61, 75, 79–80, 82, 88–89, 91

Xijiang faction, 125–26
Xu Shichang, 129
Xu Xilin, 81–82, 82n.71

Yan Fu, 102, 119
Yang Changji, 44
Yang Yulin, 55–56
Yangzi Valley, 31, 35–36, 56, 75, 90, 230
Ye Jianying, 223
yellow ancestor, 63–65
Yellow Race School, 80
Yennan, 233–34
Yingzhou, 88–89
youth, 20–22, 26, 31, 36, 42–49, 51, 56–60, 71, 95, 97, 99, 101, 104, 111–12, 114, 119, 123, 127–30, 132, 134, 137, 146–47, 151–54, 165, 175–76, 193, 196–98, 214–21, 227–28, 235–36; and Anhui Academy, 47; Chen Duxiu as leader of, 43–44, 57, 111, 193ff; and Chinese society, 20, 45, 49, 51, 97
youth groups, 45, 48, 56, 60, 101
youth movements, 21, 36, 42, 45, 59, 71, 114, 130, 146, 153, 198
Youth Army, 91n.100
Youth Communist International, 169
Youth Determination Study Society, 39
Youth League, 169
Youth Magazine, 123n.56. *See also New Youth*
Youth Society, 37–39, 51; in Japan, 51
Yu, 64, 74, 84
Yuan Mei, 28–29, 34, 54, 58

Library of Congress Cataloging in Publication Data

Feigon, Lee, 1945-
Chen Duxiu, founder of the Chinese Communist Party.

Bibliography: p.   Includes index.
1. Ch'en, Tu-hsiu, 1879-1942. 2. Communists—China—Biography.
3. Politicians—China—Biography. 4. Chung-kuo kung ch'an tang—
Biography. I. Title.
DS777.15.C5F44 1983   324.251'075'0924 [B] 83-42556
ISBN 0-691-05393-6

LEE FEIGON is Associate Professor of History at
Colby College, Waterville, Maine.